The Wide Arch

THE WIDE ARCH

Roman Values in Shakespeare

Charles Wells

Bristol Classical Press

For my sons: Michael, Richard and David

forsan et haec olim meminisse iuvabit

First published in 1993 by
Bristol Classical Press
an imprint of
Gerald Duckworth & Co. Ltd
The Old Piano Factory
48 Hoxton Square, London N1 6PB

A catalogue record for this book is available
from the British Library

ISBN 1-85399-088-4

Printed in Great Britain by
The Cromwell Press, Melksham, Wiltshire

Cover illustration: A detail from Hollar's 'Long View of London',
showing Southwark and including the Globe. [Guildhall Library,
Corporation of London.] Cover by Zeebra Design, Bristol

Contents

Acknowledgements

The writer who ventures into this particular area is doubly conscious of indebtedness since, towering over him, are the two huge and largely separate edifices of Classical and Shakespearean scholarship. I have sought, in the notes and bibliography, to apportion credit wherever it is due. Since, however, so much has been written by so many, one owes, necessarily, far more than can ever be fully paid. If a point has been left unacknowledged or unattributed the omission is inadvertent and apology tendered unreservedly.

My principal debt of gratitude is to my friend and colleague David Chandler whose classical scholarship has been the *sine qua non* of my endeavours. Without his expertise, his patience and his genial rigour this book would never have found its way to press. I would also like to record here my thanks to Alastair Wilson, William Husband and Kenneth Tricker to whose impressive knowledge of things Roman I have had frequent recourse and whose patience I must on occasion have sorely tried.

My thanks are in great measure due to the Master and Fellows of St John's College, Cambridge for electing me to the commoner fellowship that enabled me to conduct much of my Shakespearean research in the most congenial and stimulating of environments. To Professor John Crook, generous to me with his time and learning, I owe particular thanks. I am also much indebted to Guy Lee, Malcolm Schofield, John Kerrigan, Richard Beadle and many others in Cambridge without whose help and encouragement I could not have proceeded. I have, I trust, profited from the advice of all those mentioned but they are, of course, fully exonerated from blame for shortcomings and inaccuracies, responsibility for which must be mine alone.

Thanks are due to John Sennett for the generous interest he has taken in my writing over many years and to my numerous students who have, I hope, learnt as much from me as I have from them.

I am grateful to my editors in Bristol, particularly Michael Bird and Dawn Pudney, for piloting the book between the scattered rocks and into harbour – if delayed by adverse tides then at least intact above the waterline.

Acknowledgements

Finally I turn – as always – to my wife Mary from whom, over the last quarter century and more, I have learnt most of all. For her unselfish, loving support I am more grateful than any words can say.

C.H.W. 1992

Note

All line references are to the Arden Shakespeare – now published by Routledge – unless otherwise indicated.

Abbreviations

Introduction

Gerrit Gerritszoon of Rotterdam, better known as Erasmus, made his first visit to England in the autumn of 1499. His arrival, coinciding as it almost did with the new century, could be taken to symbolise the dawning of English Humanism, and the same eye for symmetry might see, in the opening of *Hamlet* one hundred years later, the culmination of that prolific age. The teaching of Greek also crossed the Channel at the end of the 15th century, pioneered by such scholars as Grocyn, Linacre and Vitelli.[1] In the colleges of Oxford and Cambridge, students were now enabled to read Plato and Aristotle in the original language, giving further stimulus to what was already a surge of interest in Classical literature as a whole. The changed climate of academic thought that followed these developments has been described by some historians as signalling a radical break with the medieval world. There was, undeniably, a marked shift of emphasis.

In the ecclesiastical, Latin culture of the medieval Schoolmen – Aquinas, Ockham, Duns Scotus and others – secular and spiritual values had been inseparable. Truth, for them, was first and foremost a matter of revelation, not to be apprehended through the intellect alone. Nothing was knowable but by the light of divine illumination. Man's relationship with God was all-important. Questions of sin and expiation hung heavily in the air, and debate tended to be excessively abstract, esoteric and meta-physical, focusing on mysteries such as Trinity or the nature of essence as the appropriate matters for learned symposia. Moreover, the Catholic Church propounded an effectively self-validating system of thought, which embraced all aspects of human morality and aspiration but which was largely directed towards the contemplation of predetermined certi-tudes. By contrast the English Humanists, such as Colet, Cheke and More, joined with Erasmus in advocating a new learning, secularised through reference to the human values they found in their study of ancient Greece and Rome. They developed the belief that man could, through empirical observation and rational understanding, take control of his circumstances and improve his lot on earth. By an act of will he might create his own future. Chaucer's 'Clerk of Oxenford' had studied Classical philosophy[2] the better that he might serve God in the office of a priest, but in the 16th century many scholars began to look towards the very different ideal typified by the *uomo universale* of Renaissance Italy. As the perceived rift between the physical and spiritual widened, so things came to seem ever more complex and variable, and this new way of seeing is summed up in an elegant passage from John Florio's translation of Montaigne:

> There is no constant existence...and we, and our judgement, and all mortall things else do uncessantly rowle, turne and passe away. Thus can nothing be certainely established,...both the judgeing and the judged being in continuall alteration and motion.... It would be even as if one should go about to graspe the water: for, how much the more he shal close and presse that, which by its owne nature is ever gliding, so much the more he shall loose what he would hold and fasten.[3]

This conception of events as random, arbitrary and contingent would have made little sense a hundred years before. If all was not bound into a closed, harmonious system by the miracle of faith then decisiveness and resolution, the larger dare of the intrepid individualist, might sway the issue. The Schoolmen had interested themselves little in statecraft but the legitimisation and just exercise of human government had become a matter of prime concern for Renaissance thinkers, linked to a growing belief in the value of action, as opposed to contemplation, and its wider social consequences. What, it was asked, can history tell us about our own nature and how can it help us to take charge of our own destiny?

These questions were addressed most famously and most candidly by Machiavelli. Fortune, he observed, is the ruler of half our actions, but she allows us to govern the other half ourselves. Whoever wishes to foresee what will happen should look to what has already taken place, for all that exists now had its counterpart in times past.[4]

Men themselves are the stuff of history, a point made cogently in Sir Thomas North's translation of Amyot's Preface to Plutarch's *Lives* (1559):

> For it is a certaine rule and instruction, which by examples past, teacheth us to judge of things present, and to foresee things to come: so as we may knowe what to like of, and what to follow, what to mislike and what to eschew.

It was, of course, not a new idea. Cicero had observed:

> Histories...are the handmaids of Prudence and Wisdome, the which

may be easily and truly purchased out of the deeds and examples of others there written.[5]

And this view itself reflects the thinking of Thucydides, writing over three centuries earlier still:

Yea, though the persons do sometyme chaunge in common welthes, neverthelesse so much as is concernynge the qualytye of mattiers, the worlde is and always abydeth lyke to hym selfe.[6]

The impact of Machiavelli's thought in 16th-century England gave further impetus to a reading of ancient history which was seen to reveal the underlying political realities that form the basis of all communities and states. His admiration for Rome, in particular, sprang from his study of its personal values which, he argued, projected themselves into the wider domain of civil life. He held that valour and high-mindedness had been enfeebled by Christian humility and deference, making rulers effete and opening the way for the ruthless to trample them down. This was, in effect, why the Roman Empire fell.

For Machiavelli, too, events were chaotic and anomalous. The outcome of even the most carefully evolved decision was never certain, its wider ramifications often labyrinthine. Erasmus urged that the prince 'should first question his own right' and then 'should carefully consider whether it should be maintained by means of catastrophes to the whole world'. 'Those who are wise', he continued, 'sometimes prefer to lose a thing rather than to gain it, because they realise that it will be less costly.... What is safe anywhere while everyone is maintaining his rights to the last ditch? We see wars arise from wars, wars following wars, and no end or limit to the upheaval. It is certainly obvious that nothing is accomplished by these means.'[7] Machiavelli, on the other hand, read very different lessons in history. 'Love is maintained by a bond of obligation which, because men are wicked, is broken when an opportunity of private advantage offers, but fear is maintained by a dread of punishment which never fails.'[8] Moral scruple, he argued, must be renounced when necessary by any ruler who wished to remain in power and influence events. 'Men do not go in the direction of Good unless forced to by necessity.'[9]

The traditional religious certitudes had of course also been brought into question by the attacks on the institutionalised Church initiated by Luther and Calvin in the name of reformation. At a time of such moral uncertainty it is not surprising that men should have found in the Classical authors a cool common sense and urbanity that they much admired. Greek and Roman patterns of conduct, since necessarily pagan, were, of course, often at variance with Church teaching, though certain attitudes, for example, Stoicism, were found to fit comfortably into either system, despite a few inconsistencies such as, in this case, the differing attitudes towards suicide. Both Christianity and Stoicism, after all, placed the highest value on inner, spiritual strength, found merit in self-denial and looked askance at any hint of uncontrolled emotion; thus Hamlet's famous words to Horatio:

> Give me that man
> That is not passion's slave, and I will wear him
> In my heart's core, aye, in my heart of heart.

> (*Ham.* III.ii.71)

could be endorsed equally from either point of view.

Shakespeare's age saw its problems mirrored in the wide glass of Roman history, staring into it for guidance as to how the stability of the state might be maintained amid the pressures that came crowding in upon it from all sides. Roman constancies appeared alluring, judged against the perplexing moral climate of the time. Referring to the earth's demotion from its place at the centre of the cosmos and the heavenly bodies,[10] John Donne wrote:

> ...new philosophy calls all in doubt.
> The element of fire is quite put out;
> The sun is lost, and th'earth, and no man's wit
> Can well direct him where to look for it...
> 'Tis all in pieces, all coherence gone;
> All just supply, and all relation.[11]

This uneasiness was compounded by the social and economic ruptures marking the end of feudalism, which were, in their immediate effects, far more destabilising than all the realignments of cosmography. The Elizabethan view of Rome thus embodied a rigour and an equilibrium that were felt to have been lost.

In 16th-century contemplations of the Classical world the dominant sense is not so much one of innovation as of restoration of an inheritance that had been shouldered aside by medieval mysticism and its excesses of piety. The growth of printing now enabled many to share in their common European legacy on a scale that had never been possible hitherto. A mood of confident optimism is discernible in the early decades of the century, for example, in a letter of 1517 from Erasmus to Pope Leo X.

I congratulate this age of ours which promises to be an age of gold if ever there was one wherein I see...three of the chief blessings of humanity are about to be restored to her, I mean first that truly Christian piety which has in many ways fallen into decay, second learning of the best sort hitherto partly neglected and partly corrupted, and third the public and lasting concord of Christendom, the source and parent of piety and erudition.[12]

This mood was destined not to last. Though More, Colet and others sought, with some success, to reconcile Classical thought with Christianity, the two very different tempers could never really be made compatible. For the medieval scholar the great ages of Greece and Rome were, despite the magnificence of their accomplishments, a part of the pre-Christian darkness. To Humanists, on the other hand, they represented a light that had been extinguished, to be reawakened after a thousand years by Petrarch and Giotto. Cicero was their shining model of wisdom and oratory; but had not St Jerome in his dream been reproved by Christ Himself for reading those same pagan meditations?[13]

With the Reformation this dichotomy became more pronounced, writers on history tending to see the past in natural rather than supernatural terms:[14] events might, for example, take an unfortunate course not on account of the unseen hand of a wrathful God so much as because those involved were misguided, stubborn, selfish or ambitious. Machiavelli again expressed this change of mood:

It is necessary that he who frames a commonwealth, and ordains laws in it, should presuppose that all men are bent to mischief, and that they have a will to put in practice the wickedness of their minds so oft as occasion shall serve.... It seemed that there was in Rome a perfect union of the people and the Senate when the Tarquins were banished, and that the nobility, having laid by their pride, were become of a popular disposition and supportable to every one, even of the meanest rank.... But no sooner were the Tarquins dead, and the nobility delivered of that fear, but they began to spit against the people the poison that all this while had lurked in their breasts, and in all sorts possible to vex and molest them: which thing confirms what I said before, that men never do good unless enforced thereto; but where choice is abundant and liberty at pleasure, confusion and disorder suddenly take place.[15]

Discord such as this between the Roman plebeians and patricians mirrored the social and political unease that ran like a dark thread through so much of Elizabeth's reign, just as the power struggles between Lancaster and

York, which paved the way for the Tudor dynasty, could be seen as a parallel to the civil wars of Caesar and Pompey, Octavius[16] and Antony. Equally, the achievements and reborn splendours of England and her Virgin Queen were felt, by enthusiasts and by sycophants alike, to echo the greatness of Rome itself. Roman history seemed more than ever relevant: the courage and tenacity of the great military leaders of Classical times found equivalents in the feats of such contemporary heroes as Frobisher, Sidney, Grenville, Essex and Blount. Through resolve and endeavour, aspiration might be turned into achievement for, as Cicero affirmed, virtue was praiseworthy only in the doing.[17] Men must, therefore, take responsibility for themselves and their own actions, thus acquiring the true moral freedom that is the essence of human dignity, an idea implicit in the word *humanitas* itself and one which can be traced back as far as Aristotle.[18] An idealisation of 'manliness' along these lines is at the heart of the Latin term '*virtus*', the central value of the Roman moral system. Machiavelli called it 'virtù', by which he intended a combination of strength of character, resolution, intelligence, courage and – above all – decisiveness. The values derived from *virtus* had a particular appeal to the Elizabethans with their cult of individualism. If heroism lay in exploits, in deeds of nobility and valour, then its essence was to be sought in that blend of austerity, firmness, dignity and action that constituted 'the high Roman fashion'. It was this, above all, that caught the imagination of so many writers of the time.

Into his own Tudor milieu of flux and ambiguity Shakespeare brought, plucked from the pages of Plutarch and Livy, stern-minded, heroic figures, possessed of a mysterious, inward power that enabled them to face life's daunting complexities with an enviable equanimity. He shared Marlowe's burning faith in the possibility of man's triumph here on earth although, unlike his passionate contemporary, he survived long enough to reach more complex judgements, often sceptical, contradictory and inconclusive. For both men moral integrity was fundamental, as we see in plays like *Tamburlaine* and *Titus Andronicus* written, it seems, within a year or two of each other. Single-mindedness and unwavering constancy clearly fascinated Shakespeare, though he was well aware that these qualities might teeter on the edge of fanaticism. There is something terrible about Shylock's refusal to be deflected by so much as a 'scruple' from his ghastly purpose. We find in it a compelling blend of the awe-inspiring and the absurd. Irresolution, on the other hand, often earns contempt.[19] Othello's words to Iago as he embarks on his sacred 'cause' contain the cold hardness of imagery which is characteristic of what might broadly be termed Shakespeare's 'Roman' attitude:

Like to the Pontic sea,
Whose icy current and compulsive course
Ne'er feels retiring ebb, but keeps due on
To the Propontic and the Hellespont:
Even so my bloody thoughts, with violent pace
Shall ne'er look back, ne'er ebb to humble love,
Till that a capable and wide revenge
Swallow them up. Now by yond marble heaven...

(*Oth.* III.iii.460)

'How terrible in constant resolution', as the French Constable says of Henry V.[20] Brutus' inescapable conclusion: 'It must be by his death'[21] contains the epitome of that uncompromising self-belief Shakespeare found so quintessentially Roman.

It is significant that Shakespeare should have written no Roman comedy. The nearest he came to one was *The Comedy of Errors*, based closely on the *Menaechmi* of Plautus and set in Ephesus on the eastern shore of the Mediterranean, an area for many years a part of the Empire. The play contains, nonetheless, not one reference to Rome or to Romans, and the presence of an abbess and a priory seems to place it in a later, Christianised world (although historical consistency was often a minor consideration, as we shall see when we turn to *Cymbeline*).

Shakespeare's six 'Roman' texts – five plays and a narrative poem – fall into three distinct pairs. There is a pattern of development in the thinking about Rome which, with one discrepancy,[22] follows the chronology of composition now broadly agreed by scholarship. It is a process which evolved over two decades, spanning almost the whole of Shakespeare's career. The two earliest of these texts, *Titus Andronicus* and *The Rape of Lucrece*, were both written, apparently, between 1590 and 1593 when Shakespeare was still in his twenties. Rome, here, is envisaged in relatively simplistic terms, and there is little attempt to question the values put forward by the protagonist despite the extremes of behaviour to which they give rise. Both Titus and Lucrece propel themselves towards the ends they have determined with a startling, unswerving, though scarcely admirable logic.

Unlike Mark Antony, Titus holds his 'visible shape' with little difficulty.[23] He is 'steel to the very back',[24] something Antony merely talks of becoming.[25] Supremely untroubled by conscience and always clear as to where his duty lies, only once throughout the play does Titus waver. Having denied life itself to his disobedient son, he further determines to refuse him his traditional funeral rites, and it is with great reluctance that he eventually yields to the entreaties of his family, allowing him burial in the ancestral tomb. When, in the final act, he tells Tamora that 'what is written shall be executed'[26] the words sum up the linearity of his mind. Lucrece shares the same uncomplicated moral stance.

> Her honour is ta'en prisoner by the foe...
> 'Few words', quoth she, 'shall fit the trespass best
> Where no excuse can give the fault amending'.

> (ll. 1608-14)

Despite her promise, however, she is, like Richardson's Pamela, unremittingly verbose on the subject of chastity. Her lengthy and over-elaborate exposition of 'The story of sweet chastity's decay' (l. 808) may at times try the patience of all but the most tolerant reader.

In both these early works Shakespeare's sense of the tragic is expressed in terms of bloody conflict between an evil that is uniformly dark and a virtue that is spotlessly pure, though there is a recognition that one world may be corrupted by the other.

In *Julius Caesar* this picture alters radically. Here, as later in *Coriolanus*, motive is complex, decision onerous, outcome equivocal, and Shakespeare enters the realm of Renaissance introspection and ambiguity so eloquently expounded by Montaigne:

> Whosoever looketh narrowly about himselfe shall hardly see himself twise in one same state.... If I speake diversly of my selfe it is because I looke diversly upon my selfe. All contrarieties are found in her, according to some turne or removing...and whosoever shall heedfully survey and consider himselfe shall finde this volubility and discordance to be in himselfe, yea and in his very judgement. I have nothing to say entirely, simply and with soliditie of my selfe without confusion, disorder, blending, mingling.[27]

Better, perhaps, than any other of Shakespeare's Romans, Brutus epitomises the late Tudor moral dilemma. In *Julius Caesar* characters are often confused and uncertain as to their proper course, a situation not encountered in *Titus* or *Lucrece*, where no one seems to have doubt about anything. Now Roman values are called into question, often by bringing a cogent irony to bear, as when the conspirators wash their hands in the blood of their fallen victim to accompanying shouts of 'peace, freedom and liberty!'[28] The contrast between Brutus' remote idealism and its catastrophic consequences forms the play's ironic core. Clearly Shakespeare had begun to have misgivings about the characteristic Roman ability to separate mind from feelings, above all in its effect on the urgings of the sentient heart.

8

He returned to this problem with still greater uneasiness a few years later in *Coriolanus*, a play which has many affinities with *Julius Caesar* and, for the purposes of this study, will be paired with it, though *Antony and Cleopatra* (rather inconveniently from the critical viewpoint) stands between them in terms of its date of composition. Few Shakespearean characters arouse stronger, more conflicting feelings in an audience than Coriolanus. In this play we find, at its starkest, the confrontation between stern Roman *virtus*, built on long tradition, and the gentler, more instinctive claims of familial love and harmony. The concept of *pietas*, which in the end prevails over the harsh warrior code, again provides an opportunity for pagan Roman values to move into line with those of Christianity.

Coriolanus is often seen as a study of Roman politics, and in this it has more in common with *Julius Caesar* than with the four other texts. Increasingly, however, critics have focused on the play's intensely human and personal elements, particularly the hero's relationship with his mother, Volumnia. At the heart of *Coriolanus* there exists the same dilemma that Shakespeare encountered when he studied Plutarch's picture of Marcus Brutus: how may a man preserve that integrity and cold self-reliance so fundamental to *romanitas* and so clearly commanding respect while, at the same time, possessing that natural, spontaneous warmth and sympathy which expresses itself in the Christian virtues of humility and forgiveness? This quandary is well illustrated by Volumnia's bewilderment. Torn between admiration for her son's resolute consistency and irritation at his pig-headed intransigence, she produces a sentence which ties itself into an impressive semantic knot:

> You are too absolute,
> Though therein you can never be too noble,
> But when extremities speak.
>
> (*Cor*. III.ii.39)

Roman values receive a very different treatment in *Antony and Cleopatra*. It is as though Shakespeare has burst out of the dark, claustrophobic tunnel of the earlier tragedies[29] into a new world of vibrant colour and exhilaration. Now, for the first time, Roman values, as embodied in Octavius, seem to have become staid and dull, exemplifying a 'squareness' which Antony, by his own admission, has failed to keep.[30] The play's central metaphor of fluidity and evanescence contrasts with a Rome that appears stolid, angular and marmoreal. The quality of *gravitas* – weighty, enduring, monumental in earlier works – is now diminished and deglamorised until it strikes us as rigid, sterile and tedious. The imagery here conveys Shakespeare's meaning to a degree unique among the Roman plays. We move, it is true, from the frivolity of Antony's 'dotage' in the opening line to the 'high order' and 'great solemnity' of the last, passing from the chaotic period of the Civil War to the beginning of the Augustan golden age, when Rome was to reach the pinnacle of its power and influence. This historical progression counts for little, however, when juxtaposed against the mercurial passion of the lovers and the music of their poetry. Antony looms larger than the Rome that bred him and which, in part, he still inhabits. As Cleopatra tells the bewildered Dolabella:

> ...his delights
> Were dolphin-like, they show'd his back above
> The element they lived in...

> (*Ant.* V.ii.88)

This is a new world of capriciousness, fluctuation and fantasy that is far distant from the solemn Rome of *Titus Andronicus*, consecrated to 'virtue...justice, continence and nobility.'[31] The way is open for *Cymbeline*, perhaps the strangest of all Shakespeare's plays.

Historically, the events behind *Cymbeline* follow on from *Antony and Cleopatra*, with Augustus now firmly established on his throne. Although geographically remote from Celtic Britain where the action largely takes place, Rome is never out of sight for long. Again its values are severely questioned, though admittedly more by implication than direct discussion, since in Arviragus' words: 'Love's reason's beyond reason'[32] – a line that would sit easily in *Antony*. In reading – or, better still, watching – *Cymbeline* we may be momentarily struck with the disturbing thought that when he embarked on *Titus* Shakespeare was unconsciously aiming towards this late romance. There is a weird, dream-like quality about it which is difficult to define. Time and again we hear half echoes of the earlier Roman texts as though Shakespeare had them, as he wrote, all jumbled in the forefront of his mind. The imagery has much in common with *Antony*, particularly in its insistence upon natural growth, fruition and renewal, and there is the same note of poignant lyricism in the verse. Aaron's attempt on Imogen's chastity sharply recalls both *Titus* and *Lucrece*. The chamber tapestry depicts Cleopatra in her barge on the River Cydnus, while there are implicit links between the typically Roman general, Lucius, and several earlier bearers of this resonant name. In the final act the two great peoples, Roman and British, come together in propitious harmony, as though Shakespeare had at last achieved a synthesis of the values each stood for, a synthesis towards which he had been moving – though he could hardly have realised it – ever since that opening speech of Saturninus two decades before.

Notes

1. Robert Grosseteste and Francis Bacon attempted to stimulate the study of Greek at Oxford as early as the 13th century but with little or no success. The first Greek grammar to be printed was Manuel Chrysoloras' edition of 1471, later used by Erasmus. For further information on this topic see *Scribes and Scholars: A Guide to the Transmission of Greek and Latin Literature*, L.D. Reynolds and N.G. Wilson (Oxford University Press, 1968).

2. Chaucer's Clerk would have read Aristotle in a Latin version, perhaps Boethius' 6th-century translation. Much Aristotelian writing reached medieval Latin via the Arabic versions of Averroes and Avicenna.

3. *An Apologie of Raymond Sebond* (1603).

4. *The Prince* (1514) ch. 18.

5. Cicero's words paraphrased in Latin by William Camden, translated into English by Abraham Darcie in 1625.

6. *History of the War between Athens and Sparta*, ca. 400 BC, trans. Walter Lynne, 1550.

7. *The Education of a Christian Prince* (1516) trans. L.K. Born (New York, 1936) p. 250.

8. *The Prince* trans. Edward Dacres (London, 1640) ch. 17.

9. *Discourses* I.3, trans. Edward Dacres (London, 1636).

10. The idea of a geocentric universe, propounded by Ptolemy in the second century, held sway until Copernicus' *De Revolutionibus*, published in 1543. The heliocentric universe was later confirmed by the researches of Galileo, born, coincidentally, in the same year as Shakespeare, 1564.

11. *An Anatomy of the World (The First Anniversary)* (1611).

12. *The Epistles of Erasmus*, F.M. Nichols (ed.) (New York, 1904) Vol. II, p. 521.

13. *Letters* xxii (to Eustochium).

14. See, for instance, Polydore Vergil's *Historiae Anglicae Libri XXVI* (1534) and William Camden's *Brittania* (1586).

15. *Discourses* op. cit., pp. 17-19.

16. Shakespeare always uses *Octavius* in preference to *Octavian*.

17. *Virtutis laus omnis in actione consistit.*

18. Cicero used the word *humanitas* to translate the Greek *paedia* – meaning both education and culture.

19. See, for example, *Mac.* II.i.52; *John* II.i.567 and *3H.VI* II.i.171.

20. II.iv.35.

21. *Caes.* II.i.10.

22. This smooth progression is disrupted by the fact that *Antony and Cleopatra* almost certainly predates *Coriolanus* by a year or so, having been written, it seems, during the winter of 1606/7. *Julius Caesar* is generally agreed to have been written in 1599, *Coriolanus* in 1608 and *Cymbeline* in 1609.

23. Cf. *Ant.* IV.iv.14.

24. *Tit. A.* IV.iii.47.

25. *Ant.* IV.iv.43.

26. V.ii.15.

27. *On the Inconstancy of our Actions.*

28. III.i.111.

29. *Othello, King Lear* and *Macbeth* were written, it is generally agreed, between 1604 and 1606.

30. II.iii.6.

31. I.i.14.

32. *Cym.* IV.ii.22.

1

Titus Andronicus and *Romanitas*

Titus Andronicus, Shakespeare's first tragedy and the earliest of the Roman plays, has never found much favour with critics, although it seems to have been hugely popular on the Elizabethan stage. Many readers have dismissed it as a farrago of mayhem and mutilation, pausing only to cast doubt upon its authorship or to smile indulgently at its immaturity, before hurrying away from such rough, unpalatable stuff towards lusher pastures such as *The Comedy of Errors* and *The Taming of the Shrew*. There is, however, good reason to take *Titus* far more seriously than has generally been the case. Simplistic though it frequently seems when compared with later plays, it nevertheless begins the debate on Roman values which was to preoccupy Shakespeare's mind for twenty years. Indeed, in its opening two dozen lines or so we find references to the patrician class, nobility, justice, patriotism, imperialism, primogeniture, and such values as *amicitia*, *virtus*, *continentia* and *pietas* – a list that embraces most of the issues that will form the substance of the plays to come.

Opinions on the date of *Titus* vary, but it may well have been written as early as 1590. Some scholars push the date back even further. Unlike the other Roman texts, it appears to have been based not upon historical source material such as Plutarch's *Lives* but on a medieval prose tale no longer extant. A version of this 'lamentable and tragical' account, translated from the original Italian, apparently found its way into an 18th-century chap-book, a single copy of which survives in the Folger Library.[1] The play is set – again uniquely for Shakespeare – in the later Roman period, seemingly at the end of the 4th century AD, when Rome was struggling to hold back the marauding Goths.

Unfocused and crude it may be, but *Titus Andronicus* conveys powerfully Shakespeare's fascination with the Roman world. He holds its values up for scrutiny, silhouetted against the barbarous red glow cast by Tamora and Aaron, finding in them a sharp, hard-edged austerity and straightforwardness which must have seemed very appealing in the more problematic moral climate of his own day. There is little attempt to analyse and discuss, as later in *Julius Caesar*, and ideas are, for the most part, clear-cut and uncomplicated. Honour, for instance, is mentioned nearly fifty times, but Shakespeare here shows little inclination to investigate the implications of a term he later explored at length in such plays as *Henry IV*, *Hamlet* and *All's Well*. Virtue and nobility, though much talked about, amount to little more than martial courage. Rome is 'a nation strong, train'd up in arms'[2] and 'the good Andronicus' its 'Patron of virtue, Rome's best champion' (I.i.64). The play is full of sententious aphorism: 'He lives in fame that died in virtue's cause' (I.i.390) pronounce the Andronici as they lay Mutius in his tomb. The words have a ponderous resonance that suggests at first hearing depths of meaning which prove, on reflection, to be illusory. Tamora speaks of that 'ingratitude which Rome reputes to be a heinous sin' (I.i.448), while Marcus reminds his brother of his moral obligations: 'Thou art a Roman; be not barbarous' (I.i.378). Both sentiments typify the shallowness of the dialectic in *Titus*.

What emerges, nonetheless, is an awareness that Rome possessed for Shakespeare, as for the Elizabethans generally, a powerful mystique. Rutilius Namatianus, traditionally the last of the Roman poets, declaimed in 416:

> Spread forth the laws that are to last throughout the ages.... Thou alone needst not dread the distaffs of the Fates.... The span which doth remain is subject to no bounds, so long as earth shall stand and heaven uphold the stars!

This eloquent tribute resonates with the assurance of one bestriding a thousand years of history, its confidence undiminished by the fact that the Visigoths were by then within Rome's gates.

In the opening scene of *Coriolanus* Menenius addresses the discontented plebeians in similar terms:

> ...you may as well
> Strike at the heaven with your staves as lift them
> Against the Roman state, whose course will on
> The way it takes, cracking ten thousand curbs
> Of more strong link asunder than can ever
> Appear in your impediment.

> (*Cor*. I.i.66)

Had not the Augustan poets insisted that Rome's very being was divinely ordained?[3]

It is surely significant that of all the plays only *Titus* should stress, on its title page,[4] that it is, specifically, a 'Romaine' tragedy, and the very words 'Rome' and 'Roman' seem in this early work to hold for the youthful playwright a potent verbal magic. Together they occur 126 times; twice as often as in *Julius Caesar* and more than three times as frequently as in *Antony and Cleopatra* (the more significant a statistic when one bears in mind that *Titus* is much the shortest of the five Roman plays). In the theatre the sound of these words is constantly in our ears, until sheer battering repetition imprints them on our minds. An almost palpable Roman aura is thus evoked by this simple device alone. Undoubtedly *romanitas* – which might be translated as 'Roman-ness'[5] – exerted a powerful influence on Shakespeare's imagination at this early, receptive stage.

It has been said that the true hero of the Roman plays is Rome itself.[6] Shakespeare presents his hero, Titus, as the embodiment of Roman ideals as he then understood them. What comes across most forcefully is the self-confidence and massive authority of high-minded men. Ruthless determination and uncompromising commitment give the Roman aristocracy an inflexibility which is both impressive and alarming. 'A stone is soft as wax, tribunes more hard than stones' (III. i. 45) declares Titus, faced with the inexorability of Roman justice and pleading as fruitlessly for the lives of his own two sons as, earlier, Tamora had with him for hers. Mercy finds no place in the all-pervasive shadow of the eagle's wing by which, as Tamora tells us, the sun is dimmed.[7]

What seems to impress Shakespeare more than anything is Rome's power of sheer endurance. 'This monument five hundred years hath stood' (I.i.350) boasts Titus fiercely of the family tomb, a place in which he seeks to deny the son who tried, ill-advisedly, to bar his father's path. Grim self-discipline and stubborn probity, though admired by some, alienate Titus from many of those around him in a manner that anticipates the much larger figure of Coriolanus some twenty years later. These early – though late – Romans possess a dignity that strikes us at every turn as monumental. They are 'high-resolved men', forthright and heroic in their single-mindedness, even though there are times when their inability to compromise pushes them to extremes and they totter on the brink of absurdity. Rigid adherence to what seems an outmoded code may take precedence over common sense, as in the episode of the severed hand. Their innate *gravitas* sustains them nevertheless and they carry in their own being something of the weight and durability of the Roman state that bred them. They themselves, in a sense, *are* Rome; time, flesh and stone made one.

Ill-defined as Shakespeare's sense of *romanitas* is, it nevertheless embraces an earnestness and a solemnity little encountered in other areas of his work. Of the eighty or so named Romans who appear in the plays only two – Menenius and Enobarbus – display a sense of humour. One might just add Mark Antony to the list, though more as a result of what others tell us about him than of what he actually says. The high seriousness Shakespeare intends is conveyed principally by the grandiloquent manner in which the characters speak. In *Titus* we sense the inexperienced playwright trying too hard to find a mode of utterance impressive enough to do justice to his lofty theme. The result is an orotund style epitomised by Bassianus' opening words:

> Romans, friends, followers, favourers of my right,
> If ever Bassianus, Caesar's son,
> Were gracious in the eyes of royal Rome,
> Keep then this passage to the Capitol,
> And suffer not dishonour to approach
> The imperial seat, to virtue consecrate,
> To justice, continence and nobility.

(Tit. A. I.i.9)

By comparison with Brutus' oration for the dead Caesar, which opens in not dissimilar fashion, we find here a stiff, bombastic manner that is characteristic of the play as a whole, although more genuine feeling does at times break through. Underlying this approach was Shakespeare's clear respect for his Roman literary models, coupled, no doubt, with a need to out-Kyd Thomas Kyd and to emulate the grandiloquence of Marlowe, considerations forced upon him by the cut-throat theatrical rivalries of the early 1590s. In consequence we find much wooden characterisation and 'operatic' attitudinising, the majority of speeches being declaimed in the general direction of the audience rather than addressed to others on the stage.

Shakespeare's classical learning[8] appears here undigested, in marked contrast with its employment in the plays to come. Latin tags, it seems, are thrown in for no better reason than to remind us that we are in Rome, unless perhaps as a riposte to so-called university wits such as Nashe and Greene, who derided the playwright for his 'unlettered' background. '*Sit fas aut nefas*',[9] remarks Demetrius to his brother Chiron. The fact that the two of them are Goths either seemed irrelevant to the writer, or perhaps escaped his attention altogether. Indeed many of the speeches are so lacking in both spontaneity and individuality that they could be delivered by almost any character, with Goths as likely to produce a stream of high-flown Latinate rhetoric as any of the *bona fide* Romans.

Shakespeare parades his classicism self-consciously in this early work, witness his coinage of the Latinate word 'palliament', a robe worn by the *candidatus* seeking political office.[10] The young playwright works, in turn, through most of the major Roman authors, but his principal source is Ovid's *Metamorphoses*. So important is this book to Shakespeare's purpose that it even appears on the stage as a hand-prop, enabling the now tongueless Lavinia to communicate her plight by indicating in Lucius' copy the page which contains 'the tragic tale of Philomel'.[11] Shakespeare's evident familiarity with the poem was probably by way of Arthur Golding's translation of 1567, although it seems likely that he was acquainted with the original Latin too, as indicated by Titus' quotation from it at the start of what might be called the 'archery' scene.[12]

Golding's colourful rendering into 'English meeter'[13] of the Tale of Procne must have been closely studied by Shakespeare, although the description of Lavinia's mutilation was more likely inspired by the translation of Book IV in which Pyramus stabs himself to death in a splendidly picturesque if somewhat messy fashion:

> ...therewithall he drew
> His sworde, the which among his guttes he thrust, and by and by
> Did draw it from the bleeding wound beginning for to die
> And caste himselfe upon his backe. The bloud did spin on hie
> As when a conduite pipe is crackt, the water bursting out
> Did shote itselfe a great way off and pierce the ayre about.

Marcus, confronted by his bleeding niece, discourses upon her misfortune in markedly similar terms:

> Why dost not speak to me?
> Alas, a crimson river of warm blood,
> Like to a bubbling fountain stirr'd with wind,
> Doth rise and fall between thy rosed lips,
> Coming and going with thy honey breath...
> And not withstanding all this loss of blood,
> As from a conduit with three issuing spouts,
> Yet do thy cheeks look red as Titan's face...

> (*Tit. A.* II.iv.21)

But the artificiality of these words in such a context is evident. The imagery is ornate, not to say incongruous, and serves merely to diminish the horrors it describes by distancing us from them, as it does, by design of course, in Bottom's famous Ovidian parody.[14] How different Cornwall's words on blinding Gloucester:

> Lest it see more, prevent it. Out vile jelly!
> Where is thy lustre now?

(Lear III.vii.82)

Here there is no empty posturing, the impact of the scene so much the more powerful for the bluntness of the language employed. Ovidian *copia* – the piling on of detail for purely decorative effect – is found throughout *Titus Andronicus*, suggesting a writer groping for what he conceives to be an appropriately 'Roman' style.[15] We find it again in *The Rape of Lucrece*[16] but by the time he wrote *Julius Caesar* such excesses had largely disappeared.

The cannibalistic banquet is taken from Seneca's *Thyestes*. Shakespeare catches something of its declamatory style in *Titus*, no doubt considering its exhortatory tone appropriate to his Roman subject matter. His hero even quotes two lines from *Phaedra* in the original Latin to the bafflement, one presumes, of the larger part of his Tudor audience.[17] The starched, rhetorical convention that he adopts also owes much to Ciceronian *eloquentia*. At the beginning of Act IV we learn that the young Lucius has been brought up – like Shakespeare himself perhaps – on a diet of *De Oratore*, as well as the Ovid he carries round with him.

The play abounds in classical allusion, much of it, as we have seen, fitting ill with the action on the stage but contributing, Shakespeare evidently felt, to the heightened style that his idea of Rome seemed to demand. A prime example of this is the awkward insertion of two lines from a Latin ode into Act IV Scene ii.

> *Demetrius*: What's here? a scroll; and written round about;
>   Let's see:
>   *Integer vitae, scelerisque purus,*
>   *Non eget Mauri iaculis, nec arcu.*[18]
> *Chiron*: O, 'tis a verse in Horace; I know it well:
>   I read it in the grammar long ago.
> *Aaron*: Ay, just; a verse in Horace; right, you have it.

(Tit. A. IV.ii.18)

These last three lines, in particular, must surely rank among Shakespeare's least successful. Virgil's *Aeneid*, too, receives attention,[19] as does Ovid's *Fasti*, source for the story of Tarquin and Lucrece referred to several times in Act IV,[20] as though in preparation for the narrative poem soon to follow.

The staging of *Titus Andronicus* also plays a major part in establishing that aura of *romanitas* Shakespeare sought to evoke. The first Quarto's elaborate stage direction at I.i.69 is worth quoting in full:

> *Sound drums and trumpets*, and then enter two of Titus' sons, and then two Men bearing a coffin covered with black; then two other sons; then TITUS ANDRONICUS; and then TAMORA, the Queen of Goths, and her sons, ALARBUS, CHIRON and DEMETRIUS, with AARON the Moor, and others as many as can be; then set down the coffin, and TITUS speaks.

Such tableaux, suggestive, Shakespeare intends, of martial pomp and imperial splendour, recur at frequent intervals throughout the play. Yet despite Tamora's contemptuous reference to 'the giddy men of Rome' and her husband's worry that 'the citizens favour Lucius And will revolt...to succour him' (IV.iv.79), we never actually hear from the assembled masses that later on take centre stage in *Julius Caesar* and *Coriolanus*. The absence of the plebeians from the argument at this point indicates that Shakespeare's view of Roman politics changed radically over the next decade. Here he shows a brief concern with the transference of power and the claims of primogeniture but little more. The play opens with Saturninus' call for his followers to 'Plead [his] successive title with [their] swords', on the grounds that he is 'first-born son' while Marcus – anxious to 'set a head on headless Rome' – argues a vaguely conceived notion of democracy as the preferable method of choosing their new leader:

> Know that the people of Rome, for whom we stand
> A special party, have by common voice
> In election for the Roman empery,
> Chosen Andronicus...

> > (*Tit. A.* I.i.20)

Indeed the tribunes are brought in briefly, but they allow Titus to defer in favour of his rival and here the matter rests, apart that is from a perfunctory reference to 'the common voice', which apparently prevails in the final scene when Lucius takes up the reins of empire.

Of far greater significance to Shakespeare than such political concerns are the personal values he associated with the Roman way of life. Chief among these is honour. The term is never clearly defined but seems to be synonymous with that 'uprightness and integrity' – *dignitas* it might be – lauded by Bassianus in the opening scene and the *fides* or good faith

19

identified in Lucius by the totally amoral Aaron, progenitor of Edmund and Iago. Aaron seeks to preserve his child's life by appealing to Lucius' *clementia*, underpinned by what he himself disclaims but recognises in the Roman as 'a thing...called conscience':

> Therefore I urge thy oath; for that I know
> An idiot holds his bauble for a god,
> And keeps the oath which by that god he swears.

> *(Tit. A.* V.i.78)

Aaron's cynicism may owe something to Shakespeare's reading of Machiavelli who noted the difficulty of enjoining oaths upon mere mercenaries:

> By what god or by what saints may I make them to swear? By those that they worship or by those that they blaspheme? Who they worship I know not any: but I know well they blaspheme all.... How can they that despise God, reverence men?[21]

Lucius readily pledges himself to spare the infant: 'Even by my god I swear to thee I will' (*Tit. A.* V.i.86). Saturninus goes a stage further, swearing 'by *all* the Roman gods' to marry Tamora, while Titus vows 'by [his] father's reverent tomb' to ensure that his sons stand trial to clear their names.[22] Such swearing is stoutly rejected by both Cassius and Brutus in the later play, the former protesting that he has no need 'to stale with ordinary oaths' his love for his friend, while Brutus insists that 'honesty to honesty engaged' is sufficient guarantee of the conspirators' faith:[23]

> What need we any spur but our own cause
> To prick us to redress? What other bond
> Than secret Romans, that have spoke the word,
> And will not palter?

> *(Caes.* II.i.123)

This straightforward approach is signally lacking in *Titus*, where some higher power is frequently evoked as a kind of moral collateral. 'Rome and the righteous heavens be my judge!' (I.i.426) protests Titus, and Tamora pledges allegiance to her new husband in equally vehement terms:

> ...the gods of Rome forfend
> I should be author to dishonour you!

> *(Tit. A.* I.i.434)

20

Titus' inflexible code of honour alienates him from the other characters and drives him towards bestial ferocity and madness. When justice, the great bulwark of polity, crumbles, Rome, epitome of civilised values, becomes its own antithesis: 'a wilderness of tigers.'[24] The imagery here anticipates Albany's horrified vision of a Britain ruled by those 'tigers, not daughters' Goneril and Regan, who unleash anarchy into the world until

> Humanity must perforce prey on itself
> Like monsters of the deep.

> > > > (*Lear* IV.ii.47)

In such an ethical desert honour is of small account. Raw courage, however, is essential and this we find exemplified throughout the play. Even the appalling Aaron goes to his hideous death – 'fast'ned in the earth' and left to 'famish' – with no hint of a tremor on his lips:

> I am no baby, I, that with base prayers
> I should repent the evils I have done;
> Ten thousand worse than ever yet I did
> Would I perform, if I might have my will.
> If one good deed in all my life I did,
> I do repent it from my very soul.

> > > > (*Tit. A.* V.iii.185)

This insentience is echoed, some fourteen years later, in the wounded Iago's mockery of Othello: 'I bleed sir; but not kill'd.' (*Oth.* V.ii.291). A capacity to endure that is scarcely human is prominent throughout *Titus Andronicus*, Shakespeare apparently perceiving it as a Roman Stoicism with its total contempt for suffering and death. The starkest example of this attitude is to be found in Titus' self-mutilation: 'Give me a sword, I'll chop off my hands too' (III.i.72). The incident was perhaps inspired by the story of Mucius Scaevola who, it is said, demonstrated his complete indifference to pain by holding his hand in the fire, saying: 'Look and see how cheap the body is.'[25]

Such fortitude was the bedrock of the *virtus* code, itself grounded in the *mos maiorum*, or way of the ancestors.[26] These normative standards, ratified by long tradition into unquestioning acceptance, bequeathed a massive self-confidence and authority to the Roman disposition as Shakespeare understood it. Titus stands four square upon custom and precedent. Violence seems to be sanctioned by its ritualisation.[27] In his opening speech he calls upon Jupiter Capitolinus to 'Stand gracious to the rites that

21

we intend' (*Tit. A.* I.i.78). These 'rites' include the dismemberment of Alarbus and the burning of his entrails that the 'shadows' of the Andronici may be appeased – a process arranged by Lucius, arguably the most temperate character in the play. When Titus serves up to Tamora the remains of her two sons in a pie the audience may feel that the distinction between 'civilised' Roman values and barbaric atrocity has become somewhat blurred. 'Roman rites' in practice seem to amount, by and large, to ritual murder, indistinguishable – if one strips away the accompanying rhetoric – from those supposedly carried out by, for instance, the Druids at Stonehenge.

Titus, the stern *paterfamilias*, slays Mutius, one of his few surviving sons, when the latter, emerging unscathed from the rigours of war, misguidedly seeks to bar his path.[28] It is a startling demonstration of the *jus patrium* or *patria potestas*, the father's sovereign authority over all members of his family which allowed him absolute discretion to punish any act that he felt impugned his honour. No matter that such a deed would clash head-on with the claims of *pietas*.[29] The incident attests to a surprisingly detailed grasp of Roman codes of conduct at this early stage of Shakespeare's career and provides a foretaste of the harsh rigidity of thought which is to figure prominently in later plays in the sequence. In certain respects Titus might even be considered as the outline sketch that led ultimately to the full portrait of King Lear. The powers of both are seen to be on the wane. Each is enraged by what he interprets as filial ingratitude and lapses into madness when the mind gives way beneath its weight of pain.[30] Titus both gives and demands unquestioning loyalty and obedience. The cold fury he displays in killing Mutius flies in the face of all normal human feeling, to say nothing of the natural ties of family affection which *pietas* should entail. Shakespeare seems, in this first exercise, to have envisaged his Romans as a race somehow apart, imagining, one can only assume, that Titus' behaviour will not forfeit the audience's sympathy for him at the outset.

Lavinia's 'spotless chastity' is, for her father, 'more dear/Than hands or tongue.'[31] To this ideal of purity she is sacrificed, Titus finding it eminently reasonable

> To slay his daughter with his own right hand
> Because she was enforc'd, stain'd and deflower'd.

(Tit. A. V.iii.38)

His action is endorsed by Saturninus, who agrees that, in such circumstances, 'the girl should not survive her shame'. In vindication of his deed Titus cites the example of Lucius Virginius Rufus who stabbed to death his daughter Virginia to save her from the concupiscent magistrate Appius Claudius, a pre-emptive strike in this case and one which, according to Livy,[32] brought to an end the power of the decemvirs. In Shakespeare's women honour is closely identified with chastity, Tamora's becoming 'spotted, detested and abominable' by her adultery with Aaron whereas Lavinia, 'Rome's rich ornament', must be killed rather than bear the stigma of its violation – a theme to which Shakespeare will return, within a year or two, in *Lucrece*. This theme of chastity under threat will recur time and again in the plays and poems and is perhaps the only one to link *Titus* with that very different play, *The Tempest*, at the opposite end of Shakespeare's career. Yet in comparison with Titus, the behaviour of such tyrannical fathers as Leontes, Egeus, Capulet, Duke Frederick and Brabantio seems relatively mild.[33]

When Titus orders the death of a Gothic prince as a sacrifice to the shades of his own slaughtered sons, Tamora springs to her children's defence with the very reasonable argument that:

> ...if to fight for king and commonweal
> Were piety in thine, it is in these.

(Tit. A. I.i.114)

Her pleas are futile, however, and Alarbus is dragged off to be torn limb from limb.

> O cruel, irreligious piety!

(Tit. A. I.i.130)

The mother's scathing irony makes clear that Titus' much vaunted *pietas* – he is, after all, 'Andronicus, surnamed Pius'[34] – is starkly at variance with his brutal actions in the play. His earlier self-reproach helps explain this seeming dichotomy:

> Unkind and careless of thine own,
> Why suffer'st thou thy sons, unburied yet,
> To hover on the dreadful shore of Styx?

(Tit. A. V.iii.86)

The passage emphasises the importance of the kinship bond in Roman thinking, whereby to be 'unkind' is to be impious, neglectful of one's duty towards family and the gods. Titus' reluctance to bury his disobedient son, Mutius, in the family tomb receives a stern rebuke from his brother, Marcus:

My lord, this is impiety in you.
My nephew Mutius' deeds do plead for him;
He must be buried with his brethren.

(*Tit. A.* I.i.355)

When Titus remains unmoved, Marcus and Martius join in appealing to the ties of blood, rejection of which violates the natural affections which hold society together.

Marcus: Brother, for in that name doth nature plead, –
Martius: Father, and in that name doth nature speak, –

(*Tit. A.* I.i.370)

Their kneeling before him, and the substance of their entreaty, prepare the way for a similar scene in *Coriolanus* many years later, as does Aaron's attitude towards his new-born child. When Demetrius seeks to 'broach the tadpole on [his] rapier's point',[35] the Moor defends him energetically:

He dies upon my scimitar's sharp point
That touches this my first-born son and heir...
My mistress is my mistress; this my self;
The vigour and the picture of my youth:
This before all the world do I prefer;
This maugre all the world will I keep safe.

(*Tit. A.* IV.ii.107)

He intends to bring him up 'To be a warrior and command a camp' (*Tit. A.* IV.ii.181). Volumnia takes Coriolanus' young son with her on her mission to save Rome, addressing the father in not dissimilar terms:

This is a poor epitome of yours,
Which by th'interpretation of full time
May show like all yourself.

(*Cor.* V.iii.68)

The idea of transmitting one's own selfhood through lineal succession loomed large in a Roman father's mind, as it seems to have done in Shakespeare's own. Lucius is a 'Brave slip, sprung from the great Andronicus' (*Tit. A.* V.i.9), a horticultural image that Shakespeare will develop at length in late plays such as *The Winter's Tale*. When Lucius is 'unkindly banished' from mother Rome, his plight again calls Coriolanus to mind. 'What hast thou done, unnatural and unkind?' (*Tit. A.* V.iii.48)

24

cries Saturninus when Titus stabs Lavinia, his own daughter, and his words here foreshadow Mark Antony's bitter jibe in his famous funeral oration:

> Through this the well-beloved Brutus stabb'd;
> And as he pluck'd his cursed steel away,
> Mark how the blood of Caesar follow'd it,
> As rushing out of doors to be resolv'd
> If Brutus so unkindly knock'd or no...

> (*Caes.* III.ii.178)

It is the hideously unnatural assault upon the associated notions of kinship and kindness which concerns Shakespeare, reaching its hysterical climax in the *Thyestean* feast when Tamora is induced 'to...swallow her own increase,'[36] 'Eating the flesh that she herself hath bred' (*Tit. A.* V.iii.62).

Even *Titus Andronicus*, for all its butchery, is not entirely negative in outlook but occasionally exalts the values of kinship in a more positive way. The ties of family sometimes hold firm in the face of all that can be hurled against them. Marcus and Lucius, for example, offer their own hands in place of Titus' when Aaron treacherously promises to accept this as a ransom for the lives of his two sons.

> *Lucius*: Sweet father, if I shall be thought thy son,
>   Let me redeem my brothers both from death.
> *Marcus*: And for our father's sake, and mother's care,
>   Now let me show a brother's love to thee.

> (*Tit. A.* III.i.179)

Quintus, similarly, joins his brother, Martius, in the pit rather than leave him to a solitary fate: 'Thou canst not come to me: I come to thee.' (*Tit. A.* II.iii.245). Many of the speeches in *Titus* are stiff and formulaic, but when the verse does quicken with the pulse of genuine emotion it is usually provoked by the touching of this kinship nerve.

Any such tender sentiments, however, are qualified by the fact that 'kind Rome' is also 'ambitious Rome',[37] and ambition is a quality towards which Shakespeare is always ambivalent. Too often it leads to the violence we experience in this play, as it does, for instance, in *Richard III* and *Macbeth*. Machiavelli pointed out that,

> Whenever men do not have to fight from necessity they fight from ambition, which is so strong in the human heart that it never leaves them, however high the station they reach. The reason is that Nature

so created men that they can desire everything yet cannot obtain everything.[38]

Excess of *ambitio* can turn men into beasts. In this blood-drenched drama with its casual callousness – exemplified by the flippant tone of remarks such as: 'his limbs are lopp'd'[39] – it is often hard to discern the difference between Roman 'nobility' and Gothic brutality. Whenever we think of *Titus Andronicus* it is the image of the raped and mutilated Lavinia that predominates. She looms before our horrified gaze as a hideous symbol of disorder, unrivalled in Shakespearean drama at least until the blinding of Gloucester in *King Lear*. At the end of the play, however, chaos gives way to a civilised order as Rome returns to strong, authoritarian government.

For all its obvious deficiencies, *Titus Andronicus* does point the way forward towards the latter, more accomplished Roman works, as the following examples illustrate. *The Rape of Lucrece*, as we have seen, has close affinities with Lavinia's story. Indeed Shakespeare three times draws the parallel directly.[40] We find *Julius Caesar* anticipated, albeit dimly, in the discussion about the political succession that begins the play. Titus' preoccupation with his sense of honour finds a distant echo in Marcus Brutus, both men experiencing the loneliness that stems from their brand of steely idealism:

> Even now I stand as one upon a rock
> Environed with a wilderness of sea.

> (*Tit. A.* III.i.93)

Brutus' attempt to ritualise Caesar's assassination – 'Let's carve him as a dish fit for the gods' (*Caes.* II.i.173) may also find its origin in the earlier play.

The seductive charms of the 'changing piece',[41] Tamora –

> ...this queen,
> This goddess, this Semiramis, this nymph,
> This siren that will charm Rome's Saturnine
> And see his shipwreck and his commonweal's –

are, of course, a pale shadow of Cleopatra's, but both women hold their Roman lovers in thrall and wield, through them, a powerful and catastrophic influence on events.

The similarity between Lucius' exile and Coriolanus' is remarked upon by Aemilius in Act IV,[42] both men returning intent on battle against ungrateful Rome. The later play seems already to be germinating in

Shakespeare's mind and Titus' sheer physical courage and battle-hardness are a still more obvious prototype for Caius Martius. Each shows a genuine reluctance to put on the traditional garb of the candidate for high political office,[43] yet each is deeply conscious that his claim to such elevation is well attested by the scars he bears:

> Hear me, grave fathers! noble tribunes, stay!
> For pity of mine age, whose youth was spent
> In dangerous wars, whilst you securely slept;
> For all my blood in Rome's great quarrel shed...

> > (*Tit. A.* III.i.1)

When, towards the end of *Titus Andronicus*, Marcus makes his speech of reconciliation before an audience of assembled Romans and Goths, another ringing call for harmony suggests itself:

> Set we forward: let
> A Roman and a British ensign wave
> Friendly together.

> > (*Cym.* V.v.480)

The words are Cymbeline's. Their longing for order and unity to spread their balm upon a nation's wounds awakens a distant echo of the first Roman play. In these two very different works, at opposite ends of Shakespeare's career, it is notable that in each case bloodshed – and even decapitation – yields at the last to concord as the *Pax Romana* is reimposed.

> You sad-fac'd men, people and sons of Rome,
> By uproars sever'd, as a flight of fowl
> Scatter'd by winds and high tempestuous gusts,
> O, let me teach you how to knit again
> This scatter'd corn into one mutual sheaf.

> > (*Tit. A.* V.iii.67)

Notes

1. See Geoffrey Bullough: *Narrative and Dramatic Sources of Shakespeare Vol. VI* (London, 1966).

2. I.i.30.

3. For example, Virgil: *Aeneid* 1.19-22, 1. 234f. and 6.756f.

4. That is to say the First Quarto edition, published in 1594.

5. *Romanitas* – 'the Roman way', as used, e.g., by Tertullian in *De Pallio* 4 (AD 209).

6. For example, by H.T. Price: *The Authorship of Titus Andronicus, Journal of English & German Philology* XLVII.

7. IV.iv.81-7.

8. For a detailed account of this subject see J.A.K. Thomson: *Shakespeare and the Classics* (Allen & Unwin, 1952).

9. 'Be it right or wrong.' Another example is *Suum cuique* ('to each his own') I.i.280.

10. See I.i.182-5. 'Candidatus' means, literally, 'dressed in white'.

11. IV.i.47.

12. *Terras Astraea reliquit* ('the goddess of justice has left the earth'). *Metamorphoses* I.150. See *Tit. A.* IV.iii.4.

13. Heptameters or 'fourteeners' as they were sometimes called.

14. *MND.* V.i.261-95.

15. Aaron's speech at the beginning of Act II provides perhaps the best example.

16. See, particularly, ll. 1734-46.

17. IV.i.81-2.

18. Horace: *Odes* I 22.1-2.

19. See, for example, V.iii.80-7. 'The fatal engine' is a literal translation of Virgil's *fatalis machina* (*Aeneid* II. 237) as J.A.K. Thomson points out.

20. For example, IV.i.62 and IV.i.90.

21. *The Art of War* Book VII, trans. Peter Whithorn (London, 1588) p. 106. I am indebted to J.C. Maxwell for this quotation.

22. II.iii.296.

23. *Caes.* II.i.127.

24. III.i.154.

25. See Livy 2.12.

26. The *mos maiorum* is discussed more fully in ch. 8.

27. A decree forbidding human sacrifice was issued as late as 97 BC (Pliny NH 30.i.12) but there is no suggestion that the practice was current towards the end of the Empire, the period where *Titus* is located.

28. I.i.291.

29. *Pietas* is discussed in ch. 7.

30. Titus' ravings about the fly (III.ii.52-67) make an interesting parallel with Lear's more cogent ramblings at IV.vi.112.

31. V.ii.175.

32. Livy 3.44-58.

33. In, respectively, *Wint., MND., Rom., AYL.* and *Oth.*

34. I.i.23.
35. IV.ii.85.
36. V.ii.190. Note the similar image in *Ham.* I.ii.144.
37. I.i.165 and I.i.132.
38. *Discourses* 1.3.
39. I.i.143.
40. II.i.108; IV.i.64; IV.i.91.
41. I.i.309.
42. IV.iv.68.
43. See *Tit. A.* I.i.82 and *Cor.* II.iii.114, for instance.

2

Lucrece and Chastity

The Rape of Lucrece, written, it would seem, in 1593, reveals Shakespeare's continuing fascination with the brutal collision between masculine lust and female chastity, a theme which will feature prominently in *Much Ado, Measure for Measure, Othello, Pericles, Cymbeline* and *The Winter's Tale. Titus Andronicus* paved the way for the narrative poem with its specific references to Lucrece[1] in addition, of course, to the hideous fate of Lavinia who survives rape and mutilation only to be murdered by her own father on the grounds that, unlike the dutiful wife of Collatine, she no longer has hands with which to turn the knife against herself.

> Die, die Lavinia, and thy shame with thee;
> And with thy shame thy father's sorrow die!

> (*Tit. A.* V.iii.46)

Collatine – like Posthumus in Shakespeare's last Roman play, *Cymbeline* – boasts of his wife's matchless chastity. Both husbands regard themselves as the keepers of this 'honour', seeing it as a precious jewel to be locked away from 'lust, the thief'.[2] Neither, however, can resist the temptation to parade the precious object in front of their companions, in what amounts to a vicarious flaunting of female charms. We are told, for example, how Collatine

> ...in Tarquin's tent
> Unlock'd the treasure of his happy state:
> What priceless wealth the heavens had him lent
> In the possession of his beauteous mate...

> (l. 15)

He appears oblivious to the well known truth that

> Honour and beauty in the owner's arms
> Are weakly fortress'd from a world of harms

(l. 28)

and unwisely becomes

> ...the publisher
> Of that rich jewel he should have kept unknown
> From thievish ears, because it is his own.

(l. 33)

Iachimo reminds Posthumus, in similar terms, that chastity is, by its very nature, highly vulnerable. A modern audience is likely to take strong exception to the stress upon property and ownership.

> You may wear her in title yours: but you know strange fowl light upon neighbouring ponds. Your ring may be stolen too: so your brace of unprizable estimations, the one is but frail and the other casual; a cunning thief, or a (that way) accomplished courtier, would hazard the winning both of first and last.

(*Cym.* I.iv.85)

Posthumus' reply – 'nothwithstanding, I fear not my ring' – is reminiscent of the quibbling couplet with which Gratiano brings *The Merchant of Venice* to a close:

> Well, while I live, I'll fear no other thing
> So sore as keeping safe Nerissa's ring.

In the latter case the husband seems less sanguine as to his prospects of success. Like Iachimo, he takes it for granted that all women are, at heart, promiscuous. Iago shares this jaundiced view of the sex, urging upon Othello the notion that a woman's

> ...honour is an essence that's not seen;
> They have it very oft that have it not.

(*Oth.* IV.i.15)

At length the Moor is persuaded of Desdemona's infidelity:

O 'tis the spite of hell, the fiend's arch-mock
To lip a wanton in a secure couch
And to suppose her chaste.

(Oth. IV.i.73)

Again the predominant image is of failed custodianship.

Throughout Shakespeare's works the contemplation of chastity's collapse provokes, in the male mind, the most violent revulsion. The maligned Hero becomes, in the eyes of her accusers, 'a rotten orange' to be cast away. As far as they are concerned

...she is fall'n
Into a pit of ink, that the wide sea
Hath drops too few to wash her clean again.

(Ado. IV.i.140)

To Lear, in his 'madness', women

But to the girdle do the gods inherit,
Beneath is all the fiends';
There's hell, there's darkness, there is the sulphurous pit –
Burning, scalding, stench, consumption...

(Lear IV.vi.124)

The tormented Leontes avers that many a husband

...holds his wife by th'arm
That little thinks she has been sluic'd in's absence
And his pond fish'd by his next neighbour...

(Wint. I.ii.190)

Most, seemingly, would agree with his terse axiom: 'No barricado for a belly!'[3]

Unbridled lust is generally depicted by Shakespeare as not only violent and predatory but also intrinsically self-deceptive and unfulfilling, as Tarquin recognises himself, though the thought does nothing to deflect him from his purpose.

What win I if I gain the thing I seek?
A dream, a breath, a froth of fleeting joy.
Who buys a minute's mirth to wail a week
Or sells eternity to get a toy?

(RL. 211)

This idea is pursued to its devastating conclusion in *Sonnet 129* in which the poet, victim of his own sexual obsession, contemplates in horrified humiliation a monstrous rebellion of the flesh that he is quite unable to control.

> The expense of spirit in a waste of shame
> Is lust in action; and, till action, lust
> Is perjured, murderous, bloody, full of blame,
> Savage, extreme, rude, cruel, not to trust;
> Enjoy'd no sooner but despised straight;
> Past reason hunted, and no sooner had,
> Past reason hated, as a swallow'd bait
> On purpose laid to make the taker mad:
> Mad in pursuit and in possession so;
> Had, having, and in quest to have, extreme;
> A bliss in proof, and proved, a very woe;
> Before a joy proposed; behind a dream.
> All this the world well knows; yet none knows well
> To shun the heaven that leads men to this hell.

Even more alarming, it might be argued, is a female propensity to endorse this savage masculine credo. Pushed to its extremest form – all logic and common sense left far behind – such self-denigration leads women to feel branded with a badge of infamy at having been raped. As far as Lucrece is concerned, pollution is pollution.

In pre-republican Rome, according to Livy, the concept of *castitas* was harshly simple.[4] What mattered was the material fact of unauthorised sexual intercourse. Such questions as motivation, culpability and volition were scarcely relevant. Coppélia Kahn points out in her essay on the poem[5] that we are in the realm of primitive taboo where codes are stark and unequivocal. Lucrece's course is clear. Like any Roman matron her honour exists not in its own right but as an extension of her husband's. Her husband's honour, in turn, is inextricably bound up with the 'purity' of his genealogy – a matter of assured patrilineal descent. Upon such interweavings of patrician lineage and kinship rests, ultimately, the stable structure of Roman society itself. Bastards must therefore be eliminated at all costs lest the stock be defiled. What, to a later age, seems a fundamental moral distinction between rape and adultery was, in this early patriarchal context, supremely irrelevant since biology declined to differentiate the outcome.[6]

Lucrece's rape is thus, in these terms, a violation of her husband Collatine's honour, just as Lavinia's impugns the honour of the Adronici.

She speaks of her 'offences', 'guilt', 'sin', 'disgrace' and 'shame' (ll. 747-56) as though she had taken an illicit lover. Having wronged her husband she must, of course, atone. Her suicide, like Cleopatra's, serves a multiple purpose. In her case, first, she exorcises her personal shame, washing away with her own blood the stigma of moral pollution. She reaffirms, thereby, her identity as a Roman wife and her validity as a vessel for the transmission of the male line and the social values this implies. In preserving her husband's status she safeguards his honour, the integrity of his family and hence posterity itself. By her death she seeks to re-establish order and thereby to buttress the foundations upon which Rome is built although, ironically, the revenge upon the House of Tarquin that it occasions is instrumental in overthrowing the monarchy and setting up the new Republic, which can hardly have been what she had in mind. Though little dwelt upon, this aspect of the poem may be said to foreshadow the central conflict of the next work in the sequence, *Julius Caesar*.

The sanctity of marriage with its contract of wifely obedience was a matter that Roman society took very seriously as we see in this passage from Livy which Shakespeare would almost certainly have read in William Painter's famous translation of 1566.[7]

> What can be wel or safe unto a woman when she hath lost her chastity? Alas Collatine, the steppes of an other man be now fixed in thy bed. But it is my bodye only that is violated, my minde God knoweth is giltles whereof my death shalbe witnesse.... Then every one of them...comforted the pensive and languishing lady...affirming that her bodye was polluted and not her minde...whereunto shee added: '...for my part, though I cleare my selfe of the offence, my body shall feel the punishment: for no unchast or ill woman shall hereafter impute no dishonest act to Lucrece'. Then she drewe out a knife, which she had hidden secretely, under her kirtle, and stabbed her selfe to the harte.

Rape and adultery are held to be indistinguishable in their physical consequences. Lucrece's mind is innocent but she regards her body as guilty and it therefore seems to her perfectly appropriate that her body should suffer the consequences. If the punishment for an adulteress was death[8] then so harsh a reprisal did not seem disproportionate to the offence. An illegitimate offspring might mean her husband's discontinuity, his severing from his own posterity, in itself a kind of death.

Chastity was a fundamental Roman value in that it validated the family, the city and the state. The word 'virtue', its common synonym, reminds us, in its derivation from *vir*, that despite pertaining exclusively to women in this context it exists within the realm of masculine power, confirming the male's physical domination of their world. It may be thought of, by anatomical analogy, as an interiorisation of the male's more 'outward' role in society. Lucrece's impassioned *eloquentia* may be seen, in its turn, as the feminine counterpart to the physical power she is denied, although in her suicide she partakes in the cult of *virtus* in a way which is, by tradition, the province of men, as does Portia, Brutus' wife, when she swallows fire.

Sexual promiscuity, on the part of women at least, threatens the idea of paternal power which underlies the larger concept of patriotism essential to the continuity of Rome. Something of its importance can be seen in the cult of Vesta, goddess of the hearth and, by extension, of the home and family. Sacrifices were made to the Penates or gods of the household, microcosm of that great family of citizens, the Roman state. The living symbol of Vesta was an eternal flame kept burning on private hearth or temple altar. Significantly the six priestesses who tended the fire at the public sanctuary in the Forum were carefully chosen for their chaste purity and sworn to virginity during their years of service. So solemn was the oath of celibacy enjoined upon them that its violation meant burial alive. And if chastity was thus sanctified, then by extension so must be the family and therefore, ultimately, the state.[9] Daily ritual reinforced these notions, being passed on down the generations until the original significances were but dimly understood.

With the advent of Christianity the idea of chastity was diverted into new channels. In part a revulsion against what Christians regarded as the sexual excesses of the Roman aristocracy, it was closely related to the doctrine of the Virgin Birth and Christ's own chosen state of celibacy. Members of Christian religious orders, like the Hindu holy men and many others, renounced the flesh as an outward expression of their spiritual dedication. As St Jerome put it:

The vow of virginity is the noblest of all vowes because the hardest: the divel's master-point lies in our loines.[10]

Indeed St Paul had asserted, three centuries earlier, that sexual intercourse was the vehicle of original sin and therefore tainted necessarily with guilt and shame. By Shakespeare's time, however, attitudes had begun to change. Castiglione wrote of using 'the bridle of reason [to] restrain the ill disposition of the sense'[11] and this thorniest of the virtues was viewed, by some at least, in a negative light. In *Hero and Leander*, Marlowe wrote:

Men foolishly do call it virtuous.
What virtue is it, that is born with us?
Much less can honour be ascribed thereto;

Honour is purchased by the deeds we *do*.

(ll. 277-80)

Venus and Adonis, another poem inspired principally by Ovid, reverses the traditional pattern of wooing and presents us with a frustrated goddess whose attempted seduction of the beautiful youth is doomed to failure:

All is imaginary she doth prove;
He will not manage her, although he mount her:
That worse than Tantalus' is her annoy,
To clip Elizium and to lack her joy.

(*V & A* ll. 597-600)

In her thwarted ardour Venus wittily invokes the iconography of the sacred cult:

Therefore, despite of fruitless chastity
Love-lacking vestals and self-loving nuns,
That on the earth would breed a scarcity
And barren dearth of daughters and of sons,
Be prodigal; the lamp that burns by night
Dries up his oil to lend the world his light.

(*V & A* ll. 751-6)

For Roman Lucrece, the 'virtuous monument',[12] the issue of chastity was unambiguous. Her course was clear and she scarcely hesitated. In a Christian ethos the dilemma is more complex. As early as the 5th century St Augustine had argued that chastity was a virtue of the mind rather than the body and that the intention to sin was therefore the determining factor. From this viewpoint Lucrece was blameworthy only in that she committed suicide. Interestingly, chastity as a moral virtue figures prominently in about a third of Shakespeare's plays and is, for the most part, seen as a positive force for good – an attitude perhaps not so surprising in a writer whose patron was the Virgin Queen herself!

Of the two quite distinct sense of the word – celibacy and faithful monogamy – it is the latter which features more frequently. However, in *Measure for Measure*, perhaps Shakespeare's most probing examination of the issue, the two great Christian virtues, *castitas* and *caritas*, are weighed up in so far as they concern a novice nun who has dedicated her virginity to God. Isabella's contract, like those that faithful wives make with their husbands, holds firm against the depredations of Angelo, the irony of whose name does not pass unnoticed. It is, in the pithy phrase of

J.W. Lever, 'a terrible encounter of absolutes'.[13] Isabella's 'consecrated wall'[14] holds firm, nevertheless, as is the case in the vast majority of Shakespearean instances. In these plays it becomes the responsibility of the women to control the rampaging sexual impulse of the male and, of the major characters, only Cressida can be said to fail, although Gertrude and Cleopatra would win few prizes for their continence. Only evil women like Goneril, as Dr French has pointed out,[15] seek to assert their right to sexual freedom by moving into the realms of male power and they pay for their temerity with their lives.

Cuckoldry is a key Shakespearean theme and the invisible horns provide the Elizabethan stage with its greatest standing joke. It is, for the unfortunate victim, the equivalent of a humiliating military defeat. Aufidius' servant remarks that 'Peace is...a getter of more bastard children than war's a destroyer of men' and his colleague endorses the viewpoint:

> 'Tis so, and as war in some sort may be said to be a ravisher, so it cannot be denied but that peace is a great maker of cuckolds.

> (*Cor.* IV.v.230-5)

Roman and Tudor attitudes to chastity as expressed in their writings – male generated in both cases – seem to have been remarkably similar, each culture seeing the issue almost exclusively in terms of masculine property and power. We find this obsession with ownership strikingly illustrated in the laments of the grieving husband and father over the much abused body of Lucrece.

> Then one doth call her his, the other his,
> Yet neither may possess the claim they lay.
> The father says, 'She's mine'. 'O mine she is',
> Replies her husband, 'do not take away
> My sorrow's interest; let no mourner say
> He weeps for her, for she was only mine,
> And only must be wail'd by Collatine'.

> 'O', quoth Lucretius, 'I did give that life
> Which she too early and too late hath spill'd'.
> 'Woe, woe', quoth Collatine, 'she was my wife;
> I ow'd her, and 'tis mine that she hath kill'd'.
> 'My daughter' and 'my wife' with clamours fill'd
> The dispers'd air, who holding Lucrece' life
> Answer'd their cries, 'my daughter' and 'my wife'.

> (*RL.* ll. 1793-806)

The exchange may strike us as ludicrous in these circumstances but elsewhere the assault upon chastity often brings with it some terrifying images. Othello's anguish reaches cosmic heights:

Methinks it should be now a huge eclipse
Of sun and moon and that the affrighted globe
Should yawn at alteration.

(*Oth.* V.ii.100)

Macbeth's walk towards Duncan's chamber, the weapon in his hand, is rendered doubly hideous by the analogy with 'Tarquin's ravishing strides' towards Lucrece's bed.[16] Yet, for all the hysteria occasioned by male contemplation of chastity's overthrow, the slandered wives all vindicate themselves, even if one of them, Desdemona, must do so posthumously.[17]

Closely linked to these issues of chastity and constancy is the point that in Shakespeare bastards are a dangerous breed. As outsiders the Don Johns and the Edmunds seek to disrupt, to break through the fabric that excludes them into the centrality they are denied. That precious natural bond uniting parent and legitimate offspring is deemed lacking in their case. 'In the lusty stealth of nature', however, they take

More composition and fierce quality
Than doth, within a dull, stale, tired bed,
Go to the creating a whole tribe of fops
Got 'tween asleep and wake.

(*Lear* I.ii.12)

It is a prospect threatening to the established order, but what Posthumus calls 'the bond of chastity'[18] in fact holds firm in nearly every instance, implying the coherence not only of the family unit but of the wider social order. Indeed in Othello's celebrated appeal to the 'chaste stars'[19] we may find this ideal of constancy extended, by implication, to embrace the physical universe as a whole.

Notes

1. See note 40, ch. 1.

2. l. 690.

3. *Wint.* I.ii.204.

4. For a detailed examination of this subject see J. Balsdon: *Roman Women* (Bodley Head, 1962) pp. 25-9.

5. *The Rape in Shakespeare's Lucrece, Shakespeare Survey* 9, p. 45.

6. There were, naturally, important *legal* distinctions between rape and adultery. Jane Gardner discusses this topic in *Women in Roman Law and Society* (Croom Helm, 1986).

7. Included in *The Pallace of Pleasure*, a miscellany of prose tales taken principally from Roman and Italian writings. The extract quoted is from I.LVIII.

8. Augustus' *Lex Iulia de Adultoriis* of 18 BC allowed a father to execute a daughter caught *in flagrante delicto*. A husband was directed to divorce an adulterous wife on pain of his own death or banishment.

9. See Pliny 4.11 on Vestal Virgins and the relationship between *castitas* and *sanctitas*.

10. The quotation is taken from Montaigne's essay *Upon some verses of Virgil* in the John Florio translation (Dent edition, 1897) Vol. V, p. 123.

11. *The Courtier* trans. Thomas Hoby (1561) Tudor Translations (London, 1905) pp. 345-6.

12. l. 391.

13. Arden edition (Methuen, 1965) p. lxix.

14. *RL*. l. 723.

15. *Shakespeare's Division of Experience* (Abacus/Sphere, 1983).

16. II.i.55.

17. One thinks in particular of Hero, Hermione and Imogen (although Hero is, of course, a few moments short of wifehood when she is wrongfully accused).

18. *Cym.* V.v.206.

19. V.ii.2.

3

Caesar and Caesarism

In the six years or so that follow the writing of *Lucrece* thoughts of Rome were never very far from Shakespeare's mind. We hear, for example, Petruchio describing Katherina as a 'Roman Lucrece for her chastity'[1] and Bassanio referring to his friend Antonio as

> ...one in whom
> The ancient Roman honour more appears
> Than any that draws breath in Italy.

> (*Mer.V*. III.ii.297)

The English history plays in particular contain dozens of Roman allusions, the majority of them to the violent end of the Republic and to those who helped to bring about its fall. There were many parallels to be drawn between the struggles of York and Lancaster and the civil wars that saw the establishment of the Empire under Octavian. When, in 1599, Shakespeare turned again to Roman history it was to this period and to these prodigious men.

Julius Caesar differs markedly from the two earlier works previously discussed. Characters now possess a three-dimensionality that we do not find in *Titus Andronicus*. They are racked with doubts. They behave with the inconsistency of the real world. It is the mature Shakespeare now at work. His attitude to his theme has become ambivalent, shot through with glittering threads of irony.

> Stoop Romans, stoop,
> And let us bathe our hands in Caesar's blood
> Up to the elbows and besmear our swords:
> Then walk we forth, even to the market place,

40

And waving our red weapon o'er our heads,
Let's all cry, 'Peace, freedom and liberty!'

(Caes. III.i.106)

From the chronicler of St Albans, Towton, Tewkesbury and Bosworth Brutus' words have a wry equivocality that would not have been lost on a Tudor audience. In the lines that follow, Shakespeare skews events towards still giddier ironies.

Stoop then and wash. How many ages hence
Shall this our lofty scene be acted over,
In states unborn and accents yet unknown!

(Caes. III.i.iii)

The effect is compounded in as much that, within a year or so, the first actor to play Caesar will appear again on the stage of the Globe Theatre, this time in the part of Polonius,[2] and will reminisce:

I did enact Julius Caesar. I was killed i' th' Capitol. Brutus killed me.

(Ham. III.ii.102)

If the actor playing the part of Hamlet was the original Brutus – as seems highly likely – then, of course, the fact that Polonius is destined soon to die on the Prince's sword must add still further layers of irony to the scene.

A similar instance of this new ironic view to the future occurs when Cleopatra fears for her reputation and for her lover's.

The quick comedians
Extemporally will stage us, and present
Our Alexandrian revels: Antony
Shall be brought drunken forth, and I shall see
Some squeaking Cleopatra boy my greatness...

(Ant. V.ii.215)

The device serves a number of purposes. In one sense it can be said to distance the event so that we see it as though from the wrong end of a telescope, the remoteness imparting to the scene an exotic glamour, a heightened sense of awe. It also helps to provide a frame which brings the characters into sharper focus, thus enhancing their heroic stature and dignity. And yet, paradoxically, there is a foreshortening effect as well. The figures are brought up close to us and, shrunk to the size of actors as

41

they are, we the more easily share in their common humanity. Shakespeare employs the tactic again in *Henry V*, the Chorus apologising to the audience for the Globe's inadequacies:

> And so our scene must to the battle fly;
> Where – o for pity! – we shall much disgrace
> With four or five most vile and ragged foils,
> Right ill-disposed in brawl ridiculous,
> The name of Agincourt. Yet sit and see,
> Minding true things by what their mock'ries be.

(H.V IV Prol. 48)*

There is about the playwright's later vision of Rome a sense of grandeur and purpose that we do not find in *Titus* or *Lucrece*. Plutarch, his principal source, believed in a divine providence protecting the City and its people[3] and Shakespeare shares his sense of the numinous. *Julius Caesar* reverberates to supernatural rhythms. Omen, presentiment, soothsaying, portent, augury, dreams and nightmares, ghosts and spirits, 'genius', storm and stars are woven into the fabric of the play. The predominant imagery suggests weight, expansiveness, quantity and stature. We see 'Tiber tremble underneath her banks' and

> Th'ambitious ocean swell and rage and foam
> To be exalted with the threat'ning clouds.

(Caes. I.iii.7)*

Men stare up at a sky which is 'painted with unnumer'd sparks.'[4] Casca has only to point his sword and

> ...the sun arises
> Which is a great way growing on the south,
> Weighing the youthful season of the year.

(Caes. II.i.106)*

Portia speaks of setting 'a huge mountain 'tween [her] heart and tongue',[5] while Antony imagines that Caesar's every wound will move 'The stones of Rome to rise and mutiny.' *(Caes.* III.ii.232). Octavius feels himself surrounded by 'millions of mischiefs'[6] while Brutus finds the sum of Cassius' faults 'as huge as high Olympus.'[7] Caesar himself is 'the foremost man of all this world'[8] and liable to 'soar above the view of men'[9] unless the feathers are plucked from out his wing. In the memorable words of Cassius:

...he doth bestride the narrow world
Like a colossus and we petty men
Walk under his huge legs and peep about...

(Caes. I.ii.133)

The night before his death we are told that

...all the sway of earth
Shakes like a thing unfirm.

(Caes. I.iii.3)

The most vivid account of these events is given by that would-be Roman, Horatio, on the battlements of Elsinore:

In the most high and palmy state of Rome,
A little ere the mightiest Julius fell,
The graves stood tenantless and the sheeted dead
Did squeak and gibber in the Roman streets;
As stars with trains of fire and dews of blood,
Disasters in the sun; and the moist star,
Upon whose influence Neptune's empire stands,
Was sick almost to doomsday with eclipse.

(Ham. I.i.116)

These and other passages convey a sense of superhuman scale. The known world is the stage. 'There is', as Brutus tells us, 'a tide in the affairs of men'.[10] Its currents push them towards a personal destiny that is also Rome's. They take on, thereby, a *gravitas*, a solemnity that at times comes close to ponderousness. There were elements of this in *Titus Andronicus* too, but in *Julius Caesar* we find as well a human dimension largely absent from the earlier play. The 'full sea' of lofty ventures now has an ironic undertow that moves us away from heroism, history and decision towards vacillation, petulance and self-deception. Even great men may prove fallible. On the verbal level we lurch between fiery rhetoric and mere verbosity. Abstract, high-sounding principle jars uncomfortably against expediency and the contingent.

Julius Caesar himself is an enigma. Few characters in Shakespeare have stirred more fierce controversy among the critics. No-one, not even Hamlet, dominates his play as comprehensively as he does. The name itself rings out more than two hundred times.[11] In the second half, Caesar dead is as potent a force as Caesar living, his *genius* controlling events as Brutus had feared it would before he killed him.

43

O that we then could come by Caesar's spirit
And not dismember Caesar.

(*Caes.* II.i.69)

On the losing field of Philippi Brutus is forced to the wry acknowledgement: 'O Julius Caesar thou art mighty yet!' (*Caes.* V.iii.94). In fact the aura surrounding Caesar is what matters in this play. He associates himelf with grandiloquent images such as lions and stars. He is surrounded by followers who talk of him with awe-struck deference. 'Peace ho! Caesar speaks!' shouts Casca and Antony tells us that 'When Caesar says 'Do this', it is perform'd' (*Caes.* I.ii.10). Caesar habitually refers to himself in the third person as though a disembodied beholder of his own vast consequence. 'Speak. Caesar is turn'd to hear' (*Caes.* I.ii.17). Of the twenty verbs he utters during his brief first appearance exactly half are in the imperative mood, a pattern that is typical of what follows. He even dies with a self-command upon his lips, as John Velz points out in his essay on the play.[12]

So huge a shadow does Caesar's presence cast it is hard to believe how small his role is in the literal sense. Of the play's eighteen scenes he appears (alive) in only three. He speaks a mere 146 lines, or less than 6% of the play's total. Brutus, by contrast, is given 679. Past and future are his elements,[13] and yet he is a kind of permanent, standing present.

For always I am Caesar.

(*Caes.* I.ii.209)

In the very next line, however, we see him as fallible man rather than disembodied principle: 'Come on my right hand for this ear is deaf' (*Caes.* I.ii.210). It may be that Shakespeare intends to undercut, ironically, the impression of political colossus established previously. We should however bear in mind the picture Plutarch gives us – one to which in general Shakespeare adheres with striking fidelity:

...he always continued all labour and hardiness, more than his body could bear...but yet therefore yielded not to the disease of his body...but...took the pains of war as a medicine...fighting always with his disease.[14]

Perhaps by his references to Caesar's deafness and epilepsy Shakespeare seeks to humanise an otherwise remote and forbidding figure. Only in Cassius' anecdotes of the Tiber swim and the Spanish fever[15] are such frailties dealt with unsympathetically. Neither occurs in Plutarch and it seems likely that Shakespeare intended them to be taken as calumnies indicative of Cassius' spite and envy rather than as a means to discredit Caesar in the eyes of the audience.

A more tenable criticism of the man concerns his apparent vacillation in Act Two. For all his claims to be 'unshak'd of motion' and 'constant as the northern star'[16] he changes his mind several times on the question of his attendance at the Senate House before deciding 'Caesar shall forth', adding that 'death, a necessary end/Will come when it will come'[17] – a sentiment which has about it the calm, acquiescent strength that one associates with Stoicism. We find a similar sentiment, a year later, in the last act of *Hamlet*, the wording of which makes it highly probable that Shakespeare still had *Julius Caesar* in mind. The circumstances too are very similar. Horatio offers to deliver the Prince's excuses for his non-appearance at court, pleading sickness on his behalf. Hamlet responds:

Not a whit. We defy augury. There is a special providence in the fall of a sparrow. If it be now, 'tis not to come; if it be not to come, it will be now; if it be not now, yet it will come. The readiness is all. Since no man, of aught he leaves, knows aught, what is't to leave betimes? Let be.

(*Ham.* V.ii.215)

Like Horatio, Hamlet seems often to be 'more an antique Roman than a Dane.'[18] Caesar too dismisses augurers, refusing to give way to superstition. He yields only when Calphurnia, who has had bad dreams, beseeches him on bended knee, to stay at home. As Shakespeare presents the scene, the change of heart stems purely from a loving concern for the sensibilities of his wife. It is 'for [her] humour'[19] and shows an unexpected tenderness in Caesar's nature endearing him to us rather than earning our scorn. As an example of *pietas* – a value that embraced the reverence due to family in admitting their rightful claims – the incident looks forward to Coriolanus' famous submission, near the end, to his wife and mother. *Pietas* was, in point of fact, personified on coins as a dignified Roman matron very much in the Calphurnia mould.

It is to Caesar's credit that, like Hamlet, he refuses to plead an imaginary illness, saying bluntly:

The cause is in my will: I will not come;
That is enough to satisfy the Senate.

(*Caes.* II.ii.71)

News of the proffered crown, however, is enough to change his mind, together with the taunt that 'Caesar is afraid.'[20] The power of *ambitio* is broached. Shakespeare seems to have accepted Plutarch's belief that ambition was Caesar's great motivating passion:

> …the chiefest cause that made him mortally hated was the covetous desire he had to be called king: which first gave the people just cause, and next his secret enemies honest colour, to bear him ill will.[21]

The word 'ambition' resonates in this text,[22] its pejorative connotations seemingly taken for granted by everyone. As Cymbeline puts it in the Romano-British play:

> Caesar's ambition
> Which swell'd so much that it did almost stretch
> The sides o'th'world, against all colour here
> Did put the yoke upon's.

> *(Cym. III.i.49)*

Tamora's sons, we recall, showed a similar distaste for 'ambitious Rome'.[23] Like the Roman commentators,[24] Shakespeare is deeply mistrustful of ambition. We find it, for the most part, in the wicked. Iago is perhaps the best illustration of what Brutus claims to be the

> …common proof
> That lowliness is young ambition's ladder.

> *(Caes. II.i.21)*

Macbeth conceded that he has

> …no spur
> To prick the sides of [his] intent, but only
> Vaulting ambition, which o'erleaps itself,
> And falls on the other.

> *(Mac. I.vii.24)*

Wolsey provides a particularly spectacular example of what can happen to the ambitious.[25] In a delightful image Buckingham claims that

> No man's pie is freed
> From his ambitious finger.

> *(H.VIII I.i.52)*

46

Later in the play the penitent Cardinal urges people to learn by his example:

> Cromwell, I charge thee, throw away ambition:
> By that sin fell the angels.

(H.VIII III.ii.440)

Rarely is ambition viewed in a favourable light – a striking difference between Shakespeare's day and ours. It is surely significant that his most celebrated creation, Hamlet, is so signally lacking in ambition, though in their conversation upon the subject it falls to Guildenstern to point out that 'the very substance of the ambitious is merely the shadow of a dream'.[26]

Looking at Roman history through Greek eyes, Plutarch saw Caesar's usurped power as *tyrannis* in that he put himself outside the law. The word 'tyranny' did not always carry the connotations we now attach to it, but many political philosophers from the time of Plato onwards, and writing after the advent of the democratic city-state, regarded such regimes as odious. Plutarch insists that Caesar deprived his fellow citizens of their rights although Caesar himself claimed to have done the precise opposite. But whatever the truth of this, his power, like that of other memorable Shakespearean characters, was both won and lost at the blade's point.

Even before defeating Pompey militarily in 48 BC[27] Caesar had become *dictator* – an office originally intended as a temporary magistracy in time of national crisis. It was not subject to veto or appeal but limited to a maximum period of six months. This stipulation Caesar ignored. In 46 BC he extended his powers for a further ten years, using the precedent set by Sulla some thirty years earlier. In 44 BC he had himself voted dictator for life, thus jeopardising the prospect of a return to constitutional rule. His enemies claimed that he sought to establish a hereditary monarchy but there seems to be little evidence for this.

The Greek concept of the 'tyrant' was rendered, rather loosely, into Latin as *rex*, a word with powerfully negative associations in rebublican Rome recalling, as it did, the hated Tarquins of long ago. This *rex*, in turn, was translated into English – again somewhat misleadingly – as 'king'. In the German language Caesar's own name has come to stand as *Kaiser* for one modern idea of 'emperor'. It is revealing that, in *Henry V* (written, it should be noted, in the same year as *Julius Caesar*) Shakespeare describes Henry's triumphant return from Agincourt in terms of a scene from Roman history:

> The mayor and all his brethren in best sort,
> Like to the senators of the antique Rome,

With the plebeians swarming at their heels,
Go forth and fetch their conquering Caesar in.

(H.V Chor. V.25)

The explicit linking together of the two great military leaders in this way suggests that Shakespeare was tempted to regard Caesar, whatever the rights and wrongs of his climb to power, as a king in all but name.

For centuries Romans had believed in a shared political wisdom. Now there came among them a man who sought to be more than *primus inter pares*. Like Marius and Sulla before him, he wielded *imperium* or supreme administrative power, taking *Imperator* as a cognomen. Indeed after his death Caesar was proclaimed a god, thus ironically vindicating Cassius' bitter jibe.[28] This apotheosis – and the stellar imagery he associated with it – had been in Shakespeare's mind for years as evidenced by a comment in an early History play when Bedford, at the funeral of Henry V, declares:

A far more glorious star thy soul will make
Than Julius Caesar...

(1H.VI I.i.55)[29]

It is not difficult to see why the Renaissance attitude towards Caesar contained unresolved inconsistencies. Erasmus, though praising Caesar for his strength of will, regarded him as a manifest despot. As far as he was concerned the only fit man to rule was one who assumed office with the greatest reluctance. Luther and Montaigne, among others, held him the enemy of liberty and a man, furthermore, greatly swayed by flattery and ambition. Once established in power, however, it was generally conceded that Caesar ruled wisely. Although his authority remained unchallenged for little more than a year, he did bring about a number of important reforms. His assassination plunged Rome into chaos and was therefore widely regarded as an appalling deed. Dante went so far as to consign Brutus and Cassius to the lowest depths of his *Inferno* along with Judas Iscariot.

Sir Thomas Elyot in *The Governor* (1531) observed:

The best and most sure governance is by one king or prince, which ruleth only for the weal of his people.

(I.ii)

As another great upholder of the monarchic principle and, therefore, the legitimate acquisition and transmission of power that this entailed, Shakespeare must have been torn in his sympathies. Though, like most of his contemporaries, clearly admiring Brutus, he seems, in the end, to condemn the conspiracy on the grounds that the toleration of a *de facto* 'king' (if he governed wisely) was preferable to civil war – for the Tudor establishment the greatest of all evils. He shows a similar attitude towards Henry Bolingbroke, coming, in due course, to regard his success in stabilising the realm as at least partial mitigation for the sin of Richard's usurpation and murder. As Charles Merbury wrote in a tract of 1581:

> It is not sufficient that...a prince be descended lineally and lawfully into his kingdom, but he must also possess and exercise such royal and princely powers therein as is most fit for his worthiness and for his subjects' happiness.[30]

Clearly Richard failed to fit the bill. Shakespeare was able, however, to combine the pragmatism of a Warwick –

> Are these things then necessities?
> Then let us meet them like necessities. –

> *(2H.IV* III.i.92)

with, when it suited him, a clear-eyed belief in the divine attributes of kingship that was the very model of Tudor orthodoxy. Thus the catastrophic consequences of Caesar's murder may be seen as in some sense analogous to those that followed Richard's killing in Pomfret Castle. He might well have gone on to draw a further parallel between the eventual triumphs of Octavius Caesar and Henry Tudor, each issuing in a long period of peace and successful government after the horrors of bloody internal strife. Suffolk's words in *Henry VI Part Two* add weight to these impressions:

> Come soldiers, show what cruelty ye can,
> That this my death may never be forgot.
> Great men oft die by vile bezonians.[31]
> A Roman sworder and banditto slave
> Murder'd sweet Tully;[32] Brutus' bastard hand[33]
> Stabb'd Julius Caesar; savage islanders
> Pompey the Great; and Suffolk dies by pirates.

> *(2H.VI* IV.i.132)

The lines, it is true, were written about 1590 and Shakespeare's perception of these complex issues evolved and deepened over the next nine years. There seem to be strong indications, however, as to where his fundamental sympathies lay.

In the person of Caesar – viewed both as man and as institution – Shakespeare identifies three particular qualities which struck him as epitomising the Roman. The first of these may be described as a combination of dignity and authority, though neither word appears in the text.[34] According to Montaigne: 'The greatest thing in the world is to know how to be sufficient unto oneself.'[35] Like Coriolanus, Caesar possesses this total self-belief and from it draws a massive *auctoritas*. The word, which has a long republican tradition behind it, finds its roots in *auctor* or 'originator', hence implying a sense of continuity that is, as we have seen, peculiarly Julian. In the constancy of his public, stellar self we may see reflected the 'eternity' of the Roman people. In its human guise, however, *constantia* is closely akin to obstinacy and pig-headedness. Again like Coriolanus, Caesar lacks the ability to compromise. Both men take pride in their intransigence:

> Hence! Wilt thou lift up Olympus?
>
> (*Caes.* III.i.74)

> I will not do't
> Lest I surcease to honour mine own truth.
>
> (*Cor.* III.ii.121)

They regard themselves as ramparts against anarchy, believing that they can distance themselves from the heat of the moment by seeking refuge in aloof, frozen solidification:

> Be not fond
> To think that Caesar bears such rebel blood
> That will be thaw'd from the true quality
> With that which melteth fools....
>
> (*Caes.* III.i.39)

They are mistaken, just as Othello is mistaken in imagining that he can dismiss his love for Desdemona and become as icily inexorable as the Pontic Sea (*Oth.* III.iii.453).

Auctoritas amounted to that innate quality of leadership bestowed by nature upon relatively few in any age. Its possessor often acquired a *dignitas* which depended, crucially, upon others' perception of his worth. This could all too easily be forfeited. Caesar crossed the Rubicon to defend his dignity, claiming that it was dearer to him than life itself.[36] Unfortunately, as Frank Adcock tellingly expresses it, 'his *dignitas* took up too much room and left too little for the *dignitas* of others.'[37] And if others fail, or cease, to accord one *dignitas* the common response is an attempt to appropriate it to oneself, rendering the aspirant peculiarly vulnerable.

Affronted dignity has, of course, enormous comic potential as we see, for example, in Mercutio's baiting of the Nurse; in Dr Caius' challenge to Sir Hugh Evans and in the debunking of Malvolio's cross-gartered posturings.[38] But the misappropriation of authority is far from a laughing matter. *Coriolanus* addresses the political aspects of this issue. In despising the tribunes or 'tongues o'th'common mouth' because 'they prank them in authority', Coriolanus does not necessarily speak for Shakespeare, but his awareness that

> ...when two authorities are up,
> Neither supreme,...confusion
> May enter 'twixt the gap of both...

> (*Cor*. III.i.109)

is one the playwright certainly endorsed, as the Roman plays illustrate with great clarity.

On a more personal – and painful – level the question of authority and its abuses is a major preoccupation of the group of plays written immediately after *Julius Caesar*, that is to say between 1599 and 1605. Hamlet's soliloquy speaks of

> The insolence of office and the spurns
> That patient merit of the unworthy takes.

> (*Ham*. III.i.73)

Lear asks Gloucester whether he has 'seen a farmer's dog bark at a beggar', adding:

> And the creature run from the cur? There thou might'st behold
> The great image of Authority:
> A dog's obeyed in office.

> (*Lear* IV.vi.152)

Measure for Measure gives the theme its sternest examination. The unfortunate Claudio declares authority to be a 'demi-god' and we may uneasily remember the deified Caesar. The most celebrated words on the subject fall to Isabella:

> But man, proud man,
> Dress'd in a little brief authority,

51

> Most ignorant of what he's most assur'd –
> His glassy essence – like an angry ape
> Plays such fantastic tricks before high heaven
> As makes the angels weep.

(Meas. II.iii.118)

The image of the ape pranked absurdly in its human garb looks forward four years to Coriolanus' tribunes and a further century or so to Jonathan Swift's Yahoos.

A second – and contrasting – value that Shakespeare associates with Caesar is *clementia*, a blend of mercy, generosity and forebearance. Unlike his autocratic predecessor Sulla, Caesar forged a reputation for clemency.[39] He would release and even promote captured troops who had fought against him and appeared unconcerned if they made war upon him a second time. Since he possessed the supreme power to be *un*forgiving if he so chose, many felt his forgiveness to be arbitrary and even condescending, amounting to a 'kingly munificence'[40] that became notorious. It was, they argued, more a matter of calculatedly ostentatious gesture than of genuine compassion. The fact that Caesar had the word *clementia* stamped upon his coinage goes some way towards substantiating the claim. Cicero described it as *insidiosa clementia* or 'treacherous mercy.'[41]

Caesar himself regarded his clemency as a strength, saying in a letter: 'Let this be the new thing in our victory, that we fortify ourselves by mercy and generosity.'[42] Shakespeare's picture of Caesar is, in fact, a lot warmer than Plutarch's.

> Good friends, go in and taste some wine with me;
> And we, like friends, will straightway go together.

(Caes. II.ii.126)

There is, of course, a sharp, unconscious irony in these words to the murderous faction arrived to escort him to the Senate House but they do not suggest the cold, austere despot that some detect in Shakespeare's characterisation of the man. Shortly afterwards we watch Caesar dismiss Artemidorus' warning letter with the words:

> What touches us ourself shall be last served.

(Caes. III.i.8)

Magnanimous or merely magniloquent? It is possible to play it either way. Caesar's largesse, however, is unequivocal. Ransomed prisoners helped to fill Rome's 'general coffers' – a *clementia* redoubled, so to speak – and his will leaves to all Romans, and to their heirs in perpetuity,

> ...his walks,
> His private arbours and new-planted orchards
> On this side Tiber.

(Caes. III.ii.249)

Clemency as flamboyant gesture is an important element in Antony's make-up too, as we see in his treatment of Enobarbus, whose treasure chest he sends on to him after his desertion, causing him to commit suicide in remorse. It is, as we noted earlier, ironic that it should be the barbarian, Tamora, who voices the sentiment that: 'Sweet mercy is nobility's true badge' (*Tit. A.* I.i.119) and the Roman Titus who rejects it out of hand. In *Timon of Athens* Alcibiades seeks to persuade the senators that

> ...pity is the virtue of the law
> And none but tyrants use it cruelly.

(Tim. III.v.8)

It is a position endorsed, it must surely be, by Shakespeare himself and two plays in particular – *The Merchant of Venice* and *Measure for Measure* – are much concerned with debating the relative claims of mercy and justice. Clemency, of its very nature, cannot be compelled. Portia tells Shylock that 'mercy...is enthroned in the hearts of kings' and indeed is 'an attribute to God himself,' giving to her words additional force with the reflection that

> ...in the course of justice, none of us
> Should see salvation.

(Mer.V. IV.i.189)

The most impassioned defence of mercy is delivered by Isabella. Angelo, reasonably enough, points out the dangers inherent in making 'a scarecrow of the law' and even concedes that

> The jury passing on the prisoner's life
> May in the sworn twelve have a thief or two
> Guiltier than him they try.

(Meas. II.i.I & 19)

Isabella accepts the logic of this argument but counters it with her own impassioned one:

No ceremony that to great ones longs,
Not the king's crown nor the deputed sword,
The marshal's truncheon, nor the judge's robe,
Become them with one half so good a grace
As mercy does.

(Meas. II.ii.59)

To Angelo's cold riposte that her brother, Claudio, is 'a forfeit of the law' and she is, therefore, simply wasting her words, Isabella calls to her aid the message of the Gospels:

Alas, alas!
Why all the souls that were were forfeit once
And He that might the vantage best have took
Found out the remedy. How would you be
If He, which is the top of judgement, should
But judge you as you are? O think on that,
And mercy then will breathe within your lips,
Like man new made.

(Meas. II.ii.72)

It is a very un-Roman sentiment, but she follows it with an aphorism that might almost have sprung from Caesar's lips:

O it is excellent
To have a giant's strength, but it is tyrannous
To use it like a giant.

(Meas. II.ii.108)

Yet condign punishment, legitimately administered, must sometimes displace mercy. This much is clear. Shakespeare's concern is with the watershed that divides the two. Law underpins social order. It is perhaps Rome's greatest single bequest to Western civilisation.[43] Nevertheless, for all its stabilising function, law can change with bewildering frequency as Montaigne, for one, observed:

Nothing is more subject unto a continuall agitation than the lawes. I have since I was borne seene those of our neighbours the Englishmen changed and rechanged three or foure times.... Nay, I have seene amongst our selves some things become lawfull which erst were deemed capitall.[44]

Isabella expresses what is presumably Shakespeare's own revulsion towards those, like Angelo, who bid

> ...the law make curtsey to their will,
> Hooking both right and wrong to th'appetite
> To follow as it draws.

(Meas. II.iv.174)

This vision of justice perverted by crooked power, with its paradoxical and terrifying implications of distorted order and toppled stability, is one that Shakespeare returns to many times but, like most such dilemmas, it is not, in the end, resolved.

The third of the great Roman values epitomised in Caesar and explored by Shakespeare was known in Latin as *fides*. It was the dictator's great boast, as Cicero tells us in *De Officiis*,[45] that he was Caesar and would keep faith. He saw himself as patron of the Roman state and *fides* as the bond of trust and loyalty that tied him to his people. It was their guarantee that his power would not be abused. This sense of duty and scrupulousness was to be expected in those endowed with *dignitas* and was maintained, Caesar declared, by an imperviousness to bribes or flattery. This is demonstrated in his contemptuous rejection of Metellus Cimber's grovelling sycophancy, which he dismisses as

> Low-crooked curtsies and base spaniel fawning.

(Caes. III.i.43)

He insists that his decree of banishment must stand since, being Caesar, he cannot go back on his pledged word – a word which, Antony reminds the citizens in his funeral oration, 'stood against the world.'

> If thou dost bend and pray and fawn for him,
> I spurn theee like a cur out of my way.

(Caes. III.i.45)

Shakespeare, it seems, loathed nothing more than flattery. It is an itch that he cannot scratch too often. Iago speaks approvingly of those (*Oth.* I.i.50)

> Who, trimm'd in forms and visages of duty,
> Keep yet their hearts attending on themselves.

All Roman aristocrats would have been familiar with obsequiousness since every morning their 'clients' – a group of officially recognised hangers-on who sought advancement from their wealthy patrons in return for ritualistic gestures of respect and other services – would assemble outside their houses for the ceremony of *salutatio*. Cassius' servile kneeling on behalf of Metellus' brother Publius earns the resonant reply:

> I could be well mov'd, if I were as you;
> If I could pray to move, prayers would move me;
> But I am constant as the northern star,
> Of whose true-fix'd and resting quality
> There is no fellow in the firmament.

> > (*Caes.* III.i.58)

In this firm resolution to keep faith Caesar resembles Brutus who had earlier rejected Cassius' demand for an oath by asking, rhetorically:

> > What other bond
> Than secret Romans that have spoke the word
> And will not palter? and what other oath
> Than honesty to honesty engag'd?

> > (*Caes.* II.i.113)

The antithesis of this fidelity may be found in that particular brand of political opportunism and expediency that the Bastard in *King John* calls 'commodity'.

> > ...that sly divel,
> That broker, that still breaks the pate of faith,
> That daily break-vow,...
> That smooth-fac'd gentleman, tickling commodity,
> Commodity the bias of the world...

> > (*John* II.i.56)

In the golden world of the romantic comedies, however, we find another sort of faith:

> Two bosoms interchained with an oath,
> So then, two bosoms and a single troth.

> > (*MND.* II.ii.48)

Through all vicissitudes Lysander's words to Hermia hold true. All too often elsewhere, however, it is the cynicism of a Pistol which prevails.

> For oaths are straws, men's faiths are wafer-cakes,
> And Holdfast is the only dog, my duck!

(H.V II.iii.52)

Fides, the Roman personification of good faith, had for her symbol a pair of clasped hands betokening consent in the just wielding of power. How ironic, therefore, that the assassins' first gesture after the murder should be to bathe their hands in Caesar's blood.

> Thus pour the stars down plagues for perjury!

(LLL. V.ii.394)

Berowne says to Rosaline, and his image calls to mind once again the stellar constancy of Julius Caesar.

Notes

1. *Shr.* II.i.298.

2. This is, admittedly, suppositional but fits well with all the available evidence.

3. See, for example, Plutarch: *Coriolanus 3*.

4. III.i.63.

5. II.iv.7.

6. IV.i.51.

7. IV.iii.91.

8. IV.iii.22.

9. I.i.74.

10. IV.iii.217.

11. In fact Caesar's name is used 209 times. By comparison Hamlet's is used about 80 times in *his* play, which is nearly twice as long.

12. *Clemency, Will and Just Cause in Julius Caesar, Shakespeare Survey* 22.

13. Note, for example, the many anecdotes about his former life (e.g., I.ii.99-127) and the importance of prophecy in the play.

14. *Life of Caesar* trans. Sir Thomas North. Modernised by W. Skeat (Macmillan, 1875) p. 57.

15. I.ii.99-127.

16. III.i.60-70.

17. II.ii.10 and 36.

18. V.iii.346.

19. II.ii.56.

20. II.ii.101.

21. As for note 14 above.

22. 'Ambition' and 'ambitious' occur, between them, a dozen times in the play.

23. *Tit. A.* I.i.32.

24. See, for example, Sallust's *Bellum Iugurthinum.*

25. Other prominent characters brought low by ambition include Lady Macbeth, Richard III, Claudius, Edmund and Malvolio.

26. II.ii.257.

27. Caesar became Dictator in 49 BC after the Battle of Ilerda.

28. I.ii.114.

29. The idea of Caesar's stellification apparently stems from Pliny. See his *Naturalis Historia* 1:94.

30. *A Brief Discourse of Royal Monarchy as of the Best Commonweal,* p. 40.

31. A 'bezonian' was an ignorant, worthless person (probably from Spanish *bisoño* – a raw recruit).

32. 'Tully' was a common Tudor name for (Marcus Tullius) Cicero. See also, for example, *Tit. A.* IV.i.14.

33. Brutus was rumoured to have been Caesar's illegitimate son since his mother, Servilia, became Caesar's mistress. The suggestion was almost certainly false. Caesar was only about fifteen when Brutus was born (ca. 85 BC).

34. Apart, that is, from 'dignities' in the sense of 'positions of importance', which occurs at III.i.178.

35. *Essays* I.xxxix.

36. See Ronald Syme: *The Roman Revolution* (Oxford University Press, 1939) p. 48.

37. *Roman Political Ideas and Practice* (University of Michigan Press, 1959) pp. 67-8.

38. *Rom.* II.iv.100-41; *Wiv.* III.i.1-116; *Tw. N.* III.iv.16-126.

39. See, for example, Plutarch's *Life of Caesar* 230-3 and 256-7. Caesar even erected a Temple of Clementia. Despite this carefully cultivated reputation, however, Caesar supposedly killed a million Gauls between 58-51 BC. (Plutarch: *Caesar*, ch. 15).

40. See L.R. Taylor: *Party Politics in the Age of Caesar* (University of California Press, 1949) p. 171.

41. *Ad Atticum* 8.16.2.

42. *Ad Atticum* 9.7.1.

43. Codified by Justinian in AD 523, Roman law forms the basis of

legal systems throughout the world.

44. *An Apologie of Raymond Sebond* (Dent, 1897 edn) Vol. IV, p. 39.

45. *De Officiis* 1.7.

4

Brutus and the Stoic Temperament

Shakespeare's picture of Brutus has stirred almost as much controversy among the critics as his portrayal of Julius Caesar, a fact which no doubt reflects the widely divergent views of the historical figure himself. By his contemporaries Brutus was much admired. Plutarch's profile is, again, the one which largely coloured Shakespeare's own.

> Brutus framed his manners of life by the rules of virtue and study of philosophy, and having employed his wit, which was gentle and constant, in attempting of great things, me thinks he was rightly made and framed unto virtue.... Brutus, being in Pompey's camp, did nothing but study all day long.... The self-same day before the great battle of Pharsalia...when others slept, or thought what would happen the morrow after, he fell to his book, and wrote all day long till night.... [He] did always incline to that which was good and honest.... By flattering him a man could never...make him do that which was unjust.... Brutus, for his virtue and valiantness, was beloved of the people...and hated of no man, not so much of his enemies.[1]

To the modern mind there is something peculiarly repellent in the idea of a man stabbing his friend – indeed the man who had spared his life and promoted him[2] – in pursuit of a political ideal. The typical Roman viewpoint was different, Brutus' actions being seen not as betrayal but rather as evidence of a lofty disinterestedness which most found admirable.

Not all, however, were equally impressed. Cicero, for one, took issue with Brutus on several important occasions, feeling that his cold intellectuality ignored the promptings of the human heart.[3] This position was endorsed by a later Roman, St Augustine, who held that reason and emotion were, properly, inseparable. To disengage the mind from the body and its feelings, as Stoicism required, was for him a very dangerous thing to attempt.[4]

By the Middle Ages literary opinion had swung against Brutus and the conspiracy. Chaucer, for instance, in *The Monk's Tale*, has nothing but praise for Caesar:

> By wisedome, manhede and by greet labour
> From humble bed to roial magestee
> Up roos he, Julius the Conquerour,
> That wan al th'occident by land and see,
> By strength of hand, or elles by tretee.

(ll. 3861, Robinson edn)

These qualities aroused in others feelings of inferiority and malice.

> Brutus...
> That ever hadde of his hye estaat envye
> Ful prively hath maad conspiracye
> Agayns this Julius in subtil wise...
> And in the Capitol anon him hente,
> This false Brutus and his oother foon,
> And striked hym with boydekyns anoon.

(ll. 3887-97)

Chaucer is here following the line expressed so vigorously by Dante.[5] Renaissance commentators, by and large, redressed the balance. Humanism brought with it a revival of interest in the old Stoic doctrines. *De Constantia*, by the Flemish thinker Justus Lipsius, was translated into English by Sir John Stradling in 1594 under the title *Two Bookes of Constancie*. It reasserted the primacy of reason, fortitude and self-reliance, qualities that fitted well with the new cult of aspiring individualism exalted by playwrights such as Marlowe and Chapman. Lipsius argued that 'the nearest man can have to God is to be immovable'.[6] Guillaume Du Vair's *Moral Philosophie of the Stoicks* was translated into English by Thomas James and published in 1598, the year before *Julius Caesar*. It may well have influenced Shakespeare's thinking about Brutus since it reaffirms the view that honour is not something external that we can gain as our reward for virtuous deeds – which is very much how Aristotle saw it – but rather something intrinsic to us, an innate regulator of conduct that is, essentially, personal and subjective.

Honour doth wholly depend on us. If we once forsake it, we do but fasten the rest of our minds upon the opinion of the vulgar…and love not virtue but as the common people do love and favour it.[7]

The French King in *All's Well That Ends Well*, speaking of Bertram's father, says:

> …his honour
> Clock to itself, knew the true minute when
> Exception bid him speak.

> (*All's W*. I.ii.39)

The mechanism here referred to is that same instinctive impulsion that motivates Brutus. It never occurs to him to doubt its validity. His soliloquy on the subject of murder is strikingly at variance with Macbeth's. 'It must be by his death', he begins, and goes on over the next two dozen lines to justify the deed, apparently believing that nothing can be evil if performed by an 'honourable' man, a self-fulfilling prophecy, as it were, that we find echoed in his tautologous words to the populace:

> Believe me for mine honour, and have respect to mine honour that you may believe.

> (*Caes*. III.ii.15)

Macbeth's agonised speech:

> If it were done when 'tis done, then 'twere well
> It were done quickly…

> (*Mac*. I.vii.i)

proceeds along very different lines containing, as it does, a sharp horror and rawness of emotion quite unknown to the cold, intellectual Roman, although the two assassins, it is true, both share the same trait of insomnia and this adds a humanising, softer touch to Brutus' somewhat flinty temperament.

Many attempts were made in the 16th century to accommodate the harsh, rigid Stoic view with Christianity and its warmer, more gentle qualities such as a stress upon forgiveness and redemptive love. To submit to reason, men argued, is, in effect, to submit to God. Certainly the Stoic idea of resignation in the face of an unyieldingly indifferent universe had much in common with the key Christian virtue of patient suffering which was held to beatify the meek. The Stoic, however, sought to make himself steel and thus become indifferent to his suffering. This squared ill with the

Christian emphasis upon conscience and the life to come. There is, for example, a hideousness about Iago's total lack of remorse and his contempt for torture at the end of *Othello*.

> Demand me nothing, what you know you know.
> From this time forth I never will speak word.

> (*Oth.* V.ii.305)

Erasmus, in *The Praise of Folly*, talks of the Stoic as 'a stony semblance of a man, void of all sense and common feeling of humanity...no more moved with love or pity than if he were a flint or rock'.[8]

Only seconds before his death Caesar points out that, in general, 'men are flesh and blood and apprehensive' (*Caes.* III.i.67), seeming to deny these qualities in himself. Ironically, his assassination shows that other men, too, seek to emulate this moral petrifaction. It is a renunciation of 'kindness' that Shakespeare will probe more deeply in *Coriolanus*.

Before the appearance of the muffled faction at his door, Brutus alludes briefly to a conflict in himself:

> Between the acting of a dreadful thing
> And the first motion, all the interim is
> Like a phantasma, or a hideous dream:
> The genius and the mortal instruments
> Are then in council; and the state of man,
> Like to a litttle kingdom, suffers then
> The nature of an insurrection.

> (*Caes.* II.i.63)

If there is a struggle, however, between mind and body, then it is never one, we feel, that the mind is in any danger of losing. Again the speech is markedly different from its counterpart in *Macbeth*.

> Why do I yield to that suggestion
> Whose horrid image doth unfix my hair
> And make my seated heart knock at my ribs,
> Against the use of nature? Present fears
> Are less than horrible imaginings.
> My thought, whose murder yet is but fantastical,
> Shakes so my single state of man
> That function is smothered in surmise,
> And nothing is but what is not.

> (*Mac.* I.iii.134)

Here the physical is very much in control. For all his murderousness, Macbeth is possessed of that lively apprehension so lacking in Brutus and is, for that reason, the more sympathetic character of the two.

This disengagement of mind from feeling is what epitomises the Stoic code. The School was founded by the philosopher Zeno towards the end of the 4th century BC. What chiefly concerned him was the pursuit of virtue as an end in itself. He had little time for the subtleties of the metaphysicians, believing that what mattered was to align the will with natural law, that Aristotelian notion of a principle of order based on reason in accordance with which the universe is regulated. The good life is thus the life led in harmony with nature or, as Christian thinkers later expressed it, the will of God. One's own personal wellbeing is of little account.

For the Stoic, perfect freedom lay in distancing oneself from bodily desires. To seek happiness is, after all, illogical since it suggests a refusal to submit oneself to the inevitable. We must die and therefore we should determine to die nobly, as Socrates taught us by example.

> Set honour in one eye and death i'th'other
> And I will look on both indifferently,

> (*Caes.* I.ii.85)

says Brutus in Act One and proves to be as good as his word. It is a heroic doctrine and from it he draws that inner, spiritual strength which Shakespeare found so characteristically Roman. Cassius sums it up:

> Nor stony tower, nor walls of beaten brass,
> Nor airless dungeon, nor strong links of iron
> Can be retentive to the strength of spirit.

> (*Caes.* I.iii.93)

The historic Brutus embraced Stoicism wholeheartedly – probably under the influence of his uncle and father-in-law Cato – even writing a treatise upon *virtus* which, unfortunately, is no longer extant.[9] Plutarch lays great stress upon Brutus' nobility, envisaging it as stemming principally from his overriding concern for the wellbeing of the Roman people as a whole. Antony's famous eulogy of him keeps very close to North's translation:

> This was the noblest Roman of them all.
> All the conspirators save only he
> Did that they did in envy of great Caesar;

He only, in a general honest thought
And common good to all, made one of them.

(Caes. V.v.68)

This lofty Roman sense of moral duty (*officium*) fitted well with the tenor of Stoic thought. Honour derived from public service in war or politics, and honour was the Roman aristocrat's principal concern. Decorum dictated that community virtues should take precedence over the cultivation of a private, self-regarding merit.[10] In Shakespeare's Brutus we find the two at odds. More inward-looking than his other Romans, Brutus confesses:

I turn the trouble of my countenance
Merely upon myself. Vexed I am
Of late with passions of some difference,
Conceptions only proper to myself...
　　　　Brutus, with himself at war,
Forgets the show of love to other men.

(Caes. I.ii.37)

A few lines later, however, he has shaken free of this reverie and is prepared to hear Cassius' proposition,

If it be aught toward the general good...
For let the gods so speed me as I love
The name of honour more than I fear death.

(Caes. I.ii.84)

In the quarrel scene of Act Four he angrily reminds his friend why Caesar had to die:

Did not great Julius bleed for justice' sake?
What villain touch'd his body, that did stab
And not for justice?...Shall we now
Contaminate our fingers with base bribes
And sell the mighty space of our large honours
For so much trash as may be grasped thus?
I had rather be a dog, and bay the moon,
Than such a Roman.

(Caes. IV.iii.19)

There is general agreement that *Henry V* and *Julius Caesar* were written in the same year – 1599 – though which is the later play is open to conjecture. It could be argued that King Henry is a reworking of the Stoic Brutus, though this time, of course, with a strong Christian overlay. Both men enjoy enormous prestige in their respective plays. Hal's words to his would-be assassins exhibit that same sense of public duty outweighing personal feeling that we find in the Roman's cast of mind:

> Touching our person seek we no revenge;
> But we our kingdom's safety must so tender,
> Whose ruin you have sought, that to her laws
> We do deliver you.

> (H.V II.11.174)

His words to Sir Thomas Erpingham in the cold dawn of Agincourt have about them a Stoic ring that recalls the battlefield of Philippi.

> 'Tis good for men to love their present pains
> Upon example; so the spirit is eased.

> (H.V IV.i.18)

In Henry, though, we find a warmth and humanity lacking in the austere Brutus whose coldness is a matter of remark. Cassius observes, not without irony, that he is glad his

> ... weak words
> Have struck but thus much show of fire from Brutus,

> (Caes. I.ii.73)

suggesting that his friend lacks the emotional spontaneity which most regard as a humanising trait. Brutus himself concedes that he

> ...carries anger as the flint bears fire
> Who, much enforced, shows a hasty spark
> And straight is cold again.

> (Caes. IV.ii.110)

Caesar too possessed an icy self-control. Cimber's 'couchings' and 'lowly courtesies' 'Might fire the blood of ordinary men' (*Caes.* III.i.37) but his own, he suggests, is not to be so easily 'thaw'd from [its] true quality.'[11] As far as Brutus is concerned it is that political abstraction, the justice of the republican cause, that must

> ...bear fire enough
To kindle cowards.

> (*Caes.* II.i.120)

His reaction to the news of his wife's violent death makes an interesting parallel with Macbeth's.

> Why farewell, Portia. We must die, Messala.
> With meditating that she must die once
> I have the patience to endure it now.

> (*Caes.* IV.iii.189)

It is an exemplary demonstration of Stoic self-control and the messenger – who had earlier enjoined him to bear the truth 'like a Roman' – is struck with admiration at his calm:

> Even so great men their losses should endure.

> (*Caes.* IV.iii.192)

Cassius declares that his own 'nature could not bear it so' and we think the better of him for the admission.

Macbeth's bleak response, on receiving similar news:

> She should have died hereafter:
> There would have been a time for such a word,

> (*Mac.* V.v.17)

leads him into the great 'tomorrow' meditation upon the meaninglessness of human existence which is, in its own way, a statement of the Stoic creed, expressing, as it does, contempt for suffering and resignation to the natural law. Yet it contains a dark grandeur and a sense of infinite weariness and pain that is totally outside Brutus' more limited emotional range.

The irony of Portia's mode of death should not escape us. Her swallowing of hot coals may be seen, symbolically, as a reproach to her husband for his cold neglect of her need for physical affection in his high-minded pursuit of abstract political truths. 'The conquerors can but make a fire of him' (*Caes.* V.v.55) says Strato, looking down at his master's corpse. Only after death, it seems, can Brutus be set aflame!

With Henry it is very different. On the eve of Agincourt he goes about the camp, talking to the common soldiers and boosting their morale with the effect

That every wretch, pining and pale before,
Beholding him, plucks comfort from his looks.
A largess universal like the sun
His liberal eye doth give to every one,
Thawing cold fear...

(*H.V* IV Chor. 41)

Unlike Brutus, Henry understands what it is to be afraid but controls his fear 'lest he, by showing it, should dishearten his army'.[12] His rejection of the 'idol ceremony',[13] with its 'poison'd flattery', is Stoical in temper, as is his determination to fight on against overwhelming odds. In his case, however, he has put his trust in a 'God of battles' to whom he has prayed fervently for deliverance.

Living, as he did, before the coming of Christ, Brutus, of course, is denied Henry's hope of salvation. He dies, like many of Shakespeare's other tragic heroes, in a hopelessness made magnificent by valour.

I merely choose what history foretells

says the Brutus of Roy Fuller's *The Ides of March*. Through his Stoic acceptance of his fate we feel an exaltation of the human spirit. There is a haunting quality about his words over Cassius' corpse:

I shall find time, Cassius, I shall find time.

(*Caes.* V.iii.103)

It is as though, with his dying, something finite is released into infinity.

Notwithstanding its heroic qualities, however, Shakespeare is aware of Stoicism's inconsistencies and limitations. It is all very well to urge that pain is of no consequence in itself and that the 'virtuous' man can rise above it, but experience teaches differently. Leonato, for one, declares that he

...will be flesh and blood;
For there was never yet philosopher
That could endure the toothache patiently,
However they have writ the style of gods
And made a push at chance and sufferance.

(*Ado.* V.i.36)

Seneca's Stoicism, with its avowed indifference to the creature comforts, did not, it seems, prevent his becoming, in Roman terms, a millionaire.

Brutus' sense of Stoic honour cuts him off from contact at the human level. His moral code shows the inflexibility of a Titus and, despite the soliloquies, there is little evidence of any genuine self-doubt. Indeed at times we detect an arrogance that is reminiscent of Julius Caesar's:

> Must I budge?
> Must I observe you? Must I stand and crouch
> Under your testy humour?...
> There is no terror, Cassius, in your threats;
> For I am arm'd so strong in honesty
> That they pass by me as the idle wind,
> Which I respect not.

> (*Caes.* IV.iii.44)

He shares Caesar's habit of referring to himself in the third person.[14] In the quarrel scene there is a priggish, self-righteous note in his protestations that he 'can raise no money by vile means'[15] although he seems quite happy to spend what Cassius has acquired in such a way. It was perhaps passages like this that led Addison's Syphax, the Numidian general, to remark:

> 'Tis pride, rank pride, and haughtiness of soul;
> I think the Romans call it Stoicism.

> (*Cato* I.iv.82)

Schopenhauer found 'the Stoic sage...a wooden, stiff lay figure [who]...does not know where to go with his wisdom and...directly contradict[s] the nature of mankind.'[16]

Shakespeare uses Brutus, in part, to illustrate the limitedness of the Stoic vision and the dangers inherent in believing that the disordered will is amenable to the strictures of the theoretician.

There are striking similarities between Brutus and Hamlet, both men being unable to separate politics from ethics. Their over-cerebral attitude to life and their stubborn idealism make it difficult for them to act decisively when circumstance so demands. Men less principled, less philosophical, might have had fewer qualms about eliminating their adversaries when opportunity presented itself. Mark Antony, in the forum, stands, as he says himself, upon 'slippery ground'[17] while the kneeling Claudius affords his nephew the perfect chance 'to do it pat, now he is praying.'[18] The volatile Hamlet, though, goes often to the edge of hysteria and beyond whereas Brutus, like the would-be Roman Horatio, is self-possessed to the point of stolidity. Cassius remarks upon his 'sober form'[19] and we feel that his admiring observation upon Caesar:

69

I have not known when his affections swayed
More than his reason

(Caes. II.i.20)

applies with equal aptness to himself. This studied reasonableness we find
reflected in his spare, laconic mode of speech. Shakespeare had clearly
made some study of *eloquentia*, the classical art of public speaking, and
knew that Brutus affected the Attic style with its bluntness and lack of
ornament. His funeral address – in prose – with its dry antitheses and
clipped rationality is very different from the rousing, florid oratory of
Mark Antony and King Hal.

Brutus' celebrated ancestor had, supposedly, led the revolt against the
Tarquins, becoming the first consul of the Republic and earning for
himself the title *liberator*. This appellation Brutus seized upon in his turn,
issuing coins showing a cap of liberty between two daggers. Unsurpris-
ingly, Antony and Octavius also laid claim to the same emotive cachet. In
Brutus' case, however, his Stoic idealism led him to suppose that his cause
was self-evidently just and would be supported by all right-minded citizens. Any member of the faction who might have second thoughts about
going through with the assassination, he declared, would thereby betray
not only his fellow conspirators but his own legitimacy as a Roman:

...every drop of blood
That every Roman bears, and nobly bears,
Is guilty of a several bastardy,
If he do break the smallest particle
Of any promise that hath pass'd from him.

(Caes. II.i.36)

For a Tudor audience this idea would have contained a particular irony
since there was a popular, though erroneous, belief that Brutus was
Caesar's own misbegotten son.[20] The reproachful 'Et tu, Brute?' – which
is not in any classical source material – suggests that Shakespeare himself
may have subscribed to this view.

Whatever his beliefs on this particular point, it is clear that Shakespeare
regarded Brutus' idealism as badly flawed. He takes his stand upon the
grounds of moral purity and spotless principle but becomes, in fact, the
butcher of his friend, plunging his country into civil war as a consequence.
Remorse in him disjoins itself from power, precisely the fault of which he
held Caesar accountable and for which he murdered him.[21]

Elizabethans, by and large, saw Brutus as a tragically misguided figure,
although there were some, such as Sir Thomas Elyot, who considered him

guilty of the grossest self-deception. Like Othello, Brutus seeks to ritualise murder as if pageantry were a means towards purification.

> Let's be sacrificers but not butchers, Cassius,...
> Let's carve him as a dish fit for the gods,
> Not hew him as a carcass fit for hounds.

(Caes. II.i.173)

In so doing, he supposes, the perpetrators will be 'call'd purgers, not murderers.' But no amount of rhetoric can formalise violence into ceremony. In the words of Imbesi: 'In order for something to become clean, something else must become dirty'.[22] To put it in more banal terms, no end, Shakespeare seems to be suggesting, can ever justify such hideous means.

Perhaps the Stoic's contempt for his own pain and suffering deadens his apprehension of these things in other people. Portia feels the need to inflict upon herself 'a voluntary wound...in the thigh' as 'strong proof of [her] constancy'.[23] Such masochistic ritual, she hopes, will be something that her husband will understand. The incident is taken from Plutarch:

> This young lady, being excellently well seen in philosophy...and of a noble courage, because she would not ask her husband what he ailed before she had made some proof of herself – she took a little razor such as barbers use to pare men's nails and, causing her maids and women to go out of the chamber, gave herself a great gash withal in her thigh, that she was straight all of a gore blood; and, incontinently after, a vehement fever took her, by reason of the pain of her wound. [She said:]...'good education and the company of virtuous men have some power to reform the defect of nature. As for myself, I have this benefit moreover: that I am the daughter of Cato and wife of Brutus. This notwithstanding, I did not trust to any of these things before, until that now I have found by experience that no pain nor grief whatsoever can overcome me'.; ...Brutus was amazed...and besought the gods to give him the grace...that he might be found a husband worthy of so noble a wife.[24]

Portia's death is even more bizarre. Plutarch tells us that 'determining to kill herself...[she] took hot burning coals and cast them into her mouth and kept her mouth so close that she choked herself.'[25]

The two episodes seem to have more in common with the frenetic immolation of *Titus Andronicus* than the austere sobriety of *Julius Caesar*. By comparison the suicides of Cassius and Brutus are restrained, almost decorous affairs. Cassius shows again his fine sense of irony in utilising the very sword 'that ran through Caesar's bowels'[26] to encompass his own end. Pindarus, who holds the weapon, is enjoined rather to 'guide' the blade and to 'search' his master's bosom with it, the very different verbs suggesting a studied, dispassionate frame of mind remarkable at such a juncture. Brutus, for his part, meets his death with appropriately Stoic mien.

> Night hangs upon mine eyes; my bones would rest,
> That have but labour'd to attain this hour...
> Farewell good Strato. – Caesar, now be still;
> I kill'd not thee with half so good a will.

(*Caes.* V.v.41-51)

The Roman code of military honour was rigid and merciless, the defeated general often preferring death to public humiliation.[27] There are striking similarities with the Bushido code that evolved with the rise of the Samurai class in 12th-century Japan. Both cultures took a deep pride in their Stoicism, venerating courage and personal loyalty above life itself. Bushido – 'the way of the warrior' – fostered frugal living and the martial spirit. 'Seppuku', or ceremonial suicide by disembowelment (known, colloquially, as 'hara-kiri') was institutionalised as a respected alternative to dishonour or defeat. Only noblemen were granted this dubious privilege, the complex and hideously painful series of cuts with the Roman-style short sword demonstrating the icy self-control and almost superhuman courage of the exponent. Motives for such ritual self-slaughter included the shaming of one's enemies, a calculation not absent from the minds of Romans on a losing field. Another consideration was the need for aristocrats to exemplify virtue to the inferior classes. Confucian ethics equated the Samurai with perfect breeding, much as Renaissance humanism held up *l'uomo universale* as the ideal to which one might aspire.

Although arising from what is an essentially masculine value system, suicide was, as we have seen, by no means the exclusive province of the male. Of the sixteen instances in Shakespeare, half are carried out by women.[28] Lucrece has no doubt as to the course that she should follow:

> My honour I'll bequeath unto the knife
> That wounds my body so dishonoured.
> 'Tis honour to deprive dishonour'd life.

(*RL.* 1184)

There is, nevertheless, a feeling that the act of suicide involves, in some sense, a renunciation of the feminine. Portia's 'I grant I am a woman'[29] seems to be as much an apology for the circumstance as a concession and her subsequent actions contain an element of atonement as though, by her ghastly death, she aligns herself with her husband's machismo. Lady Macbeth and Goneril, too, renounce their genders,[30] both making away with themselves in the final scenes of their respective plays, while Cleopatra declares:

> I have nothing
> Of woman in me: now from head to foot
> I am marble constant.

> (*Ant.* V.ii.237)

Like Portia, she consciously embraces her partner's values.

> What's brave, what's noble,
> Let's do it after the high Roman fashion,
> And make death proud to take us.

> (*Ant.* IV.xv.86)

Her enemies find nothing surprising in such high-mindedness.

> Bravest at the last,
> She levell'd at our purpose, and, being royal,
> Took her own way.

> (*Ant.* V.ii.333)

Cleopatra's suicide, like those of Brutus and Cassius, contains in it a nobility which robs Octavius of his triumph. The news of her supposed death earlier shames Antony into asserting both his *romanitas* and his masculinity:

> Since Cleopatra died,
> I have liv'd in such dishonour that the gods
> Detest my baseness. I, that with my sword
> Quarter'd the world, and o'er green Neptune's back
> With ships made cities, condemn myself, to lack
> The courage of a woman.

> (*Ant.* IV.xiv.55)

Hamlet poses similar questions in his most famous speech, agonising over whether it is

> ...nobler in the mind to suffer
> The slings and arrows of outrageous fortune
> Or to take arms against a sea of troubles
> And, by opposing, end them.

(Ham. III.i.57)

Attitudes towards suicide have varied widely. The Greeks and Romans, for the most part, found it a noble deed, a proof of courage and resolution that was magnificently unequivocal. Hindu widows, by custom, once sacrificed themselves upon their husbands' funeral pyres[31] while Buddhist monks have been known to burn themselves alive as a form of social protest. Islam, Judaism and Christianity, on the other hand, all condemn suicide, believing it to be against the will of God. The early Fathers, Augustine prominent among them, evolved the canon law which decreed it sinful. In *Cymbeline* Imogen tells Pisanio:

> Against self-slaughter
> There is a prohibition so divine
> That cravens my weak hand.

(Cym. III.iv.77)

The passage is reminiscent of Hamlet's first soliloquy:

> O that this too too sullied flesh would melt,
> Thaw and resolve itself into a dew,
> Or that the Everlasting had not fix'd
> His canon 'gainst self-slaughter.

(Ham. I.ii.129)

Even Cleopatra pauses to wonder whether it might not be

>   ...sin
> To rush into the secret house of death
> Ere death dare come to us.

(Ant. IV.xv.80)

Suicide came, in due course, to infringe the criminal law as well.[32] The diggers of Ophelia's grave argue out at some length both the moral and the legal implications of the deed, entangling themselves in the bewildering technicalities of 'se offendendo' and 'crowner's quest law.'[33] Their confusion reminds us that suicide, by its very nature, has always carried with it a plethora of contradiction.

Among the ancients, some held the view that suicide was ignoble in that it sought a cowardly release from suffering. Plato, for example, condemned it in his *Phaedo*. Hamlet's central soliloquy examines two widely held but contrasting Stoic views. Should a man endure all patiently or had he, as Seneca argued,[34] the right to end his life whenever he chose? Brutus illustrates the inconsistencies in Stoic thinking. He tells Cassius that he finds it

> ...cowardly and vile,
> For fear of what might fall, so to prevent
> The time of life, arming myself with patience
> To stay the providence of some high powers
> That govern us below.

(*Caes.* V.i.106)

His next words, however, make clear that suicide is preferable to capture by his enemies.

> No, Cassius, no: think not, thou noble Roman,
> That ever Brutus will go bound to Rome;
> He bears too great a mind.

(*Caes.* V.i.III)

At the last the traditional code of the defeated general proves stronger than his determinism. 'This', as Titinius says, 'is a Roman's part.' In her despair at Antony's death, Cleopatra rejects both alternatives, neatly encapsulating the Stoic dilemma:

> Patience is sottish and impatience does
> Become a dog that's mad.

(*Ant.* IV.xv.79)

Either suicide is the supremely rational act or it is a shameful retreat under fire. Montaigne argued that it is not the length of our life that matters. 'It consists not in number of yeeres, but in your will, that you have lived long enough.'[35] As Edgar tells his father: 'Ripeness is all' (*Lear* V.ii.11).

For some, suicide is primarily a public gesture of self-vindication. In front of his horror-struck audience, Othello seeks to ritualise his own death, much as he sought to purify through ceremony the killing of Desdemona. Cleopatra meets her end dressed in her 'best attires...crown and all,' her regal pose causing Octavius to exclaim, in admiration:

> ...she looks like sleep,
> As she would catch another Antony
> In her strong toil of grace.

(Ant. V.ii.344)

Even Lucrece's blood gives an ostentatious performance.

> ...bubbling from her breast, it doth divide
> In two slow rivers, that the crimson blood
> Circles her body in on every side...

(RL. 1737)

Seneca believed suicide to be the highest expression of self-determination, the assertion of the ultimate freedom of man's will. 'One may open the road to liberty with a lancet and gain tranquillity at the cost of a mere pinprick.'[36] It is, perhaps, the *only* act that is genuinely free. As Epictetus said: 'If there is too much smoke in the house, then walk out'.[37] To the Stoic, death is not evil but an escape into, quite literally, nothing.

Shakespeare lays great stress upon this idea of suicide as liberation and peace. Lucrece's death is presented in just such terms:

> Even here she sheathed in her harmless breast
> A harmful knife, that thence her soul unsheathed;
> That blow did bail it from the deep unrest
> Of that polluted prison where it breathed.
> Her contrite sighs unto the clouds bequeathed
> Her winged sprite, and through her wounds doth fly
> Life's lasting date from cancell'd destiny.

(RL. 1723)

Juliet's breast, likewise, becomes sheath for her 'happy dagger' and Cassius is another to understand the powers of sharp steel:

> I know where I will wear this dagger then;
> Cassius from bondage will deliver Cassius.

Hamlet is well aware that

(Caes. I.iii.89)

> ...he himself might his quietus make
> With a bare bodkin.

(Ham. III.i.76)

Death for him is a 'consummation devoutly to be wished'. 'Absent thee from felicity awhile', he adjures Horatio, as though to continue living 'in this harsh world' were pain indeed.[38] Others, too, are, in Keats' words, 'half in love with easeful Death.'[39]

In *Antony and Cleopatra* dying takes on a strongly erotic connotation.[40] Antony will be

> A bridegroom in [his] death and run into't
> As to a lover's bed.

> (*Ant.* IV.xiv.95)

To Cleopatra

> The stroke of death is as a lover's pinch
> Which hurts and is desir'd.

> (*Ant.* V.ii.294)

Suffolk, faced with exile, tells Queen Margaret:

> If I depart from thee, I cannot live;
> And in thy sight to die, what were it else
> But like a pleasant slumber in thy lap?

> (*2H.VI* III.ii.387)

Suicide is the one strong, decisive, unambiguous act. It hurls defiance at fortune or, in the words of Marcus Andronicus, 'triumphs over chance in honour's bed'.[41] Death is the irrevocable absolute that so many seek. It seals for Romeo 'a dateless bargain'.[42] With the dagger Juliet takes, for the first time, power over her own life. To the Stoic the greatest thing was to be the controller of one's self. As Seneca put it: 'Let us thank God that no one can be held in life; we can trample down our constraints.'[43] Through his death Enobarbus snatches a kind of victory from what would be else ignominious betrayal and defeat. His action, like Cleopatra's, shows at last 'the cinders of [his] spirits/Through the ashes of [his] chance.'[44] Thus is our soul sealed, the heroic figure throwing down to annihilation the challenge of his or her greatness.[45]

> Be absolute for death.

> (*Meas.* III.i.5)

Vincentio's words sum up the Stoic spirit for, as Cleopatra tells us,

> ...it is great
> To do that thing that ends all other deeds,
> Which shackles accidents and bolts up change.

(Ant. V.ii.4)

It is an embracing of eternity, like Brutus' at Philippi.

Notes

1. *Shakespeare's Plutarch* edn Walter Skeat (Macmillan, 1875) *Life of Brutus*, pp. 105-30.

2. Brutus fought on Pompey's side in the Civil War but was pardoned after Caesar's victory at Pharsalus (48 BC).

3. Cicero: *Letters. Ad Brut.* (edn H. Sjögren, Uppsala, 1910).

4. See *The City of God* XIV 5.

5. See p. 48 below

6. *Two Bookes of Constancie* I.vi.

7. Edn Rudolph Kirk (New Brunswick, 1951) pp. 78-9. My attention was drawn to this passage by Norman Council's *When Honour's at the Stake* (Allen & Unwin, 1973).

8. Trans. John Wilson (Ann Arbor, 1958) pp. 46-7.

9. A few fragments of Brutus' treatise survive, such as his comment that 'it is better to be master of no-one than a slave to anyone'. See Donald Earl: *The Moral and Political Tradition of Rome* (Thames & Hudson, 1967) p. 61.

10. In practice, of course, the two would usually be linked. *Officium* came to imply an obligation and *beneficium* a favour. Reciprocity would frequently be involved.

11. III.i.41.

12. IV.i.112.

13. IV.i.246.

14. For example, at IV.iii.79 and 113.

15. IV.ii.71.

16. *The World as Will and Representation* trans. E.F.J. Payne (Gloucester, MA, 1958) p. 91. My attention was drawn to this passage by Michael Long: *The Unnatural Scene* (Methuen, 1976).

17. *Caes.* III.i.191.

18. *Ham.* III.iii.73.

19. *Caes.* IV.ii.39.

20. See note 33, ch. 3.

21. See II.i.18.

22. Quoted in *Oxymoron* by P. Hughes (Cape, 1984) p. 113.

23. II.i.300.

24. *Life of Brutus* trans. Sir Thomas North (edn George Wyndham, London, 1895) pp. 116-8.

25. Op. cit., pp. 151-2.

26. V.iii.42.

27. For example Cato after Thapsos (46 BC).

28. Lucrece, Portia, Juliet, Goneril, Lady Macbeth, Cleopatra, Iras, Charmian. (Some might add Ophelia to the list.)

29. II.i.292.

30. *Mac.* I.v.41 and *Lear* IV.ii.17.

31. This practice, known as *suttee*, was made illegal in 1829 but continued long after that date.

32. England was, in fact, the last European country to decriminalise suicide, the legislation not being passed until 1961.

33. *Ham.* V.i.9-22.

34. See, for example, *Epistles* lxx.

35. *Essays* op. cit., I.112.

36. *Epistles* 65.21.

37. *Disc.* 4.10.27.

38. V.ii.352.

39. *Ode to a Nightingale*.

40. 'Dying' was a common metaphor for sexual climax in the poetry of Shakespeare's day.

41. *Tit. A.* I.i.178.

42. *Rom.* V.iii.115.

43. *Epistles* 12.10.

44. *Ant.* V.ii.172.

45. The words are Henri Fluchère's. See *Shakespeare* (Longman, 1953) p. 51.

5

Brutus, Cassius and the Friendship Cult

Friendship, or *amicitia*, was a key Roman value both in private and in public life. Cicero's affection for Atticus is justly famous, the pair corresponding for some twenty-five years.[1] 'A singular and principall friendship dissolveth all other duties and freeth all obligations.' Montaigne, in his essay on the subject, chooses the relationship between Gracchus and Blossius to exemplify this ideal of amity.[2] 'There is nothing', Horace claims, 'that may be compared with a cheerful friend.'[3]

In its political context *amicitia* established broad communities of interest among men of affairs, imposing obligations of mutual support upon the members of each group. Roman politics was built upon such alliances of influential individuals and families, success in the quest for office depending very largely upon the number of 'friends' the aspirant could muster. Litigation, too, entailed a rallying round of one's pledged supporters, who operated much as a freemasonry network might do today, though with less secrecy and subterfuge. Such friendships were even inheritable across the generations, carrying with them bonds and duties that were regarded as sacrosanct. Often the ties were further strengthened by marriage – Antony's, for example, to Octavia and Cassius' to Tertulla, Brutus' sister.

Perhaps the most famous treatise on the subject is Cicero's dialogue *De Amicitia*, a work widely studied in Tudor grammar schools. 'Without friendship neither house nor state will endure,' he wrote,[4] and criticised the Stoic idea that the wise man seeks to cut himself off from the ties of friends and family in the belief that he should rely upon himself alone. Though recognising the importance of friends in political life, Cicero insisted that true friendship should not be based upon the giving and receiving of *beneficia*: that is to say, favours or benefits. These were no mere empty precepts. His letters to his freedman Tiro, fallen ill in Greece, reveal a painful anxiety for his humble friend's wellbeing which shows beyond question that considerations of personal advantage could not have been further from his mind.[5]

For Cassius the Epicurean,[6] *amicitia* is of central importance.

> You bear too stubborn and too strange a hand
> Over your friend that loves you,

> (*Caes.* I.ii.35)

he says reproachfully to Brutus at one point and it is clear throughout the play that, for all his 'waspish' disposition, he is the more devoted of the two. It is, significantly, the capture of his friend Titinius that prompts his suicide.

> O coward that I am, to live so long
> To see my best friend ta'en before my face.

> (*Caes.* V.iii.34)

Stoicism held far greater sway in Rome but Epicurus' philosophy won favour with a cultivated minority. The Athenian teacher spent a contented existence surrounded by his friends and pupils. Friendship, he taught, was essential if one were to live the quiet, temperate life, secure and free from fear, that he advocated as the goal of every prudent man. The physical appetites were treacherous and to be indulged – if at all – with cautious moderation. The only safe social pleasure lay in companionship and conversation.

It is perhaps for this reason that the 'spare Cassius' has 'a lean and hungry look'. Unlike Antony who 'revels long a-nights', he 'loves no plays' and 'hears no music'. He is most certainly not what Dromio, in *The Comedy of Errors*, calls 'a back-friend, a shoulder-clapper'.[7] Malcontent he may be, and bearer of a personal grudge towards Caesar that is less admirable than Brutus' loftier, more dispassionate stance, but he has in him a warmth and spontaneity that his companion lacks. Shrewd realist as he is, he is well aware that his friend walks a knife-edge between idealism and naivety. Nevertheless he allows himself, time after time, to be overruled against his better judgement, deferring to Brutus' moral authority even though his own instincts are invariably the sounder, as we see in retrospect. Is this, we may ask, the measure of true friendship? It is a question that *Julius Caesar* is at pains to explore.

The theme of friendship permeates the text, the word itself, in its various forms, occurring fifty times. The play's most famous speech opens with the pivotal words 'Friends' and 'Romans' juxtaposed. The two funeral orations contain, between them, more than twenty references to amity and love. There are many such ironies, as one would expect of a play about a man who kills his 'friend'. The most striking of these, perhaps, is Brutus' claim to have done Caesar a favour murdering him:

> So are we Caesar's friends, that have abridg'd
> His time of fearing death.

> (*Caes.* III.i.104)

A little earlier, we recall, Caesar had greeted the conspirators with the words:

> Good friends, go in, and taste some wine with me;
> And we, like friends, will straightway go together.

> (*Caes.* II.ii.126)

Even Brutus can appreciate the ironic connotations of the welcome.

> That every 'like' is not the same, O Caesar,
> The heart of Brutus yearns to think upon.

> (*Caes.* II.ii.128)

His friendship with Caesar is of the political variety whereas his relationship with Cassius has elements of both the political and the personal.

Mark Antony bears towards Caesar an 'ingrafted love'[8] which is, for Cassius, cause enough to fear him. Brutus, however, declares: 'I know that we shall have him well to friend' (*Caes.* III.i.43). There is a sharpness to Cassius' question of Antony: 'Will you be prick'd in number of our friends?' (*Caes.* III.i.216) which reverberates ominously. Did not the 'well-beloved' Brutus bestow upon his 'best lover', Caesar, 'the most unkindest cut of all'? It is, in the circumstances, hardly surprising that Antony's response should be thickened with the treacle of insincerity: 'Friends am I with you all, and love you all...' (*Caes.* III.i.220). The ironies continue to the end. Impersonating his leader amid the carnage of a bitter civil war, Lucilius proclaims:

> I am Brutus, Marcus Brutus, I !
> Brutus, my country's friend !

> (*Caes.* V.iv.8)

The battle lost, Volumnius refuses Brutus' request – 'even for that our love of old' – to turn his sword's point against him. 'That's not an office for a friend, my lord' (*Caes.* V.v.29). We may catch in the gentle reproof an echo of 'Et tu, Brute?'. Nor may we forget the Ides of March when Brutus declares, just moments before his death:

> My heart doth joy that yet in all my life
> I found no man but he was true to me.

> (*Caes.* V.v.34)

Fortunate the man, we feel, who can die with such a sentiment on his lips.

The quarrel scene of Act IV is masterly. Shakespeare presents this picture of friendship under stress in considerable detail and the variation of tone is remarkable, ranging from self-righteousness, injured innocence, pomposity and posturing through furious insult, empty rhetoric and childish contradiction to its culmination in climbdown, reasonableness and reconciliation. 'You should love your friend after you have appraised him; you should not appraise him after you have begun to love him', observed Cicero shrewdly in the *De Amicitia*.[9] 'A friend should bear his friend's infirmities' (*Caes.* IV.iii.85) points out Cassius, but Brutus replies coldly that the two are separable: 'I do not like your faults' (*Caes.* IV.iii.90). When Cassius retorts that 'A friendly eye could never see such faults,' Brutus declares such a person to be a flatterer rather than a friend. Significantly it is the choleric Cassius who backs down first.

> I said, an elder soldier, not a better:
> Did I say better?

> (*Caes.* IV.iii.56)

His face saved, Brutus is now prepared to make concessions, attributing Cassius' insults to capriciousness rather than to malice. He even shows a certain magnanimity. 'When I spoke that I was ill-tempered too' (*Caes.* IV.iii.115). It is the gesture of atonement that Cassius has been waiting for and he seizes it eagerly. 'Do you confess so much? Give me your hand' (*Caes.* IV.iii.116). Brutus' reply: 'And my heart too' resembles in its touching simplicity Miranda's to Ferdinand.[10]

The scene has been highly praised. Johnson, in his edition of the play, comments that 'the contention and reconcilement of Brutus and Cassius is universally celebrated', while Coleridge pays this glowing tribute: 'I know no part of Shakespeare that more impresses on me the belief of his genius being superhuman.'[11]

It is clear that the issue of friendship and its attendant problems fascinated Shakespeare. It is a major theme in a third of the plays and the Sonnets are largely preoccupied with exploring the poet's relationship with the Friend.

Roman moralists regarded friendship as an ultimate good in itself, particularly the camaraderie that was the exclusive province of the male. For Cicero the demands of masculine friendship were a serious matter and far outweighed the trivial concerns of womanhood. Shakespeare reflects this imbalance in the five Roman plays which feature among them only one friendship between women and even here the pair concerned – Virgilia and Valeria – are afforded just one conversation together on the stage.[12]

In Classical literature friendship and romantic love, *amicitia* and *amor*, were often felt to be in opposition one with another, a view that went back at least as far as Epicurus. Such conflicts between masculine solidarity and the seductions of the female sex appear again in medieval literature, as exemplified by Chaucer's *Knight's Tale*. Here the bond of eternal brotherhood between Palamon and Arcite survives the competition for Emily's hand. Arcite devotedly nurses his sick rival back to health before the formal combat can take place and each insists that the other have first choice of the best armour and weaponry.

> Everich of hem heelp to armen oother
> As freendly as he were his owene brother.

> (ll. 793-4)

It is a strange way of beginning a duel to the death! The dying Arcite advocates his friend's suit to Emily and we feel, at the end, that *amicitia* has triumphed over *amor*. The story, one assumes, appealed to Shakespeare since, in collaboration with John Fletcher, he dramatised it as *The Two Noble Kinsmen* (1613).

The so-called 'Friendship Cult' of Renaissance literature looks back to classical tradition, though the medieval courtly love ethic, with its very un-Roman idolatry of women, had by Shakespeare's time tilted the balance towards *amor*.

'Do not that wrong to the settled friendship of man', says Eumenides in John Lyly's *Endimion* (1591), 'as to compare it with the light affection of a woman.' But *Much Ado* tells a different tale, Claudio declaring that

> Friendship is constant in all other things
> Save in the office and affairs of love.

> (*Ado*. II.i.163)

In *The Merchant of Venice*, however, masculine friendship proves more powerful than romantic love. Bassanio's tribute to Antonio expresses the primacy of this relationship and, by implication, acknowledges the classical antecedents of the Cult.

> The dearest friend to me, the kindest man,
> The best conditioned and unwearied spirit
> In doing courtesies; and one in whom
> The ancient Roman honour more appears
> Than any that draws breath in Italy.

> (*Mer.V.* III.ii.294)

Bassanio makes his feeling still clearer when he abandons his wife on his wedding day to be with his stricken friend, assuring him that

> ...life itself, my wife, and all the world,
> Are not with me esteem'd above thy life.

> (*Mer.V.* IV.i.285)

Antonio reciprocates his feelings, causing Solanio to remark: 'I think he only loves the world for him' (*Mer.V.* II.viii.50). As A.C. Spearing puts it: '*Amor* is an all-powerful force operating on men from outside but *amicitia* is a willed human response by which man may achieve a spiritual triumph.'[13]

Implicit in such masculine comradeship as we find, for example, among the Montague entourage in Verona and the soldierly worlds of Messina and Navarre is a nervous distrust of women and the power of their sexuality,

> ...for beauty is a witch
> Against whose charms faith melteth into blood

> (*Ado.* II.i.58)

as the disconsolate Claudio affirms.

Montaigne, in his essay *Of Friendship*, sums up the difference between the two emotions:

> Her fire, I confesse it to be more active, more fervent, and more sharpe. But it is a rash and wavering fire, waving and divers: the fire of an ague subject to fits and stints and that hath but slender hold-fast of us. In true friendship it is a generall and universall heat, and equally tempered, a constant and setled heat, all pleasure and

smoothness, that hath no pricking or stinging in it, which the more it is in lustfull love, the more is it but a ranging and mad desire in following that which flies us.[14]

In *The Winter's Tale* we see the 'rash and wavering fire' of sexual jealousy overwhelm the 'constant and setled heat' of true friendship.

> Too hot, too hot!
> To mingle friendship far is mingling bloods,
>
> *(Wint.* I.ii.108)

Leontes mutters as his wife, Hermione, takes the hand of his boyhood friend, Polixenes. 'We were as twinn'd lambs that did frisk i'the sun' *(Wint.* I.ii.67), Polixenes recalls, his image carrying with it the connotations of innocence and gentle warmth that spoke the ideal of friendship in Shakespeare's mind.

The Two Gentlemen of Verona focuses upon the conflicting claims of friendship and sexual love. With elegant sophistry the aptly-named Proteus seeks to reconcile two powerful impulses, his loyalty towards his friend Valentine and his awakening lust for Silvia, Valentine's beloved.

> I to myself am dearer than a friend
> For love is still most precious in itself...
> I cannot now prove constant to myself
> Without some treachery us'd to Valentine.
>
> *(Gent.* II.vi.23)

Such a sentiment is, of course, arrant blasphemy by all the tenets of the Friendship Cult whose devotees averred that the Other must always take precedence.

> Who should be trusted now, when one's right hand
> Is perjured to the bosom?
>
> *(Gent.* V.iv.67)

demands Valentine, bitterly, and the imagery of self-alienation suggests a striking passage from Lyly's *Euphues* which sums up the value the Elizabethans placed upon friendship.

> A friend is in prosperitie a pleasure, a solace in adversity, in grief a comfort, in joy a merry companion, at all times another I.[15]

Certain of the Sonnets reveal Shakespeare himself caught painfully within a triangular situation in which he feels betrayed both by his friend and by his mistress. We find again a sense of radical dislocation as he addresses the duplicitous woman.

> Me from myself thy cruel eye has taken,
> And my next self thou harder hast engrossed.
> Of him, myself, and thee, I am forsaken;
> A torment thrice threefold thus to be crossed.

(S. 133)

Sonnet 144 deals in the harshest language with the same bifold perfidy. It is perhaps the sourest poem Shakespeare ever wrote.

> Two loves I have, of comfort and despair,
> Which like two spirits do suggest me still:
> The better angel is a man right fair,
> The worser spirit a woman colour'd ill.
> To win me soon to hell, my female evil
> Tempteth my better angel from my side,
> And would corrupt my saint to be a devil,
> Wooing his purity with her foul pride.
> And whether that my angel be turn'd fiend
> Suspect I may, yet not directly tell;
> But being both from me, both to each friend,
> I guess one angel in another's hell:
> Yet this shall I ne'er know, but live in doubt,
> Till my bad angel fire my good one out.

The sonnet is full of the coarsest *double entendre*, even suggesting, in the last three lines, that the betrayal will be revealed, in time, by the Friend's contracting syphilis from their encounter – with the added implication 'serve him right for getting involved with women!'.

For the most part, however, the Sonnets celebrate an ideal masculine friendship. Scholars have argued interminably as to whether or not the relationship was one that we would, in today's terminology, call homosexual. There can be no clear answer and the issue, in the end, is probably unimportant. What matters far more is that the poet seeks to express a union of minds which goes beyond the sensual.

> O how thy worth with manners may I sing
> When thou art all the better part of me?

87

What can mine own praise to mine own self bring
And what is't but mine own when I praise thee?

(*S. 39*)

The idea is taken, it may be, from Ovid's *Metamorphoses*[16] and derives
ultimately from Plato's belief that such partners are in themselves each
one half of a perfect totality. Portia, for example, reminds Brutus of the
'great vow' which 'did incorporate and make [them] one', referring to
herself as 'your self, your half'[17] and, in a moving account of female
friendship, Helena describes her feelings towards Hermia in similar, if
more elaborate, terms:

> We Hermia, like two artificial gods,
> Have with our needles created both one flower,
> Both on one sampler, sitting on one cushion,
> Both warbling of one song, both in one key,
> As if our hands, our sides, voices and minds,
> Had been incorporate. So we grew together,
> Like to a double cherry, seeming parted,
> But yet an union in partition,
> Two lovely berries moulded on one stem...

(*MND*. III.ii.203)

Rosalind and Celia are likewise 'coupled and inseparable' friends[18] and it
is clear that such relationships are by no means the exclusive province of
the male as far as Shakespeare is concerned.

Cicero, in *De Amicitia*, insists that friendship must be based upon an
essential parity whatever the difference in rank and status. This we find
exemplified in *Hamlet* where Horatio's devotion is unwavering despite
the fact that he is rarely given to understand the Prince's mind. The
measure of Hamlet's regard for this one rock in his turbulent 'sea of
troubles' is eloquently conveyed in the tribute he pays his friend:

> Since my dear soul was mistress of her choice
> And could of men distinguish her election,
> Sh'hath seal'd thee for herself; for thou hast been
> As one, in suff'ring all, that suffers nothing,
> A man that Fortune's buffets and rewards
> Hast ta'en with equal thanks.

(*Ham*. III.ii.63)

Other such friendships between those of widely different standing include

Hal's with Poins and Mark Antony's with Enobarbus.

There is testimony, from Ben Jonson and others,[19] as to Shakespeare's own loyalty as a friend. 'I loved the man, and do honour his memory (on this side idolatry) as much as any. He was indeed honest and of an open and free nature.'[20] No one knew better than Shakespeare the value inherent in such comradeship. We find it expressed countless times throughout the plays. 'Keep thy friend/Under thy own life's key', the Countess tells Bertram[21] and Polonius' advice to his departing son is equally cogent:

> Those friends thou hast, and their adoption tried,
> Grapple them unto thy soul with hoops of steel.

> (*Ham.* I.iii.62)

Octavius uses a similar metaphor in his discussion with Agrippa on the means to maintain concord with Antony:

> ...if I knew
> What hoop should hold us staunch from edge to edge
> O' the world, I would pursue it.

> (*Ant.* II.ii.118)

Agrippa proposes the very Roman solution of 'knitting [their] hearts with an unslipping knot'[22] through marriage with Octavia, the shortcomings of which device are shrewdly recognised by Enorbarbus, who tells Menas, with fine irony: '...you shall find the band that seems to tie their friendship together will be the very strangler of their amity.'[23]

The classical scholar Sir Thomas Elyot points out in his *Boke Named the Governour* (1531) that 'it were better to have a constant enemye than an inconstant frende.'[24]

> Blow, blow, thou winter wind
> Thou art not so unkind
> As man's ingratitude,

sings Amiens in the Forest of Arden.

> Thy sting is not so sharp
> As friend remember'd not.

> (*AYL.* II.vii.174)

It is the bitter lesson that Timon of Athens must learn. In this harsh world 'most friendship' is indeed 'feigning', as he discovers.[25] Plutarch, on whose account Shakespeare's play is based, wrote an essay entitled *How to Tell a Flatterer from a Friend*, and the distinction between the two is one that Timon fails to grasp until it is too late. The spotlight shines coldly upon one central theme, the collapse of friendship, a subject which Shakespeare must have found intensely painful for this is, surely, his most depressing play.

> Tis not enough to give:
> Methinks I could deal kingdoms to my friends
> And ne'er be weary,

(Tim. I.i.218)

announces Timon, expansively, and indulges in an orgy of wild philanthropy which is almost as alarming as its antithesis in the latter scenes. 'I am wealthy in my friends', he insists, confident that they will aid him in his hour of need. After all, as he says,

> What need we have any friends if we should ne'er have need of 'em? They were the most needless creatures living should we ne'er have use for 'em, and would most resemble sweet instruments hung up in cases, that keep their sounds to themselves.

(Tim. I.ii.93)

Like Lear, Timon must come to understand the nature of 'need'. Friendships built upon utility, as Cicero made clear, are not the most lasting kind. 'One thing can generally be said of all men: that they are ungrateful, fickle, dissimulating, cowardly, greedy of gain', wrote Machiavelli.[26] A jaundiced view, but one fully endorsed by the outcome of this play. Magnanimity, that greatest of gentlemanly virtues, collapses into overwhelming misanthropy in the last two acts as Timon's friends desert him in his bankruptcy. A chaos opens up for Timon which is even more appalling than for Othello, Lear or Macbeth because unrelieved by any gain of self-knowledge.

The betrayal of friendship is, for Timon, like the eclipsing of the sun, as though light, warmth and renewal were all to disappear from human experience.

'Men shut their doors against a setting sun' *(Tim.* I.i.141) warned Apemantus in Act One, and by Act Four Timon sees the grim significance of his words. He tells Alcibiades that he gave of himself, unstintingly, until he lacked light to give.

> But then renew I could not like the moon;

There were no suns to borrow of.

(Tim. IV.iii.69)

The summer of his generosity has turned to 'deepest winter' and all is now dark and cold. Shakespeare may again have had in mind the *De Amicitia*. 'They seem to take the sun out of the universe when they deprive life of friendship.'[27]

For Timon, in his bleak mood of hideous nihilism, once friendship fails then everything is theft.

> The sun's a thief, and with his great attraction
> Robs the vast sea; the moon's an arrant thief,
> And her pale fire she snatches from the sun;
> The sea's a thief, whose liquid surge resolves
> The moon into salt tears; the earth's a thief,
> That feeds and breeds by a composture stol'n
> From gen'ral excrement; each things a thief.
> The laws, your curb and whip, in their rough power
> Has uncheck'd theft. Love not yourselves; away,
> Rob one another!

(Tim. IV.iii.439)

A world lacking the warm light of friendship was, for the convivial Shakespeare, a prospect terrible indeed. It is a situation he had confronted in one of the early Sonnets.

> Even so my sun one early morn did shine
> With all triumphant splendour on my brow;
> But out alack! he was but one hour mine –
> The region cloud hath mask'd him from me now.

(S. 33)

All that is left Timon, at the end, is oblivion.

> Graves only be men's works and death their gain;
> Sun, hide thy beams, Timon hath done his reign.

(Tim. V.i.221)

Few things were more abhorrent to Shakespeare than the false friend, the 'glass-faced flatterer'[28] who merely reflected back the feelings directed towards him. One of the functions of a friend, of course, is to be critical when occasion demands. Feste complains to Orsino that his friends praise him whereas his enemies tell him to his face he is an ass.

91

...so that by my foes, sir, I profit in the knowledge of myself, and by my friends I am abused.

(Tw. N. V.i.18)

Hamlet speaks contemptuously of 'the candied tongue'[29] and, like Hotspur, rejects 'candy...courtesy' as the mark of the 'fawning greyhound'[30] rather than the friend. Timon, his eyes opened, speaks of 'mouth-friends...smiling, smooth, detestable parasites...time's flies.'[31]

The 'mouth-friend' and the 'parasite' played a significant rôle in Roman life. The system of *clientela* obliged the less affluent to show assiduous adulation to a patron whose status depended upon the size and obsequiousness of his entourage. Sallust writes tellingly of the sycophant who keeps his thoughts locked inside his heart while summoning honeyed words readily to his lips.[32] Martial and Juvenal owed much of their meagre income to their client duties and satirise the ostentatious parades of hypocrisy they entailed.

Caesar himself affects contempt for 'sweet words,/Low-crooked curtsies and base spaniel fawning'[33] although Decius finds otherwise, deriving a wry amusement from his susceptibility to such blandishment.

> ...when I tell him he hates flatterers
> He says he does, being then most flattered.

(Caes. II.i.203)

Brutus insists that when he kisses Caesar's hand it is 'not in flattery', but Antony's view of events is very different.

> You show'd your teeth like apes, and fawn'd like hounds,
> And bow'd like bondmen, kissing Caesar's feet:
> Whilst damned Casca, like a cur, behind
> Struck Caesar on the neck. O you flatterers!

(Caes. V.i.41)

Brutus tells Lucilius that a sure sign of cooling friendship is the resort to elaborate courtesy and fine words.

> When love begins to sicken and decay
> It useth an enforced ceremony.
> There are no tricks in plain and simple faith...

(Caes. IV.ii.20)

As Timon explains to his banquet guests:

Where there is true friendship there needs none.

(*Tim.* I.ii.18)

Such natural straightforwardness is the mark of true friendship. Montaigne's description of what the word meant to the Renaissance Humanist is surely unsurpassed.

In the amitie I speake of, they intermixe and confound themselves one in the other, with so universall a commixture, that they weare out, and can no more finde the seame that hath conjoyned them together. If a man urge me to tell wherefore I loved him, I feele it cannot be expressed but by answering: Because it was he, because it was my selfe.[34]

Shakespeare encapsulates the thought in three lines of *Sonnet 125.*

...take thou my oblation, poor but free,–
Which is not mix'd with seconds, knows no art
But mutual render, only me for thee.

Notes

1. Cicero's letters *ad Atticum* survive to fill sixteen books. Atticus' side of the correspondence is unfortunately lost.

2. *Essays* I.xxvii.

3. Horace I. Sat. v.44.

4. VI. 23.

5. See H.R. Barrow: *The Romans* (Penguin, 1949) pp. 76-7.

6. See V.i.77.

7. IV.ii.37.

8. II.i.183. The imagery of deep-rootedness and organic growth attests, it might be argued, to the value Shakespeare placed upon such relationships.

9. xxii.

10. *Temp.* III.i.90.

11. *Lectures and Notes upon Shakespeare's Julius Caesar*, published by Thomas Ashe in 1883.

12. *Cor.* I.iii.48-110.

13. See Preface to *The Knight's Tale* (Cambridge University Press, 1966).

14. *Essays* II.6.

15. *Euphues: the Anatomy of Wit* (1578) I.97.

16. XV. 875.

17. II.i.272.

18. *AYL.* I.iii.69.

19. Such as William Barksted, Henry Chettle and Antony Scoloker.

20. Ben Jonson: *Timber* (Works, 1640) pp. 97-8.

21. *All's W.* I.i.62.

22. II.ii.127.

23. II.vi.117.

24. Everyman Library (Dent, 1907) p. 321.

25. *AYL.* II.vii.181.

26. *The Prince* XVII.

27. The passage is paraphrased by Sir Thomas Elyot in *The Boke Named the Governour* (Dent, 1907) p. 159.

28. *Tim.* I.i.59.

29. III.ii.60.

30. *1H.IV* I.iii.251

31. III.vi.85.

32. *Bellum Catilinae* 10.35.

33. III.i.42.

34. *Essays* II.10.

6

Coriolanus and the Code of *Virtus*

In the later plays Shakespeare looks more critically at Roman values, holding them up for measure against their alternatives. This is especially true of *Coriolanus*, last of the tragedies and most incisive dissection of the moral imperatives that constituted *romanitas*. Anatomising this body of decorum and dogmatism, Shakespeare found at its heart the code of *virtus* or manliness.[1] In his *Life of Coriolanus* Plutarch explains the significance of the word.

> Now in those dayes, valliantness was honoured in Rome above all other vertues: which they called *virtus*, by the name of vertue selfe, as including in that generall name, all other speciall vertues besides. So that *virtus*, in the Latin, was as muche as valliantness.[2]

Courage in battle, however, was not in itself sufficient. *Virtus* stood at the summit of the Roman hierarchy of values in that it lauded the spirit of self-sacrificing patriotism. Only through service to the state might personal glory be acquired. Without such service military prowess was merely vainglorious exhibitionism or that unfocused ferocity encountered in Caithness' contemptuous description of Macbeth:

> Some say he's mad; others, that lesser hate him,
> Do call it valiant fury: but for certain,
> He cannot buckle his distempered cause
> Within the belt of rule.

> (*Mac.* V.ii.13)

The Romans regarded themselves as a disciplined people. To live and die for his country was held to be the highest ambition of its citizen.

95

Aristocratic privilege carried with it the essential concomitants of service and responsibility to a cause larger than the individual himself. The belt of civic duty, in other words, must be buckled tightly around a temperate cause. Anchises, in the *Aeneid*,[3] foretelling the fortunes of the Roman people, declares that their victories will be achieved through 'love of the fatherland and unmeasurable hunger for renown.'

In talk of *virtus* always the stress is upon deeds and conduct. The consul Gaius Marius, according to Sallust,[4] claimed that men were born equal and alike and therefore nobility was won by bravery and not inherited. Each man must seek fame afresh through his own actions. What is history, after all, but *res gestae*, things carried out? The exploits of the early Roman heroes – who were, to a large extent, the creation of Livy – were extolled with a view to increasing the general sense of patriotism. Scorning 'policy',[5] Marcius hurls himself single-handedly at the gates of Corioli, expecting his men to follow. 'Foolhardiness, not I!' is one soldier's not unreasonable response.[6] We are reminded of Young Clifford's words to his demoralised army on St Albans Field.

> Let no soldier fly!
> He that is truly dedicate to war
> Hath no self-love; nor he that loves himself
> Hath not essentially, but by circumstance,
> The name of valour.

> (*2H.VI* V.ii.36)

In the martial exploits of this early play there is little sense of irony any more than in *Titus Andronicus* its near contemporary.[7] Coriolanus however – surely more 'truly dedicate to war' than any other of Shakespeare's characters with the possible exception of the 'wasp-stung'[8] Harry Hotspur – takes the idea of Roman military honour to excessive lengths. At times it verges on the ridiculous. 'O me alone! Make you a sword of me!' (*Cor.* I.vi.75) he cries ecstatically to his men as he stands before them drenched in blood the loss of which he declares to be 'rather physical than dangerous'.[9]

The *virtus* code had a tendency to dehumanise its adherents as Shakespeare, in the later plays, so clearly saw.[10] Cominius' account depicts Marcius as a huge, unstoppable war machine, not unlike a modern tank crushing infantrymen beneath its tracks.

> As weeds before
> A vessel under sail, so men obeyed
> And fell below his stem. His sword, death's stamp,

Where it did mark, it took; from face to foot
He was a thing of blood, whose every motion
Was tim'd with dying cries...

(*Cor.* II.ii.105)

Later in the speech we hear how he 'struck Corioli like a planet'[11] and ran
'reeking o'er the lives of men.'[12] It is a horrifying picture. 'He was a *thing.*'
The reification is a calculated device. We may well recall Brutus' words
about the disjunction of remorse from power.[13] Coriolanus is the Roman
warrior ethic writ large, the logical extension of a culture founded upon
and sustained by force of arms. Like Titus he is both the product and the
victim of the system that he serves.

Rome, I have been thy soldier forty years,
And led my country's strength successfully,
And buried one and twenty valiant sons,
Knighted in field, slain manfully in arms,
In right and service of their noble country.

(*Tit. A.* I.i.193)

Though written some sixteen years earlier the words could be easily
mistaken for a passage from *Coriolanus.* The crucial difference is that
Shakespeare can now see the cramped and sterile limitation of such a code.
It is wide open, here, to parody, as in the account of the hero's young son
following in his father's footsteps.

I saw him run after a gilded butterfly and when he caught it, he let
it go again, and after it again, and over and over he comes and up
again, catched it again; or whether his fall enraged him, or how
'twas, he did so set his teeth and tear it. Oh I warrant how he
mammocked it![14]

(*Cor.* I.iii.60)

The irony is underlined, lest we miss it, by Volumnia's approbatory
comment: 'One on's father's moods!'[15] In another scene she recalls with
pride how she sent off her only son, at a tender age, 'to a cruel war'[16] in
order that he might prove himself a man. Strength of will and decisive
action are what count in this masculine value-system. The alternative, as
she points out contemptuously, is 'picture-like to hang by the wall',[17] a
state of decorative quiescence with which, in the late romances, Shakespeare finds much sympathy.[18] She would, she tells us, had she a dozen
sons, rather have 'eleven die nobly for their country than one voluptuously

surfeit out of action.'[19] When, on his return, she cries out exultantly: 'O, he is wounded, I thank the gods for't!' (*Cor.* II.i.116) there seems to be something so hideously unnatural, not to say unhealthy, in her glee that we can be in little doubt as to where Shakespeare's own feelings lie.

The contrast with *Henry V*, Shakespeare's other great military play, could not be more marked. For all the King's prowess in battle – and it is comparably heroic, as we see when he leads his men through the breached walls of Harfleur – there is in him a horror of bloodshed that we never find in Coriolanus. Whereas the Roman general seizes eagerly upon the chance to capture Antium, Henry, on the other hand, beseeches the Archbishop to be certain that the claim to France is a legitimate one.

> For God doth know how many now in health
> Shall drop their blood in approbation
> Of what your reverence shall incite us to.
> Therefore take heed how you impawn our person,
> How you awake our sleeping sword of war;
> We charge you, in the name of God, take heed;
> For never two such kingdoms did contend
> Without much fall of blood; whose guiltless drops
> Are every one a woe, a sore complaint
> 'Gainst him whose wrongs give edge unto the swords
> That make such waste of brief mortality.

(*H.V* I.ii.18)

Despite the martial language of the famous set speeches this is, in fact, the prevailing tenor of the play. As Williams says by the camp fire at Agincourt: 'I am afeard there are few die well that die in a battle; for how can they charitably dispose of anything when blood is their argument?'[20] There is, too, a mildness about that other great general, Othello (who has also 'done the state some service')[21] for all that his soldierly career is as long and illustrious as Marcius' own.

> For since these arms of mine had seven years' pith
> Till now some nine moons wasted, they have us'd
> Their dearest action in the tented field
> And little of this great world can I speak
> More than pertains to feats of broil and battle.

(*Oth.* I.iii.83)

Despite – or perhaps because of – his vast experience of war Othello, like Henry, would rather settle amicably than fight.[22] 'Keep up your bright swords for the dew will rust 'em!' (*Oth.* I.ii.59) is his calm response to the armed onslaught of Brabantio and his men. We find in the Roman play a very different response to such a challenge. 'Lay hands upon him!' shouts the tribune, Brutus, to his followers. Coriolanus immediately draws his sword.

> No, I'll die here.
> There's some among you have beheld me fighting:
> Come, try upon yourselves what you have seen me.

> (*Cor.* III.i.223)

Aufidius, his Volscian counterpart, rehearses such aggression in his dreams:

> We have been down together in my sleep,
> Unbuckling helms, fisting each other's throat,
> And wak'd half dead with nothing.

> (*Cor.* IV.v.129)

In the world of *Coriolanus* peace is viewed as, at best, a dubious blessing, an ethos reflected even at servant level.

> This peace is nothing but to rust iron, increase tailors and breed ballad-makers.... Let me have war, say I, it exceeds peace as far as day does night; it's sprightly walking, audible and full of vent. Peace is a very apoplexy, lethargy, mull'd, deaf, sleepy, insensible, a getter of more bastard children than war's a destroyer of men....

> (*Cor.* IV.v.226)

Again *Henry V* presents a striking counter-view. Burgundy, addressing the assembled royalty of two nations, demands to know

> What rub or what impediment there is,
> Why that the naked, poor and mangled Peace,
> Dear nurse of arts, plenties and joyful births,
> Should not in this best garden of the world,
> Our fertile France, put up her lovely visage.
> ...our vineyards, fallows, meads and hedges,
> Defective in their natures, grow to wildness,
> Even so our houses and ourselves and children
> Have lost, or do not learn for want of time,
> The sciences that should become our country,
> But grow like savages, as soldiers will

That nothing do but meditate on blood,
To swearing and stern looks, diffus'd attire
And every thing that seems unnatural.

(H.V V.ii.33-62)

Unlike the Christian Hal, however, Coriolanus – in the words of North's version of Plutarch – 'strained still to passe him selfe in manliness.'[23] He collects scars as others do medals, each one a tangible sign of his uncompromising commitment to his country's service. Significantly it is the taunt of 'traitor' that, on two separate occasions, reduces him to apopleptic rage.[24]

What North calls 'manliness' – known latterly as *machismo* – degenerates all too easily into a cult of extravagant toughness which brings with it, necessarily, a degree of insensitivity that can be emotionally crippling. The Stoics held that physical courage brought with it ultimate freedom. As Seneca observed: 'He who has first despised death is in awe of nobody.'[25] For Coriolanus, as for Cominius, valour

> ...is the chiefest virtue and
> Most dignifies the haver.

(Cor. II.ii.82)

He epitomises the heroic age and, of course, as Aufidius points out,

> ...our virtues
> Lie in the interpretation of the time.

(Cor. IV.vii.49)

The words remind us that even values as permanent-seeming as those of Rome are, in the long term, merely relative as later ages were to appreciate. It is a theme that Shakespeare explores at great depth in *Troilus and Cressida*. To the question: 'What's aught but as 'tis valued?' (*Troil.* II.ii.53) Hector retorts that 'value dwells not in particular will', but his attempt to assert absolute standards proves fatuous and futile. Words such as 'constancy', 'integrity', 'purity' and 'truth' saturate the text but the message of the play is inescapable. All human values will be overthrown by time and the concept of constancy is therefore meaningless.

> The will is infinite and the execution confined...the desire is boundless and the act a slave to limit.

(Troil. III.ii.80)

Shakespeare habitually dealt in ambiguities and, not surprisingly, Coriolanus' stubborn adherence to an absolute, unambiguous value system grows increasingly absurd as the play progresses, setting him at odds with the world in which he moves. Even Volumnia and Aufidius, stiff though they are, know when it is expedient – or politic – to bend. Supreme in his imagined self-sufficiency, Coriolanus is 'the rock, the oak not to be wind-shaken'[26] (*Cor.* V.ii.109). Like Browning's *Duke of Ferrara*[27] he chooses never to stoop. Aufidius, that kindred spirit, admires his 'constant temper'[28] before he kills him.

Such uncompromising and total commitment was, for Shakespeare, quintessentially Roman. After all was not *constantia*, or firmness of purpose, the foundation stone upon which the colossal edifice of Roman government rested? A metallic unyieldingness is the play's central metaphor, conveying the hero's iron-hard determination to preserve what he sees as his integrity. T.S. Eliot's poem *Coriolan* begins: 'Stone, bronze, stone, steel, stone...' and the words encapsulate the ethos of flint-like austerity that Shakespeare associated with the Roman temperament. In earlier works, such as *Titus* and *Lucrece*, its sheer straightforwardness held much appeal for him, especially when set against the labyrinthine world of Tudor politics. We find his approval lingering on through *Julius Caesar*, though now more qualified. In *Coriolanus*, however, there is a major change of mood. Cassius' talk of 'beaten brass' and 'links of iron'[29] reflected values that one could admire. Now, nine years later, the viewpoint has altered and Shakespeare suggests instead a stubbornness and a rigidity that are difficult to stomach. 'Churlish, uncivill and altogether unfit for any man's conversation,' as North's translation puts it,[30] Coriolanus shows nothing but contempt for the feelings of others. His opening words are a scathing attack upon the fickleness of the common people – and crowds, it should be noted, throng the stage in all but four of the twenty-nine scenes that follow.

> What's the matter you dissentious rogues
> That, rubbing the poor itch of your opinion,
> Make yourselves scabs?

> (*Cor.* I.i.163)

The speech immediately establishes the negative tone that dominates the play and contrasts markedly with our first impressions of Shakespeare's other Roman protagonists.

Brutus is conciliatory, politely declining Cassius' invitation to watch the sports. Titus enters with a dignified oration in praise of Rome upon his lips. Lucrece is first pictured in terms of her mingled beauty and purity while Antony's opening line is a flamboyant protestation of his immeasurable love for Cleopatra.

Although he takes great pride in serving his country, Coriolanus seems never to equate the Roman state with the people who make up its citizenry. He loses no opportunity to remind the 'Mutable, rank-scented many'[31] of its capriciousness. Whereas Rome 'sits safe and still'[32] on its seven hills, the very epitome of endurance and immovability, its inhabitants are

> ...no surer, no,
> Than is the coal of fire upon the ice
> Or hailstone in the sun.

(Cor. I.i.171)

Coriolanus sees himself as a lonely turret bastioning Rome's walls, the embodiment of fixed values or their distillation, rather. Thus distanced and depersonalised, he speaks not of 'what's meet' but of 'what must be',[33] a mode of utterance mimicked by his enemies who hurl back in his teeth the 'absolute shall'[34] of his arrogance.

> You speak o' the people
> As if you were a god to punish, not
> A man of their infirmity.

(Cor. III.i.79)

Junius Brutus' comment goes to the heart of the problem. The man's cherished integrity, seen from across the great social divide, is 'soaring insolence'[35] and monstrous egotism. He has become his own self-myth and must at all times sustain the image he has created, saying to his mother:

> Would you have me
> False to my nature? Rather say I play
> The man I am.

(Cor. III.ii.14)

He thus acts out the part of a man whose proudest boast is that he can never play a role, purporting to find the threat of his own banishment so preposterous that, ludicrously, he banishes his banishers as though, in leaving Rome, he somehow takes Rome with him. We are reminded of Falstaff's breathtaking hubris in the Boar's Head tavern: 'Banish plump Jack and banish all the world!' *(1H.IV* II.iv.473) and Gaunt's advice to his son, Bolingbroke:

Think not the king did banish thee,
But thou the king.

(*R.II* I.iii.279)

Like Hardy's Michael Henchard, Coriolanus seems hell bent upon his own destruction. This trait he inherits from his combative mother, Volumnia, who declares:

Anger's my meat: I sup upon myself
And so shall starve with feeding.

(*Cor.* IV.ii.50)

Yet nowhere, perhaps, is Shakespeare's attitude towards a character more equivocal. 'His nature is too noble for the world' (*Cor.* III.i.253) Menenius tells us and this nobility is insisted upon time and again throughout the play. Not even his sworn opponents will deny it. Coriolanus is a man who cannot compromise his honour. What is seen, so often, as stubborn intransigence becomes, if we shift the angle of vision slightly, an admirable integrity that is wholly consistent in its imperviousness to flattery, bribes and double-dealing. It arises from his deep-seated sense of his own identity, a quality that Shakespeare found peculiarly Roman.

For always I am Caesar.

(*Caes.* I.ii.209)

Never for a moment does the Dictator feel any doubts upon this score. Brutus' confidence in his own credentials is equally strong, being firmly located in his lineage.

My ancestors did from the streets of Rome
The Tarquin drive.

(*Caes.* II.i.53)

Portia too asserts her selfhood in resounding terms, declaring herself 'A woman well reputed, Cato's daughter' (*Caes.* II.i.295). Titus has an authenticity that derives from half a millenium of service to the state.

This monument five hundred years hath stood
Which I have sumptuously re-edified:
Here none but soldiers and Rome's servitors
Repose in fame.

(*Tit. A.* I.i.350)

Even the defeated Mark Antony can rally himself with defiant affirmations of who he is.

> I am Antony yet...I, that with my sword
> Quarter'd the world and o'er green Neptune's back
> With ships made cities...

> > *(Ant.* III.xiii.93 & IV.xiv.52)

It is not a quality that we meet with much in the non-Roman plays.

> Who is is that can tell me who I am?

> > *(Lear* I.iv.226)

demands Lear, plaintively. Othello, again, is riddled with self-doubt.

> > Haply, for I am black,
> And have not those soft parts of conversation
> That chamberers have, or for I am declin'd
> Into the vale of years – yet that's not much...

> > *(Oth.* III.iii.267)

Hamlet has problems with his self-esteem that would be incomprehensible to most of Shakespeare's Romans.

> O what a rogue and peasant slave am I...
> ...A dull and muddy-mettled rascal...

> > *(Ham.* II.ii.543)

Not until his return from the sea voyage can he, well into Act Five, pronounce: 'This is I, Hamlet the Dane.'[36] It is hardly the stuff of a Coriolanus, who, for all his change of name at the end of the first act, always has the keenest sense of what he is.

For Shakespeare this absolute conviction of one's personal identity lay at the very roots of Rome's survival: *civis Romanus sum.* The proud claim held the bearer free of indignity. The man who was entire within himself despised the fruits of ambition such as wealth and political office. The Greek historian Polybius writes in glowing terms of the high standard of honesty and incorruptibility that characterised Rome's ruling nobility and Sallust laments its later decline, which he ascribes to the perversion of *virtus* by *ambitio.* In the true patrician manner Coriolanus expresses scorn for material gain as Cominius admiringly points out:

> Our spoils he kick'd at,
> And look'd upon things precious as they were
> The common muck of the world. He covets less
> Than misery itself would give, rewards
> His deeds with doing them, and is content
> To spend the time to end it.

(Cor. II.ii.124)

His reluctance to honour ancient custom by standing in the market place wearing the gown of humility and seeking the people's acclaim for the consulship stems from this same sense of wholeness.

> I will not do't
> Lest I surcease to honour mine own truth
> And by my body's action teach my mind
> A most inherent baseness.

(Cor. III.ii.120)

Here we see the true meaning of integrity as Shakespeare understood it. Body, mind and personality are integral elements one of another, inseparable and mutually inclusive. Integrity is therefore that soundness of principle which binds the individual together as a coherent entity just as, by extension, society is unified by firm, consistent government.

> When two authorities are up,
> Neither supreme, how soon confusion
> May enter 'twixt the gap of both, and take
> The one by th'other.

(Cor. III.i.108)

This imagery of rift and disintegration is met with frequently. Troilus feels his whole being shatter in the face of Cressida's inconstancy.

> Within my soul there doth conduce a fight
> Of this strange nature, that a thing inseparate
> Divides more wider than the sky and earth....

(Troil. V.ii.145)

Isabella – who, with her simplistic but tenacious rectitude, is herself in the Coriolanus mould – tells her condemned brother, Claudio, that the one way to save his life is at the cost of her own degradation, although

> ...you consenting to't
> Would bark your honour from that trunk you bear
> And leave you naked.

(*Meas.* III.i.71)

When the idea of killing Duncan first enters Macbeth's mind the imploding of his integrity is conveyed in equally vivid terms:

> My thought, whose murder yet is but fantastical,
> Shakes so my single state of man
> That function is smother'd in surmise,
> And nothing is but what is not.

(*Mac.* I.iii.139)

Tarquin's assault upon Lucrece's chastity involves the same radical dislocation of the self.

> Such hazard now must doting Tarquin make,
> Pawning his honour to obtain his lust;
> And for himself himself he must forsake.
> Then where is truth if there be no self-trust?

(*RL.* ll. 155)

Coriolanus' fanatical commitment to a self-reliance and consistency that is frightening in its all-or-nothingness sets him apart from the rest of Shakespeare's heroes. No other figure, not even Hamlet, is so isolated and estranged. His fierce contempt for all the norms of political life, with its compromise and prevarication, makes him 'stand as if...author of himself',[37] cut off from all around him like a craggy summit thrusting above the mist. Not even Othello is less given to self-analysis and reflection and it is significant that, uniquely among the tragic heroes, Shakespeare affords him but one soliloquy worth the name. Leaving Rome behind him, he goes

> ...alone,
> Like to a lonely dragon that his fen
> Makes fear'd and talk'd of more than seen.

(*Cor.* IV.i.29)

In a sense he has the entire play to himself. With the arguable exception of Volumnia, who exerts a hideous fascination, no other character is of any real interest to the audience.[38] We find here no Claudius, Mercutio,

Goneril or Iago to take the centre stage. Nor is there a Fool or a Porter to lighten the mood of what is, in many ways, a remarkably sombre play. It is as though Shakespeare envisaged his hero as an embodiment of the embattled Roman state itself, stern and implacable, confronting its enemies within and without its gates and beating them back before being finally engulfed by the barbarian.

Some critics have seen Coriolanus as the fascist spirit incarnate. He is peremptory, ruthless, callous, insensitive and yet, as the fixed point in a seething, devious world, not wholly, we may feel, unadmirable.

Notes

1. The word *virtus* is derived from *vir*, a man, and signified, originally, 'manly excellence' before developing its diverse later meanings.

2. Trans. Sir Thomas North 1579 (reprinted by Shakespeare Head Press, 1928) p. 2.

3. *Aeneid* VI.823.

4. Sallust: *Bellum Iugurthinum* 85.15.

5. Notwithstanding Volumnia's observations at III.ii.41-61. In Shakespeare's early plays the word 'policy' has Machiavellian overtones and is used pejoratively in nearly every instance (e.g., *Tit. A.* II.i.104 and *2H.VI* IV.i.83) but it later comes to assume the more neutral, or even approbatory sense of 'statesmanship' or 'diplomacy' (e.g., *H.V* I.ii.220 and *Oth.* II.iii.266).

6. *Cor.* I.iv.46.

7. There is, of course, irony to be found in other aspects of the play.

8. *1H.IV* I.iii.233.

9. I.v.18.

10. It should be said that the idea of *virtus* evolved over the centuries. In the early books of the *Aeneid*, for example, we see a hero prone to *furor* (impulsive behaviour) in the old Homeric mould. In the later books, however, Aeneas learns to temper instinct with reason since sheer survival is now his primary objective in order that he may fulfil his destiny.

11. II.ii.114.

12. II.ii.119.

13. *Caes.* II.i.18.

14. 'Mammocked' means 'tore to pieces'.

15. I.iii.66.

16. I.iii.14.

17. I.iii.11.

18. See, for example, *Cym.* V.v.263.

19. I.iii.22.

20. IV.i.143.

21. V.ii.340.

22. Note how Henry talks the city of Harfleur into surrendering (*H.V* III.iii.).

23. This excerpt from North's Plutarch is quoted in the appendix to the Arden edition of *Coriolanus*, p. 137.

24. III.iii.66 and V.vi.85.

25. *Hercules Oetaeus.*

26. Interestingly, Aeneas is also compared to an oak buffeted by winds (4.441f.).

27. In the dramatic monologue *My Last Duchess.*

28. V.ii.92.

29. *Caes.* I.iii.93.

30. See *Arden* appendix p. 314.

31. III.i.65.

32. IV.vi.45.

33. III.i.168.

34. III.i.88.

35. II.i.252.

36. V.i.251.

37. V.iii.36.

38. This is, on reflection, perhaps a little unfair to Menenius who provides most of the humour in the play.

7

Pietas and the Kinship Bond

A man that is accustomed to proceed in one manner never alters, as it is said, and must of necessity, when the times disagree with his way, go to wrack.[1]

Machiavelli's remark is one of many such observations upon human nature to appear in his 'Discourses' upon Livy's great history of Rome – *ab urbe condita libri* – an English translation of which was made a few years before the writing of *Coriolanus* and may well have influenced the playwright's deliberations.[2] Clearly Shakespeare endorsed the Italian's disparagement of those professional soldiers for whom blood was the only argument worth pursuing. In fact the inflexible man of all kinds – Malvolio, Shylock, Jaques, Ajax and Angelo are examples – was, in Shakespeare's mind, mechanical and dehumanised, often becoming, through his rigid adherence to outmoded codes and orthodoxies, a stock figure of ridicule.

It is in pursuit of the total consistency which he equates with integrity that Coriolanus seeks to deny affection, steeling himself against any softening of the heart. Even his one humanitarian gesture, a perfunctory attempt to secure the release of a Volscian prisoner who had once befriended him, comes to nothing. Asked the man's name he replies: 'By Jupiter, forgot!'[3] and turns his mind to more immediate matters. Coriolanus insists that he will

>   ...never
> Be such a gosling to obey instinct, but stand
> As if a man were author of himself
> And knew no other kin.

> (Cor. V.iii.34)

And yet, within 150 lines, he has yielded to his mother's pleading and torn up his treaty with Aufidius. Rome is spared and his own death warrant thereby sealed. It is, of course, the crux of the play. How is it that the man who, for so long, has flaunted his inviolable self-sufficiency and virile hardness can, finally, 'melt' and make the startling discovery that he is, as he puts it, 'not of stronger earth than others'?[4] The answer may lie in a consideration of another key Roman value – *pietas*.

The attitude of mind that *pietas* represents will, ultimately, prove more powerful than the *virtus* cult which motivates Coriolanus' words and actions for all but the latter section of Act Five.

Pietas is not an easy concept to define. Described by R.H. Barrow as 'a massive and unwritten code of feeling and behaviour',[5] the idea involves, at heart, the notion of dutifully subordinating the will to exterior forces more powerful than oneself. It is fundamental to that religious outlook on life which, for Romans, tended to be synonymous with propriety, social order and self restraint. Religion, morality and the well-being of society were scarcely separable hence the proliferation of temples and ritual observances, designed, apparently, to bind these elements together into a formal synthesis, one which, over the centuries, acquired the weight of custom and helped to ensure the continuity of the state.

Augustus especially, like Queen Victoria after him, saw it as his duty to re-emphasise traditional moral values and, by example, foster them in his subjects. He took *pietas* as his watchword and the court poets Virgil and Horace[6] enshrined the sentiment in their writing. *Pietas* is a driving force in *The Aeneid*. The hero's loyalty to the gods and his sense of divine destiny inspire all his actions in his mission to found the city and the race. This piety is shown most clearly in two dramatic episodes from the poem. By deserting Dido, *pius* Aeneas sacrifices his own personal happiness in love for the solemn cause to which he has dedicated himself.[7] In carrying his aged father Anchises from the flaming ruins of Troy – bearing him on his shoulders like a helpless child[8] – he not only leads the Trojans out onto the long road towards the glorious future the gods hold in store for Rome but, in addition, affirms his reverence for family and the kinship bond, which is the other great element of the *pietas* ideal. The same word, in fact, denoted devotion to the gods, to one's parents and to one's country, the pious man being mindful of his duty towards each. All three laid obligations upon him which were to be discharged with punctilious respect. *Coriolanus* contains numerous references to the gods but – in so far as the two are separable – it is this second element of *pietas* that must concern us here.

The family, after all, is older than the state itself and kinship loyalties imposed solemn obligations upon its members. Sometimes these led to blood feud and vendetta hence, incongruous as it might seem, both the Pompeian and the Caesarean parties could take *pietas* as their battle cry. How better, asks Cicero, can piety towards the gods be shown than by gratitude and zealous respect towards one's parents?[9] In the *De Inventione*[10] he writes of *pietas* as that virtue which 'enjoins us to do our duty towards our country, our parents and our other blood relations'[11] and, later in the same work, reverses the order, giving blood relations precedence.[12] 'A man who beats his wife and children lays hands upon what is most sacred' declared Cato,[13] reflecting the Roman belief that piety was often better exemplified in the conscientiousness of the parent and the gratitude of the child than in religious rites and ceremonies, important though the latter may have been.

Roman religion was very much the religion of the home, a divine presence, or *numen*, being felt to infuse all aspects of the daily domestic round. Piety and filial duty were thus, to a large degree, synonymous, as were *pietas* and parental love. This we find illustrated in the term *pietà* which has come, in religious painting and sculpture, to denote the Virgin enbracing the dead body of her Son. The importance of this concept to the Romans appears in the institution by the emperor Claudius of annual ceremonies to commemorate his parents and in the depiction of the empress Sabina, wife of Hadrian, on coins above the inscription '*pietas*'. These, and many other such devices, were intended to reinforce in the popular mind the inalienable relationship between dynastic continuity and godliness.

Piety, as the Romans understood it, involved an offering up, a sacrifice the value of which was proportionate to the suffering involved. Portia's self-inflicted thigh wound and the suicide of Lucrece both exemplify the resolute self-abnegation in the service of family and the wider interests of the state that characterises the *pietas* ideal.

In Renaissance iconography the depiction of Anchises childlike in Aeneas' arms was a popular emblem of *pietas*. The image suggests the idea of a natural cycle of familial reciprocity, a closed circle of giving and receiving which helps us to grasp what is perhaps the most essential feature of piety – the glad offering back of life towards the source from which it comes, one's parents, one's family and the gods.[14] Cassius, we may remember, makes ironic allusion to this celebrated illustration of filial piety in his account to Brutus of how he saved the tired Caesar from drowning.

Another such emblem with powerfully emotive connotations was the pelican, a bird which was erroneously supposed to feed its young with its own blood. This 'pelican in her piety' – to use the heraldic terminology – may still be seen, for example, on the arms of the Corpus Christi Colleges at Oxford and Cambridge.

The Temple of Pietas in the Forum Holitorium was built, as early as 181 BC it is said, upon a spot where, according to legend, a daughter had kept alive her imprisoned father by nourishing him with her own milk.[15]

These associations between blood and milk bring us back to Volumnia's words to Virgilia in Act One.

> The breasts of Hecuba
> When she did suckle Hector, look'd not lovelier
> Than Hector's forehead when it spit forth blood
> At Grecian sword contemning.

(Cor. I.iii.40)

This blood/milk dichotomy lies at the heart of the play. Both liquids are highly ambivalent in their implications. Milk suggests weakness and dependency but also cherishing, nourishment and strength while blood, besides its violent associations, may also imply health and vigour as it does, for instance, in Menenius' fable of the belly and the limbs. Volumnia seemingly rejects milk and its connotations for her of childish vulnerability in favour of blood and the aggressive qualities it conjures up in her pugnacious mind. It is hard to imagine the young Marcius at her breast. All but the poorest Roman mothers would normally, in fact, have had their babies suckled by wet nurses but, setting this aside in the interests of poetic licence, we might, nevertheless, contemplate the disturbing properties such virago milk might possess, recalling perhaps Lavinia's words to Tamora's sons, her ravishers, in *Titus Andronicus*:

> When did the tiger's young ones teach the dam?
> O, do not learn her wrath; she taught it thee;
> The milk thou suck'st from her did turn to marble;
> Even at thy teat thou hadst thy tyranny.

(Tit. A. II.iii.142)

Titus himself declares Rome to have become 'a wilderness of tigers'[16] and it is significant that Shakespeare should link the two ideas in Act V of *Coriolanus* when even Menenius can make the confident pronouncement that Rome is doomed, declaring there to be, in his friend, 'no more mercy…than there is milk in a male tiger.' (V.iv.28).

Aggressive masculinity and maternal milk are clearly at odds. Coriolanus scorns what he regards as soft, feminine values, referring contemptuously to harlots, eunuchs, virgins, babies and blubbering schoolboys in voicing his self-disgust at having yielded to Volumnia's entreaty to act 'mildly' in the market place.[17]

> You might have been enough the man you are
> With striving less to be so!

(Cor. III.ii.19)

declares his mother shrewdly if somewhat hyprocritically. Her words are, in a sense, the reverse of Lady Macbeth's to her husband when she insists that only by killing Duncan can he enhance his masculine status in her eyes.

> When you durst do it, then you were a man;
> And to be more than what you were, you would
> Be so much more the man.

(Mac. I.vii.49)

With a vehemence even more hideous than Volumnia's she rejects her own femininity. In so doing she repudiates her concomitant powers of generation, and ultimately human kindness – or indeed 'humankind-ness', the different punctuation helping to point up the layers of meaning in the word.

> Make thick my blood.
> Stop up the access and passage to remorse;
> That no compunctious visitings of Nature
> Shake my fell purpose, nor keep peace between
> The effect and it! Come to my woman's breasts
> And take my milk for gall...

(Mac. I.v.43)

Her menstrual blood, prime symbol of her procreativity, must thicken and cease to flow, the nurturing milk turning to bitter, unpalatable bile in harsh rebuttal of the maternal instinct natural to all women. Macbeth, she feels, is 'too full of the milk of human kindness'[18] – what Malcolm later calls 'The sweet milk of concord'[19] – to assassinate the King. Few passages in Shakespeare are more horrifying than the one in which she asserts – if only in theory – her readiness to violate the most sacred rite of motherhood.

> I have given suck, and know
> How tender 'tis to love the babe that milks me:
> I would, while it was smiling in my face,

113

Have pluck'd my nipple from his boneless gums
And dash'd the brains out, had I so sworn
As you have done to this.

(Mac. I.vii.54)

This appalling denial of the kinship bond, of the most fundamental ties of nature itself, paves the way for Macbeth's furious onslaught upon Duncan, Banquo, Macduff and Siward and their 'seed', their lines of continuity. A 'barren sceptre' in his own grip, a 'fruitless crown'[20] upon his own head, he launches an assault against kindness and kinship. Duncan's sons Malcolm and Donalbain having fled his reach, he orphans Fleance instead, destroys all Macduff's 'pretty chickens and their dam,'[21] and, in the last act, slays Siward's 'born of woman' son.[22]

Duncan's 'gash'd stabs' appear to the murderer's horrified gaze 'a breach in nature/For ruin's wasteful entrance'.[23] Antony, we remember, described Brutus' knife thrust as 'the most unkindest cut of all.'[24] Chaos rushes in through the rent in the fabric of the natural universe represented by Duncan's 'silver skin'.[25] 'Kindness' rushes out in the form of Duncan's horses bursting from their stalls amidst wild storm and eating one another in hideous violation of natural order.

Antony, in his funeral oration, describes Caesar's death in very similar terms.

See what a rent the envious Casca made:
Through this the well-beloved Brutus stabb'd;
And, as he pluck'd his cursed steel away,
Mark how the blood of Caesar follow'd it,
As rushing out of doors to be resolv'd
If Brutus so unkindly knock'd or no...

(Caes. III.ii.177)

' 'Gainst nature still',[26] as Ross puts it, commenting upon the Scottish princes' supposed parricide.

The events surrounding Duncan's death resemble those disruptions of nature that presaged the assassination of Caesar. Casca tells Cassius:

...birds and beasts from quality and kind
...change from their ordinance,
Their natures and pre-formed faculties
To monstrous quality...

(Caes. I.iii.64)

Monstrousness is a central image in *King Lear*, the play in which father turns against daughter, daughter against father, brother against brother, sister against sister, father against son and son against father.

> Here I disclaim all my paternal care,
> Propinquity and property of blood!

(*Lear* I.i.116)

declares the old King resoundingly, as though the kinship bond may be abrogated at will. He disowns all three daughters, just as Gloucester rejects his own true son Edgar. The children in their turn – or three of them – brutally repudiate 'The offices of nature, bond of childhood' (*Lear* II.iv.176). Derided by his wife, Goneril, for his 'milky gentleness' and 'milk-liver'd' temperament, Albany makes ingenious use of horticultural imagery to analyse the source of the evil within her.

> That nature which contemns its origin
> Cannot be border'd certain in itself;
> She that herself will sliver and disbranch
> From her material sap, perforce must wither
> And come to deadly use.

(*Lear* IV.ii.32)

Her treatment of Lear, he argues, has mutilated the tree of kinship – or kindness – and she has thus cut herself off from the nourishment of its roots.

This is precisely Coriolanus' situation. The price of the consulship, as a citizen points out, is merely 'to ask it kindly.'[27] Editors disagree as to the punctuation of his answer, but Johnson's 'Kindly, sir? I pray let me ha't!' makes better sense, I feel, than the alternatives suggested since, until his final encounter with the women, he stoutly rejects all that the word 'kindly' implies. The consulship, he insists, is rightly his by merit, hard earned by loss of blood – his and others' – on numerous battlefields in the cause of Rome. Asking 'kindly' would be to undermine that autonomy to which he clings so stubbornly throughout the play. As 'author of himself' he knows 'no other kin'. 'Kindliness', therefore, with its implications of mutual interdependence and compassion, is something that he cannot countenance. Only 'a gosling', he tells us, 'obey[s] instinct.'[28] Yet even this is a concession in that an instinct must be recognised as existing in order that it may be denied. Goslings, of course, represent just that softness and vulnerability which Coriolanus is terrified of locating in himself since it is the antithesis of the hardened belligerence that has become his persona and to which he must at all times conform. Significantly it is Aufidius' taunt: 'boy of tears!'[29] that triggers the explosion of fury which brings about his death. The effectiveness of an insult tends to be in direct proportion to the recipient's recognition of its truth.

'Alone', 'boy' and 'sword' are the last three words of any consequence that Coriolanus utters in the play and they sum up his character with admirable succinctness.

Coriolanus takes great pride in his wounds as the visible marks of his courageous service to his country. He is, however, reluctant to show them to the people in the market-place. 'Poor dumb mouths', as Antony says of Caesar's,[30] they reveal not only his vulnerability in the literal sense of the word but, it could be argued, an openness that is feminine in its implications, like Lady Macbeth's 'access and passage to remorse.'[31] Both must be stopped up, covered and denied. Coriolanus identifies himself with the sword and not the wound it makes.[32]

No true Roman, though, could be indifferent to certain 'softer' values. Inculcated in every Roman child, as we have seen, was the idea of *pietas* towards one's parents, particularly one's mother. Indeed the Roman matron was something of a cult figure, perhaps as a counterbalance to the *patria potestas*, the enormous, life-and-death power invested in the father by Roman law.[33]

There were many notable examples of powerful, honoured mothers. Brutus' mother, Servilia, was held in high esteem, as Cicero tells us,[34] and Julia Domna, mother of the Emperor Caracalla, was given the title 'mother of the senate and the fatherland'. Widowhood gave mothers still greater authority. The fact that this influence was moral rather than legally underwritten like the father's if anything made their prestige stronger still. So too, in certain cases, did their power to bequeath considerable wealth. Agrippina, with her successful efforts to establish her son Nero on the throne, is another celebrated case in point.

It is, then, not surprising that Coriolanus should show great deference towards Volumnia, a matron very much in the traditional Roman mould, not to say a termagant of the Tamora school. When, with Virgilia, Valeria and her little grandson in train, she visits her son at the Volscian camp, knowing that the failure of her mission will mean the sack of Rome, she tells him in unequivocal terms that his hostility towards his native land is tantamount to denying his own birth, his very nature (*Cor.* V.iii.122).

> …thou shalt no sooner
> March to assault thy country than to tread –
> Trust to't, thou shalt not – on thy mother's womb
> That brought thee to this world.

Coriolanus has already, in watching their approach, made reference to

> ...the honour'd mould
> Wherein this trunk was fram'd.

(Cor. V.iii.22)

Nevertheless he still seeks to deny natural instinct and the claims of *pietas*.

> But out, affection!
> All bond and privilege of nature break!

(Cor. V.iii.24)

The precise wording is important here. 'Bond' and 'privilege' suggest opposites of freedom and restraint. As in *King Lear* the 'bond of childhood'[35] is, on the one hand, a powerful tie of natural affinity and love, uniting families and strengthening relationships which extend out into society as a whole. On the other it represents a system of duties and obligations which, though supposedly reciprocal, often has the effect in practice of binding people to the will of others in situations of dependence, becoming an oppressive or even tyrannical bondage that renders one impotent and vulnerable. 'Privilege', similarly, has connotations that are powerfully ambivalent.

In denying the bond of filial *pietas* Coriolanus can see only its negative, inhibiting elements. He needs to be free to assert his autonomy and to honour the new compact entered into with Aufidius, another bond of major consequence. When Volumnia kneels to him, however, he is shamed and humiliated as a Roman son. 'Quite athwart goes all decorum', to borrow Vincentio's words from *Measure for Measure*.[36] The natural order of things is turned upside down.

> What's this?
> Your knees to me? to your corrected son?
> Then let the pebbles on the hungry beach
> Fillip the stars. Then let the mutinous winds
> Strike the proud cedars 'gainst the fiery sun,
> Murd'ring impossibility, to make
> What cannot be, slight work!

(Cor. V.iii.57)

There is a marked similarity with the descriptions of disrupted nature in *Julius Caesar*, *King Lear* and *Macbeth* quoted above. Volumnia then turns the screw, bringing forward her little grandson, Coriolanus' 'poor epitome' who, in time, she says, 'May show like all yourself' (*Cor.* V.iii.69). Virgilia points out that, as a dutiful Roman wife, she

> ...brought you forth this boy to keep your name
> Living to time.

(*Cor.* V.iii.126)

It is another powerful appeal. Lineage is of crucial importance to Coriolanus, as to all aristocratic Romans. Drawing his nobility from ancestors, it is necessary to perpetuate the family name and reputation, passing it on down the generations. He may deny his own personal needs but can scarcely trample upon the verdict of history which, he is told, will make his name 'to the ensuing age abhorr'd'[37] if he does not turn back and spare his native Rome.

Volumnia's final throw is to unite the appeal to kinship with the wider family of the state itself and her son's own sense of honour. 'The mother, wife and child', she tells him, 'shake with fear and sorrow' at the prospect of watching

> The son, the husband and the father, tearing
> His country's bowels out.

(*Cor.* V.iii.101)

Her imagery chimes with the pictures of the son treading the mother's womb and the conqueror treading upon his country's ruin.[38] Now two of the principal elements of *pietas* combine: duty to family and dedication to the future wellbeing of the state. With Volumnia's warning that the gods will plague him if he destroys Rome[39] the appeal to his piety is complete.

'Exit pursued by bear' is probably Shakespeare's most celebrated stage direction,[40] but the one that follows Volumnia's long speech surely rivals it: 'Holds her by the hand, silent.'[41] *Pietas* prevails. The kinship bond proves stronger than the new alliance made with Aufidius, indeed stronger than life itself since there can be little doubt that, in turning back from Rome, Coriolanus' own fate is determined, as he himself is well aware.

> You have won a happy victory to Rome;
> But for your son, believe it, O believe it,
> Most dangerously you have with him prevail'd,
> If not most mortal to him. But let it come.

(*Cor.* V.iii.186)

'If you drive nature out with a pitchfork she will soon find a way back' wrote Horace in his *Epistles*.[42] So it proves here. Like Lear, Coriolanus is forced to the recognition that no man can be 'author of himself',[43] fully self-sufficient and self-contained. There is indeed 'a world elsewhere'[44] – the world of common humanity. Wordsworth, in *The Prelude*, writes of

> The gravitation and the filial bond
> Of nature that connects [us] to the world.[45]

In *Coriolanus* this bond is reaffirmed and the hero achieves, like the other tragic protagonists, a belated self-knowledge. Not for nothing was Volumnia celebrated as the saviour of Rome and, as Plutarch tells us, a temple – dedicated to *Fortuna Muliebris* – erected in her honour.[46]

The Tudor mind, like the Roman, was much preoccupied with matters of ancestry and lineal descent. Property, titles and status were shuttled through the kinship networks and transmitted on down the line by judiciously arranged marriages which, in both societies, were rarely solemnised with romantic rather than material and political considerations principally in view. Just as in Rome, the Tudor family structure rested upon paternal authority and filial obedience. Children learnt deference in their catechisms, the recalcitrant offspring arousing great indignation, a point underlined in Shakespeare's imagery. Often infant fractiousness is employed as a metaphor of disorder in the realm.

> Go bind thou up young dangling apricocks
> Which, like unruly children, make their sire
> Stoop with oppression of their prodigal weight

> (*R.II* III.iv.29)

says the gardener in *Richard II*. Ulysses' vision of the universal chaos that follows the collapse of 'degree' – or respect for precedence – is likewise couched in terms of the rebellious child.

> Strength should be lord of imbecility[47]
> And the rude son should strike his father dead.

> (*Troil.* I.iii.114)

The advent of Protestantism in England brought with it a still further extension of paternal authority. It was not quite the Roman *patria potestas*, but the new doctrine of the priesthood of all believers gave the father a spiritual role which underpinned his economic and dynastic powers. The Roman principle of *agnatio*, or descent through the male line only, had its counterpart in Shakespeare's society, new laws enacted in Henry VIII's day having given men still greater scope in the bestowal of their patrimony.

In the Histories, of course, this principle is of crucial importance, as is the supposedly 'natural' law of primogeniture. The issue of birthright dominates both tetralogies with the appalling carnage of the Roses wars as the result. Carlisle prophesies:

> Peace shall go live with Turks and infidels,
> And, in this seat of peace, tumultuous wars
> Shall kin with kin and kind with kind confound.

> (*R.II* IV.i.137)

His vision proves all too accurate, the guilt of Richard's murder being transmitted down the family line through nearly a century of civil war with catastrophic rupturing of familial loyalties. Shakespeare, with his own deep personal concern for family survival,[48] must have felt the horror with particular force. Richard of York rejects the harmonies of the kinship bond with a vehemence unrivalled throughout the history cycle.

> I have no brother, I am like no brother,
> And this word 'love' which greybeards call divine
> Be resident in men like one another
> And not in me: I am myself alone.

> (*3H.VI* V.vi.80)

Like Coriolanus he is convinced that a man may indeed be 'author of himself' although in his case there is to be no belated escape from his harsh, self-inflicted alienation. As Henry Tudor says over Richard's body:

> England hath long been mad and scarr'd herself,
> The brother blindly shed the brother's blood;
> The father rashly slaughtered his own son;
> The son, compell'd, been butcher to the sire.

> (*R.III* V.v.23)

Of all Shakespeare's fratricides Claudius, the 'kindless villain',[49] is perhaps the most evil. His deed has the 'primal eldest curse upon it.'[50] What is left for humanity if one cannot show 'kindness' to one's own 'kindred'? Hamlet's opening remark makes the point with an irony all the bitterer for its punning urbanity:

> A little more than kin and less than kind.

> (*Ham.* I.ii.65)

As Montaigne wrote:

> If there be any truly naturall law...any instinct universally and
> perpetually imprinted both in beasts and us...[it is] the affection
> which the engenderer beareth his offspring.[51]

Notwithstanding his 'Surname Pius',[52] Titus is rebuked by his brother
for his lack of piety as early as the opening scene.[53] His slaying of his own
son and daughter is 'unnatural and unkind'[54] and the ghastly sight of
Tamora 'Eating the flesh that she herself hath bred' (*Tit. A.* V.iii.62) is still
more horrific. As Menenius tells the tribunes:

> ...the good gods forbid
> That our renowned Rome, whose gratitude
> Towards her deserved children is enroll'd
> In Jove's own book, like an unnatural dam
> Should now eat up her own!

> (*Cor.* III.i.287)

We are reminded of King Lear's tirade upon the heath.

> Is it not as this mouth should tear this hand
> For lifting food to't?

> (*Lear* III.iv.15)

he asks, rhetorically, his mind tormented by the impiety of his daughters'
'filial ingratitude'.[55]

Yet, for all its crude butchery, even in *Titus Andronicus* the altar flame
of *pietas* is never wholly extinguished. We find, for example, Aaron
defending the 'tadpole', his infant son, and declaring his intention to keep
him safe 'maugre all the world'[56] although, lest the point be overstated, we
note that the limit of his ambition for the boy's future is to bring him up,
like the young Coriolanus, 'To be a warrior and command a camp' (*Tit.
A.* IV.ii.181).

Lear, darkest of the tragedies, tells what happens when nature turns in
upon itself and people are cut off from the well-spring of love and
nourishment, from that 'kindness' which the family pieties entail. Nothing
indeed comes of nothing[57] and the play ends with a wordless howl of agony
that echoes through sterile emptiness at the world's end.

In the comedies, too, threats to the stability of the kinship edifice
abound but here the plays end with the healing of fracture and an
outward movement towards marriage and the planting of new roots. As

in *Coriolanus*, it is the women who restore the bonds that men have ruptured, the plays celebrating in their close, with music and dance, the rediscovered harmonies implicit in *pietas* – the willing subordination of self to the wider claims of family and the gods. In such reunion lies the mysterious power of nature to direct our onward path and to underpin those universal values that the Romans believed to be embodied in their state.

Notes

1. *Discourses* trans. Edward Dacres (London, 1636).

2. Though written in 1531, Machiavelli's *Discorsi* were not published in English until 1636, twenty years after Shakespeare's death. Translations were, however, widely available in manuscript, as Anne Barton has demonstrated in her essay *Livy, Machiavelli and Shakespeare's Coriolanus, Shakespeare Survey* 38 (1985).

3. I.ix.88.

4. V.iii.29.

5. *The Romans* (Penguin, 1949) p. 22.

6. See, for example, Horace's *Odes* iii, i-vi.

7. Aeneas tells Dido that his goal is Italy: *hic amor, haec patria est.* (4.34) His firmness is seen by Virgil to constitute another aspect of his *pietas*. See, particularly, 4.393.

8. *Aeneid* 2.707ff.

9. *Quid est pietas nisi voluntas grata in parentes?* (*Pro Plancio* 80).

10. *De Inventione* II.65.

11. II 22, 66.

12. II 53, 161.

13. I am indebted, for this quotation, to R.H. Barrow. See *The Romans* p. 64.

14. For a fuller discussion see C.R. Kerenyi: *The Religion of the Romans* (Thames & Hudson, 1962) p. 119.

15. Livy 40.34.

16. *Tit. A.* III.i.54. Dido accuses Aeneas of having been suckled by Hyrcanian tigers (*Aeneid* 4.367). See also *Mac.* III.iv.122.

17. III.ii.110-23.

18. I.v.17.

19. IV.iii.98.

20. III.i.60.

21. IV.iii.218.

22. V.vii.12.

23. II.iii.113.

24. III.ii.185.
25. II.iii.112.
26. II.iv.27.
27. II.iii.75.
28. V.iii.35.
29. V.vi.100.
30. III.ii.227.
31. I.v.44.
32. I.vi.76. There is, it should be pointed out, some dispute amongst editors as to whether this line should be given to Coriolanus himself, as in the Folio, or to the soldiers generally. Philip Brockbank discusses the matter very thoroughly in the Arden edition of the play.
33. For further information see Susan Dixon: *The Roman Mother* (Croom Helm, 1988).
34. *Ad Atticum* 15.11.
35. II.iv.176.
36. *Meas.* I.iii.30.
37. V.iii.148.
38. IV.iii.116.
39. V.iii.166.
40. *Wint.* III.iii.58.
41. V.iii.183.
42. x.24.
43. V.iii.36.
44. III.iii.135.
45. II 243-4.
46. Plutarch: *Life of Coriolanus* c.37.
47. 'Imbecility' in Shakespeare's day generally referred to physical rather than to mental enfeeblement. In this passage the reference is to the weakness of old age.
48. We find this concern expressed in the early Sonnets, particularly those numbered 1-17. The Shakespeare family's anxiety to acquire a coat of arms is well known. After much delay this was finally granted in 1596.
49. *Ham.* II.ii.577.
50. III.iii.37.
51. *Essays* II.viii.
52. I.i.23.
53. I.i.355.
54. V.iii.48.
55. III.iv.14.
56. IV.ii.110.
57. Compare, for example, I.i.86-9 with V.iii.307.

8

Coriolanus and the *Mos Maiorum*

'The Roman state stands upon its ancient customs and the men of old' wrote Quintus Ennius the so-called father of Latin poetry.[1] These famous words reflect the colossal confidence of Rome, built of the experience and practice acculumated over so many years.

The *mos maiorum* – the standards and traditions of the ancestors – came to imply, quite simply, 'the Roman way'. They constituted a norm of behaviour that needed no additional justification. The precedent established by Rome's great progenitors informed the collective consciousness of the whole community and against this criterion was each new generation to be measured.

No writer was more strongly grounded in these values than Cicero whose *De Officiis*,[2] dedicated to his son Marcus, spoke of the duties and obligations of a Roman gentleman. Foremost among these was the need to do what was 'right' as opposed to merely expedient. This rectitude was synonymous with that civic spirit and patriotism which, having served the Republic for so long, formed the solid basis of Roman life. By such devices might the *status quo* be preserved and the nobility, 'the helms of the state', in Menenius' phrase,[3] maintained in power.

Augustus in particular, as we have seen, sought to revive ancestral custom, or his own version of it. He reconstituted priesthoods long defunct, rebuilt ruined temples and revived old festivals fallen into abeyance. All this was done in the hope that old moral values would be resurrected after the years of civil war along with the institutions that had underpinned them in the past. Such efforts were, of course, in large measure fraudulent. *Mos maiorum* – ancestral custom – was idealised by historians such as Tacitus who purported to find in the abandonment of the ancient values the root cause of what he took to be Rome's decline. In practice, as Ronald Syme points out,[4] the 'Roman way' meant little more than the sentiments of the oldest and most influential senators of the day.

Successive generations of aristocratic Romans, in other words, accumulated a set of notions about the behaviour of their predecessors which it was convenient for them to believe in and sustain. In so doing they created a new mythology that owed little to historical record. Periodically *mos maiorum* was readjusted and modified to suit what Aufidius calls 'the interpretation of the time'.[5] The fiction of their immutability, however, was zealously guarded. Even the tribunes, once secure in office, start 'insisting on the old prerogative'[6] and accuse Coriolanus of being an 'innovator' who contrives 'to take/From Rome all season'd office',[7] thereby, with a splendid irony, undermining his position with their appeal to those *mores maiorum* which he, supposedly, espouses and they, by the very nature of their office, are deemed to reject.

'Innovation' and 'novelty' were very dubious concepts to a Roman aristocrat. The word *novus* itself had especially pejorative connotations, being applied, for example, to those men who made their way to the top of the political system without benefit of noble birth and illustrious ancestors. The establishment tended to look askance at these rootless climbers and often voiced its disapproval when the consulship or other high office went to such *novi homines* as Cicero and Marius.[8]

Arrivistes in Shakespeare, though mettlesome and dynamic, nearly always come to grief as witness Aaron, Angelo, Edmund and Macbeth. An exception is the Bastard in *King John* who goes from strength to strength, always gleefully alert to the ironies that accompany the parvenu up the ladder of social success.

> Well now can I make any Joan a lady.
> 'Good den, Sir Richard!' – 'God-a-mercy, fellow!'
> And if his name be George, I'll call him Peter;
> For new-made honour doth forget men's names;
> 'Tis too respective and too sociable
> For your conversation.

> (*John* I.i.184)

If the name of Rome stood for permanence then all that helped to maintain the existing order must necessarily be good. Petronius, Nero's 'arbiter of taste', expresses this innate conservatism in his *Satyricon*:

> We trained hard, but it seemed that every time we were beginning to form up into teams we would be reorganised. I was to learn in life that we tend to meet any new situation by reorganising – and a wonderful method it can be for creating the illusion of progress

while producing confusion, inefficiency and demoralisation.[9]

When disaster threatened, the Romans tended to seek salvation in their traditions, looking back to see how their ancestors had dealt with similar crises rather than questioning the assumptions that had brought them to such a pass or looking at how their rivals had dealt with similar threats. Foreign influences, in fact, were particularly suspect and could not be permitted to violate the conventions of the state.

For all their admiration of Greek culture the Romans viewed their neighbours with misgiving, suspecting them of a certain frivolity, very much in the manner of the English towards the French. 'It was Greek to me', says Casca contemptuously,[10] meaning that Cicero's words were – to use a more modern equivalent – double Dutch. This chauvinism doubtless appealed to Shakespeare's audiences. 'The chopping French we do not understand!' (*R.II* V.iii.124) protests the Duchess of York while, for Jack Cade, the ability to speak so alien a language at all is sufficient proof of Lord Say's treachery.[11] There are many such slighting references to France. Boyet, Le Beau and Dr Caius, among others,[12] all parody the Frenchman's proverbial excesses of flamboyance and 'apish courtesy'.[13] The French are frequently portrayed as 'a fickle, wavering nation' who 'turn and turn again'[14] – the very antithesis of English (and Roman) constancy. Nor does England's other near neighbour, Scotland, escape such censure. The 'weasel Scots' are variously described, in the Hal plays, as 'sprightly', 'furious', 'hot' and 'giddy'.[15]

One particular 'weasel Scot', King James, had the temerity to tamper with England's parliamentary privileges. Sir Henry Yelverton, in 1606, when Shakespeare was about to embark upon *Coriolanus*, condemned such iniquitous conduct, describing it as 'against the practice and action of our commonwealth, *contra morem maiorum.*'[16] The King's coronation oath had pledged him to resist such change, and something of Shakespeare's own attitude may perhaps be seen in Salisbury's consternation at King John's flouting of convention by undergoing a second coronation.

> In this the antique and well-noted face
> Of plain old form is much disfigured;
> And, like a shifted wind unto a sail,
> It makes the course of thoughts to fetch about,
> Startles and frights consideration,
> Makes sound opinion sick and truth suspected
> For putting on so new a fashion'd robe.

> (*John* IV.ii.21)

This concern with 'plain old form', as Salisbury calls it, is much in evidence in *Coriolanus*. Candidates for the consulship, by long tradition, stood before the people in humble garb. Plutarch describes the procedure in his *Moralia*:

> To the end, therefore, that [their] scarres might be better exposed to their sight whom they met or talked withall, they went in this maner downe to the place of election, without inward coates in their plaine gownes. Or haply, because they would seem by this nuditie and nakedness of theirs, in humilitie to debase themselves, the sooner thereby to curry favor and win the good grace of the commons.[17]

Coriolanus pleads with Menenius and the tribunes to be allowed to 'o'erleap that custom', but to no avail.

Sicinius: Sir the people
    Must have their voices; neither will they bate
    One jot of ceremony.
Menenius: Put them not to't.
    Pray you go fit you to the custom and
    Take to you, as your predecessors have,
    Your honour with your form.

(Cor. II.ii.139)

Eventually he puts on 'the customary gown', sardonically referring to it as 'this woolvish toge' since the people prefer 'to have [his] hat than [his] heart.'[18]

It might be supposed that a man so obsessed with his own integrity and so scornful of the fickleness and vacillation of the plebeians would approve the stabilising qualities of 'aged custom'[19] and its role as a bastion of order in human affairs. After all, the custom whereby would-be consuls donned the gown of humility stemmed from that same matrix of Roman tradition that bred his own highly honed sense of honour. However he sees, as Shakespeare himself surely saw, that the appeal to normative values is often spurious. Men such as Varro, Scaevola and Cicero, for example, thought it necessary to persist with the empty forms of worship laid down by the *mos maiorum* even though, to any thinking person, much of this ceremonial was plainly nonsensical. Certain rites were even conducted in gibberish, the language used being so ancient – and doubtless corrupted over time – that its meaning had been irretrievably lost.[20] Through such means, the traditionalists argued, the common people retained their awe of the gods' mysterious powers and their disaffection was thereby held in check.

Cicero, a member of the College of Augurs, took part himself in the ancient ritual of divination since this was what the public wellbeing demanded, though he clearly had no faith in its efficacy.[21] We find similar preoccupations in *Julius Caesar*. The play begins with the festival of Lupercalia. Caesar solemnly instructs Mark Antony to touch Calphurnia, as he runs past, in hope of curing her sterility. According to Cassius,

> ...he is superstitious grown of late,
> Quite from the main opinion he held once
> Of fantasy, of dreams and ceremonies.

> (*Caes.* II.i.195)

Even Cassius himself, that most sceptical of men, is obliged to entertain doubts 'And partly credit things that do presage' (*Caes.* V.i.85) when, on his march from Sardis, two eagles fly down to take food from his soldiers' hands and 'ravens, crows and kites' hover above the army like 'a canopy most fatal.'[22]

The notion that Rome's prosperity was safeguarded by the gods in return for a sedulous adherence to the rites and ceremonies they demanded in propitiation was widespread and enduring. Titus Andronicus, in his opening speech, calls upon Jupiter, 'great defender of this Capitol', to 'stand gracious to the rites that we intend', proceeding to lop off Alarbus' limbs and with his

> ...entrails feed the sacrificing fire
> Whose smoke like incense doth perfume the sky.

> (*Tit. A.* I.ii.78 & 143)

Like Coriolanus, however, he shows great reluctance to put on the ceremonial garment of the candidate for office.[23]

The way to destroy a society is to undermine its institutions, as Timon understands. Turning his back upon Athens, he calls upon 'degrees, observances, customs and laws' to decline to their 'confounding contraries' and 'bring confusion in.'[24] We are reminded of Richard's bitter words to his few remaining supporters:

> ...throw away respect,
> Tradition, form and ceremonious duty.

> (*R.II* III.ii.172)

Ironically his usurper, Bolingbroke, comes himself eventually to a similar pass. Waking from sleep, he finds his son, Hal, trying on the crown and upbraids him with biting sarcasm:

> Pluck down my offices, break my decrees:
> For now a time is come to mock at form.

(2H.IV IV.v.118)

The Romans had ceremonies for every eventuality. There was, for example, an elaborate formula for declaring war, the envoy arriving at the enemy frontier and covering his head with a woollen bonnet before calling upon Jupiter to hear and approve his demands. Thirty-three days were set aside for a satisfactory answer.[25]

Such ceremonial, of course, had a clear political purpose, being intended to provide an element of stability in troubled times. Shakespeare, with both feet firmly on the Elizabethan social ladder, well understood the importance of tradition and precedent. Moulds are not to be idly broken: 'Stick to your journal course', Imogen tells her brothers,

> The breach of custom
> Is breach of all.

(Cym. IV.ii.10)

Ulysses' 'degree' speech,[26] as is well known, sets out the orthodox Tudor view of a social harmony dependent upon hierarchy, due prerogative and natural law.

> The heavens themselves, the planets and this centre
> Observe degree, priority and place,
> Insisture, course, proportion, season, form,
> Office and custom, in all line of order.

(Troil. I.iii.85)

Canterbury's analogy of the hive in *Henry V* argues along similar lines. His honey-bees are

> Creatures that by a rule in nature teach
> The act of order to a peopled kingdom.

(H.V I.ii.188)

In other words, established institutions, if left to evolve quietly over sufficient years, will resolve themselves into a shape which reflects the fundamental pattern of nature itself. Man's duty is, by the application of his intelligence, to conform to the truth of his own inner self, to what

Richard Hooker called 'the law by which human nature knoweth itself in reason universally bound unto by the light of its natural understanding.'[27] Everywhere, Hooker insisted, natural law is self-evident and readily accessible to human enquiry.

In following custom we allow ourselves to go with, rather than against, the grain. Laertes tries unavailingly to hold back his tears on the news of his sister's death. In weeping he yields to instinct and acknowledges nature's primacy.

> It is our trick; nature her custom holds,
> Let shame say what it will.

> (*Ham.* IV.vii.186)

The idea can be traced back to the Aristotelian notion of a principle of order, based on reason, by the light of which the universe is regulated, although Montaigne, for one, was not persuaded that this concept was of any particular use:

> It is credible that there be naturall lawes; as may be seene in other creatures, but in us they are lost: this goodly humane reason engrafting it selfe among all men, to sway and command, confounding and topsi-turving the visage of all things, according to her inconstant vanitie and vaine inconstancy.[28]

The Romans codified their laws as early as the 5th century BC, setting up a commission of ten eminent men to enshrine ancient custom in twelve 'tables' which were first published in the Forum inscribed on tablets of bronze.[29] In Cicero's day schoolboys were obliged to learn them by heart.[30] Whenever – as sometimes happened – these laws came into conflict with the *mos maiorum* they were interpreted with custom and precedent very much in mind.

'Let the laws of Rome determine all,' declares Bassianus airily, but adds: 'Meanwhile I am possess'd of that is mine,' (*Tit. A.* I.i.407) endorsing Marcus' observation some lines earlier:

> *Suum cuique*[31] is our Roman justice:
> This prince in justice seizes but his own.

> (*Tit. A.* I.i.280)

Sicinius the tribune, in equally cavalier fashion, declares himself 'peremptory to dispatch' Coriolanus, the 'viperous traitor', pointing out, with devastating simplicity:

...he hath resisted law
And therefore law shall scorn him further trial.

(*Cor.* III.i.265)

All too easily, Caesar tells Metellus Cimber, may we

...turn pre-ordinance and first decree
Into the law of children.

(*Caes.* III.i.38)

The dispute between established custom, with its roots in principle, and a common sense pragmatism grounded upon expediency is frequently encountered in Renaissance writing. Erasmus argued that the Christian prince must be educated 'in accordance with established principles' and that he should 'gain his knowledge from theory and not experience'. Better, he said, to learn of the horrors of war 'from the stories of old men' than by participating in it.[32]

Machiavelli, on the other hand, was a great believer in accident as the generator of history. The world, he held, was arbitrary and contingent, not neatly ordered as Hooker would have us believe. The political act carries with it its own internal morality which hinges solely upon estimates of its likely failure or success. Rules and precepts formulated under different circumstances by previous generations are therefore of dubious worth. Our reading of history teaches us, he claimed, that commitment and determination are more valuable than reliance upon any supposed laws of nature in human dealings. Systems of government 'grew by chance among men' according to the needs of the moment, which were principally to keep the wicked under control. 'Men', he was convinced, 'never do good unless they are enforced thereto.'[33]

Like Machiavelli, Shakespeare was profoundly impressed by Rome's sheer capacity to endure and sought for the secret of her huge success. Machiavelli believed it to lie in what he termed *virtù*, the ability to carry out in practice abstract schemes. Shakespeare, while admitting the force of this argument, felt with Erasmus that the integrity of leaders was of crucial importance. His ideal king, therefore, is Henry V who, perhaps uniquely, manages to combine high moral principle with military effectiveness.

Coriolanus shares Machiavelli's pessimism about human nature. 'One thing can generally be said of all men: that they are ungrateful, fickle, dissimulating, cowardly, greedy of gain', wrote Machiavelli in *Il Principe*.[34]

131

> He that trusts you,
> Where he should find you lions, finds you hares;
> Where foxes, geese.... He that depends
> Upon your favours swims with fins of lead,
> And hews down oaks with rushes...
> With every minute you do change a mind,
> And call him noble that was now your hate,
> Him vile that was your garland.

> *(Cor.* I.i.169)

says Coriolanus to the fractious mob, believing with Machiavelli that men are essentially corrupt and must be coerced into doing 'good', by which they both mean that which furthers the interests of the state. Strong leadership is needed to achieve this and this is where the two part company.

For, Coriolanus, leadership arises out of firm principle and this, in turn, derives from the example handed down by the great precursors of Rome's past. Machiavelli, on the other hand, believed that firm leadership stemmed from a lack of scruple and a preparedness to compromise one's beliefs that owed little to what had gone before, a view pithily encapsulated in the Stranger's observation in *Timon of Athens*: 'policy sits above conscience'.[35]

In Act III of *Coriolanus* realism and idealism collide head on. Infuriated at her son's refusal to sacrifice his integrity by 'stoop[ing] to the herd,'[36] Volmunia declares, in sheer frustration:

> You are too absolute.
> Though therein you can never be too noble,
> But when extremities speak.

> *(Cor.* III.ii.39)

Here we find the paradox – some might prefer the Orwellian term 'double-think' – that makes *Coriolanus* the endlessly fascinating play that it is. As Volumnia readily concedes, it is her son's uncompromising integrity that gives him his towering stature, making him a heroic figure, grudgingly admired even by his enemies. It was through the agency of such men, we are led to believe, that Rome rose on its seven hills and reached out across the world. The nation, like the man, acknowledges no authority external to itself, deriving its strength from its accumulated centuries of existence whose distillation, custom, became woven into the fabric of its daily life.

Yet sheer survival sometimes requires that, in a crisis, honour must give place to deviousness. The wellbeing of the state demands that principle be sacrificed as well as blood. 'Honour and policy, like unsever'd friends' must 'grow together.'[37] He must, in other words, seem what he is not, speaking words

> ...that are but roted in
> [His] tongue, though but bastards and syllables
> Of no allowance to [his] bosom's truth.

(*Cor.* III.ii.55)

Volumnia assures him that she herself would be willing to 'dissemble with [her] nature' were so much at stake.

> Must I
> With my base tongue give to my noble heart
> A lie that it must bear?

(*Cor.* III.ii.99)

It is an agonising dilemma. Expediency apparently prevails.

> Well, I must do't.
> Away my disposition and possess me
> Some harlot's spirit!

(*Cor.* III.ii.110)

'Put...to choler straight'[38] by the tribunes, Coriolanus' resolve lasts less than thirty lines. His integrity – if that is what it is – holds firm, unlike his temper.

Shakespeare's own attitude towards those values and procedures sanctified by long usage and example is, itself, a highly ambivalent one. 'Give up yourself to form!' (*STM.* II.iv.170) pleads Sir Thomas More, encapsulating in five words the very essence of a Tudor orthodoxy which Shakespeare would almost certainly have endorsed. In More's *Utopia*[39] diversity is frowned upon. All private houses are identical. Fashion is unknown. Clothes do not vary with the season. This lack of variety, for all its benefits, makes for a life of intolerable dullness. This is the problem with conservatism, as Shakespeare understood. However much he respected established institutions and recognised the need for their continuance, he became increasingly uneasy about the stultifying effects of a stubborn clinging to accepted values. How, after all, is progress to be made if our lives are governed wholly by precedent? Coriolanus expresses this idea in one of the play's rare flashes of vivid poetry.

What custom wills, in all things should we do't,

133

The dust on antique time would lie unswept
And mountainous error be too highly heap'd
For truth to o'erpeer.

(*Cor.* II.iii.116)

Is stability worth having, he asks, if the price we pay for it is stagnation? 'Proceed by process,'[40] Menenius urges the tribunes, ignoring the fact that the tribunate itself came into being only when people challenged the status quo. 'Aged custom'[41] insists that Coriolanus take part in what he regards as a farcical charade which humiliates rather than humbles, and ensures that

> ...gentry, title, wisdom
> Cannot conclude but by the yea and no
> Of general ignorance.

(*Cor.* III.i.143)

The Roman veto system presupposed that 'no' always overcame 'yea'. In this way progressive proposals were often nullified and conservative propensities reinforced. Antiquity and custom are, according to the Danish messenger, 'The ratifiers and props of every word' (*Ham.* IV.v.105) and all too liable to become impediments to advancement. For Edmund, in *King Lear*, custom is irrational, arbitrary and inhibiting. Why, after all, should he 'stand in the plague of custom' and be deprived of his inheritance merely for being, by a year or so, the younger son, to say nothing of his having been conceived 'in the lusty stealth of nature' rather than in the legitimising but 'dull, stale, tired bed' of wedlock?[42] This is 'the curiosity of nations',[43] an absurd, logic-chopping pedantry which flies in the face of common sense and natural justice.

Custom can easily become a tyrant, as Othello reminds the Duke of Venice.[44] Sheer repetition is apt to deaden our responses making us hard and unfeeling. This seems to Hamlet to have happened in his mother's case. Sitting on Gertrude's bed, he shows her his father's portrait, promising to wring her heart

> If it be made of penetrable stuff,
> If damned custom have not braz'd it so,
> That it be proof and bulwark against sense.

(*Ham.* III.iv.36)

He goes on to warn her about

134

> That monster custom, who all sense doth eat
> Of habits evil,

(Ham. III.iv.163)

pointing out that 'use almost can change the stamp of nature'.[45] Even his own 'customary suit of solemn black'[46] has now become a habit in both senses of the word and he finds himself trapped inside an attitude. Like that other social misfit, Coriolanus, he discovers that

> …habit…too much o'erleavens
> The form of plausive manners…

(Ham. I.iv.29)

Hamlet is a battleground upon which is fought out a conflict between spontaneous, genuine emotion and the ritualisation of feeling into decorum and, ultimately, game – as epitomised by the professional 'players' who arrive at Elsinore.

Antony and Cleopatra, too, is much concerned with the flouting of convention. Here the 'game' is played out with the known world as its arena and according to two very different sets of rules. Antony delights in confounding expectation. Against all advice and experience to the contrary he chooses to fight Octavius at sea. He sends Enobarbus' treasure-chest on after him in the teeth of normal treatment of deserters. Here love is not containable within the established 'bourn' but 'find[s] out new heaven, new earth'. The stultifying effects of over-familiarity find no place in Cleopatra.

> Age cannot wither her, nor custom stale
> Her infinite variety.

(Ant. II.ii.240)

Shakespeare, in these later Roman plays, suggests that perhaps greatness may legitimately override that dour respect for traditional values so dear to Octavius and Volumnia.

> You were us'd to load me
> With precepts that would make invincible
> The heart that conn'd them,

(Cor. IV.i.9)

Coriolanus reminds his mother, not without irony. Their weight has been a heavy burden to him. Decorum must yield place from time to time, since, as Henry assures Princess Katherine: 'Nice customs curtsy to great kings' (*H.V* V.ii.293). Coriolanus, like Caesar and Antony, 'will be himself',[47] faithful, in the end, to his own sense of who he is rather than to the image bequeathed to him by others. Arguably Menenius is right and 'his nature' really *is* 'too noble for the world' in which he finds himself.[48] Infirmities he possesses in good measure but they are not, on the whole, those of common men for all the sneering of the wretched Junius Brutus.[49]

In the end, as Cominius says admiringly, he 'rewards his deeds with doing them'.[50] Appropriately in a play so concerned with the *mos maiorum*, the final words, as his body leaves the stage, assure us that '...he shall have a noble memory.'

Notes

1. Quintus Ennius (239-169 BC) *Annals* fr. 467 ROL. 1.

2. It may be seen as ironic that, for all its certitudes, the *De Officiis* was written just before the final collapse of the Republic (44 BC).

3. I.i.76.

4. Op. cit., p. 315.

5. *Cor.* IV.vii.49.

6. *Cor.* III.iii.17.

7. III.i.173 and III.iii.64.

8. See, for instance, Sallust: *Bellum Iugurthinum* 4.7-8. Sallust was himself a *novus homo*.

9. Petronius Arbiter: *Petronii Arbitri Satyricon* ca. AD 66. The work survives only in fragmentary state and, though generally attributed to Petronius, there is disagreement as to its authorship.

10. *Caes.* I.ii.281.

11. *2H.VI* IV.ii.159.

12. In *LLL.*, *AYL.* and *Meas.*

13. *R.III* I.iii.49.

14. *1H.VI* IV.i.138 and III.iii.85.

15. *H.V* I.ii.170; *1H.IV* II.iv.377; *2H.IV* I.i.126; *1H.IV* V.iv.114; *2H.IV* I.ii.144

16. M.A. Judson: *The Crisis of the Constitution: an Essay in Constitutional and Political Thought in England 1603-45* (New Brunswick, 1949) p. 37.

17. Trans. Philemon Holland (1603) p. 867.

18. II.iii.85; II.iii.114; II.iii.98.

19. II.iii.166.

20. For example, the ancient *carmen* of the Fratres Arvales, preserved in an inscription of AD 218. See J.E. Sandys: *Latin Epigraphy* (Cambridge University Press, 1927) p. 165.

21. See *De Divinatione* and *De Legibus* 2.

22. V.i.81.

23. I.i.189.

24. IV.i.19.

25. Livy I, xxxii.

26. *Troil.* I.iii. 75-137.

27. *On the Laws of Ecclesiastical Polity* (1594) Everyman Library edition (Dent, 1907) Vol. I., p. 182.

28. *An Apologie of Raymond Sebond, Essays* IV (Dent, 1897) pp. 39-45.

29. See N. Lewis and M. Reinhold: *Roman Civilization* (Harper & Row, 1966) I 101-9.

30. *De Legibus* II.xxiii 59.

31. 'To each his own'.

32. *The Education of a Christian Prince* (1576) trans. L.K. Born (New York, 1936) pp. 156 and 250.

33. *Discourses* trans. Edward Dacres (London, 1636) pp. 11 and 19.

34. Ch. XVII.

35. II.ii.89.

36. III.11.32.

37. III.ii.42.

38. III.iii.25.

39. Published, in Latin, 1516. First English translation, 1556.

40. II.i.311.

41. II.iii.166.

42. *Lear* I.ii. 3-15.

43. *Lear* I.ii.4.

44. I.iii.229.

45. III.iv.170.

46. I.ii.78.

47. *Ant.* I.i.40.

48. III.i.253.

49. III.i.81.

50. II.ii.127.

9

Antony and Cleopatra –
Duty, Service and Betrayal

Central to *Antony and Cleopatra* is the theme of loyal service and betrayal. It is this which connects the protagonists' fevered passion with the political and military aspects of the play. Breaches of trust abound. The opening scenes in Egypt show us both Antony's deception of Fulvia, his wife, in Cleopatra's bed and hers of him through duplicitous wars in Italy. Antony's defection to the East has broken the articles of his faith with his two co-rulers, while Pompey's opportunism threatens the Triumvirate as a whole. Antony then abandons Cleopatra for Octavia, the tactical marriage playing his lover false. When Pompey concludes a truce, Menas regards him as a traitor to his great father's memory, but nevertheless contemplates cutting the galley's cable and the throats of the 'three world-sharers', thereby making his master 'lord of all'.[1] Pompey reluctantly declines the offer.

> In me 'tis villainy,
> In thee 't had been good service.

(Ant. II.vii.73)

Menas responds with yet another dereliction: 'I'll never follow thy pall'd fortune more' (*Ant.* II.vii.81). Octavia is doubly betrayed, her new husband abandoning her to return to Egypt and to make war against her brother. Octavius tears up his compacts with Pompey and Lepidus,

> Breaking his oath and resolution, like
> A twist of rotten silk,

(Cor. V.vi.95)

as Aufidius said of Coriolanus' change of heart.[2] When Cleopatra's fleet turns sail at Actium, the breach of faith is compounded by her spurious suicide. Antony's defeat brings about the defections of Canidius, Enobarbus and Alexas, though far from winning Octavius' 'honourable trust'[3] by changing sides they succeed merely in hastening their own ignominious ends. Betrayals continue through the final act, notably by Proculeius, Gallus and Seleucus, to say nothing of Octavius' scheme to take Cleopatra prisoner and, for all his smooth assurances, parade her through the streets of Rome.

Yet surprisingly, despite this sordid catalogue of deviousness and perfidy, our overriding impression is of loyalty put to the test and holding firm. The dutifulness and dependability shown by the many servants and followers shine out all the brighter against the dark background of their 'betters' ' venality. This devotion is, for the most part, taken for granted by those they wait upon, as illustrated by Pompey's off-hand remark to Menas: 'Thou hast served me with much faith: what's else to say?' (*Ant.* II.vii.57). Such complacency is predictable perhaps, when one bears in mind the staunchness exhibited by so many of the play's subordinates. Eros takes his own life rather than hold the sword for his master's suicide, earning Antony's heart-felt tribute: 'Thrice nobler than myself!' (*Ant.* IV.xiv.95). In her choice of pronoun Iras makes it clear that she expects, quite simply, to follow her mistress to the end, as indeed she does, with Charmian her fellow handmaiden:

> Finish, good lady, the bright day is done,
> And we are for the dark.

> (*Ant.* V.ii.192)

Decretas is another whose faith has been unswerving, as he reminds Octavius, his duty done:

> Mark Antony I serv'd, who best was worthy
> Best to be serv'd: whilst he stood up and spoke
> He was my master, and I wore my life
> To spend upon his haters.

> (*Ant.* V.i.6)

Even Enobarbus, the play's most notable defector, is quickly shamed by Antony's flamboyant magnanimity in sending his treasure on after him. Mindful of that

> …ingratitude,

139

Which Rome reputes to be a heinous sin

(Tit. A. I.i.448)

he dies in an agony of remorse, pathetically begging forgiveness for his
infamous revolt and calling upon history to record him as a self-stig-
matised 'master-leaver and a fugitive'.[4] So powerful is this scene of
atonement that Enobarbus more than redeems himself in the audience's
eyes and stands, despite his transgression, with Eros, Charmian and the
others as a model of sterling service and proven constancy.

Only the most remarkable of men can inspire such allegiance. The
more military reversals Antony suffers the greater grows his followers'
devotion. It is as though he is setting them a test of their loyalty. Octavius
speaks shrewdly of 'the ebb'd man, ne'er lov'd till ne'er worth love'[5] and,
as if in illustration, we watch Antony's charisma increase with defeat and
decadence in a manner that seems oddly un-Roman, especially when
judged by the standards of the earlier plays. He inspires fidelity through
his sheer straightforwardness. As with Coriolanus, 'his heart's his
mouth'.[6] The more desperate his situation, the more outspoken he
becomes. At Alexandria he refers frankly to the likelihood of imminent
overthrow, insisting upon shaking hands with his household servants and
praising them for the service they have given. Warmed even at his dying
flame, they are reduced to tears by his generous words.

<blockquote>
Give me thy hand,
Thou hast been rightly honest: – so hast thou, –
Thou, – and thou, – and thou: you have serv'd me well...
I wish I could be made so many men,
And all of you clapp'd up together in
An Antony; that I might do you service
So good as you have done.
</blockquote>

(Ant. IV.ii.10-31)

This relationship between servants and their master or mistress is
crucially important in *Antony and Cleopatra*. A dozen or so have speaking
parts and, between them, around three hundred lines to say. In fact, in the
Roman plays taken together, Shakespeare employs some thirty-five servants, putting into their mouths rather more than 800 lines of text. These
figures do not take into account the broader category of 'follower' which,
if included, would of course increase the figure very substantially. Five
suicides from among this number may be cited should the importance of
servants require any further statistical vindication.[7]

How closely Shakespeare interested himself in the social aspects of

140

Roman history is problematical. Presumably he was well aware that Rome relied heavily upon slaves as opposed to servants in the Tudor sense, but the important distinction between the two categories either escaped him or, more probably, bothered him about as much as the celebratedly anachronistic chiming clock in *Julius Caesar*.

For many Roman slaves, particularly the chained gangs in mines and quarries, the agricultural workers and those forced into gladiatorial combat, life was grim in the extreme. A large number, however, perhaps even the majority, were in domestic service and treated, on the whole, humanely, if only because such methods paid off better from the owner's point of view. Cato was notorious for his harsh treatment of slaves, killing supposed malefactors with his own hands it is said,[8] but such extreme conduct seems to have been most untypical.

Slaves often became an integral part of the family they served. Pliny (the Younger) and Seneca, for example, claimed to enjoy the best of relations with their slaves, championing their rights and relying on kindness in their dealings with them rather than severity.[9] Shakespeare reflects such enlightened attitudes in his picture of Brutus' concern for the young Lucius. On two separate occasions he declines to awaken him, preferring to let him 'Enjoy the honey-heavy dew of slumber' (*Caes.* II.i.230). When, in his tent near Sardis, he asks the lad to play for him, he apologises for the lateness of the hour.

> *Brutus*: I trouble thee too much, but thou art willing.
> *Lucius*: It is my duty, sir.
> *Brutus*: I should not urge thy duty past thy might.

> (*Caes.* IV.iii.258)

Perhaps Shakespeare had read Seneca's Fifth Dialogue,[10] in which he wrote:

> How vile it is to hate a slave because he is exhausted by the need to keep alert at all times and so falls asleep.

Cicero's friendship with his slave Tiro was almost proverbial, the man eventually receiving his freedom and becoming his former master's secretary and biographer.[11]

Slaves were, for the most part, prisoners of war or the victims of piracy. Many were well educated, even learned men and served in capacities such as family doctor, or as tutor to their masters' children. Romans sometimes paid their domestic slaves, many of whom, in due course, saved enough of this *peculium* to purchase their freedom and become full citizens.[12]

In the early Empire slaves formed the bulk of the civil service, in some cases gaining promotion to the secretaryship of a government department and wielding considerable power, to the annoyance of the senatorial aristocracy. Licinus, originally a slave of Julius Caesar, rose to become a procurator in Gaul.[13]

We need not, therefore, think it surprising that there might exist, by all accounts, a mutual respect between slaves – or newly freed men – and their masters not unlike that between servant and master in Shakespeare's day. Freedmen often remained with their former owners, showing them an *obsequium* – a combination of deference, obedience and respect – not unlike that traditionally shown by the Roman son towards his father. They were, after all, vital cogs in the great machine of state. Organisation was crucial to the Roman way and required unquestioning acceptance of legitimate authority at all levels. Discipline, responsibility and a willingness to serve were key elements of *officium*, the importance of which was inculcated into every Roman child. This dutifulness and sense of moral obligation formed the theme of such treatises as Cicero's *De Officiis*, a work of enormous influence throughout Europe for many centuries. 'No-one will ever write anything more wise', claimed Voltaire.

To Shakespeare's age the Roman's devotion to duty was legendary, and nowhere better exemplified than in the lower orders of society. Only in the cases of Caliban and the Dromios[14] do we find the word 'slave' employed by Shakespeare in anything like its normal Roman sense. Elsewhere, when used at all, it is generally as an insult, implying a servile, cringing cast of mind. Since there was often, in the domestic sphere at least, little or no distinction in practice between the work done by the slave and the freedman, Shakespeare's failure to differentiate is understandable.

Servants are the only category of people to appear in all thirty-seven plays, a fact which, in itself, attests to their importance in Tudor society. In England, as in Rome, a huge underclass – estimated, in both cases, at between a third and a half of the total population – supported the superstructure of economic prosperity.

Slavery was taken for granted by Romans and little discussed in the abstract, even after Christianity took hold in the later stages of the Empire. In so far as men wrote of it at all in moral terms, they viewed it as one of life's natural misfortunes rather than as a glaring wrong inflicted upon one human being by another. Augustine conceded that servitude was 'filled with bitterness' but argued that the Christian could find a joyful freedom in service if he also served the greater Master uncomplainingly.[15]

To a Roman civilian the thought of being at the bidding of another was degrading, as the words 'servile' and 'subservient' remind us in their etymology. Seneca, however, pointed out that no-one was, as it were, a slave by nature,[16] and Florentinus, a century later, declared that, although slavery was an institution common to all peoples, the subjection of one person to another was contrary to natural law.[17]

Domestic service was not felt to be in the least degrading in Shakespeare's day. Indeed many wealthy people sent their children to be pages in the houses of others, believing that learning to serve was a preparation for leadership in later life. A thousand years and more of Christian teaching, accounts, one supposes, for this changed view of deference and humility.

Service in Shakespeare's time was much debated. The dedication of the faithful family retainer was held to reflect, in microcosm, the wider sense of service to the state that motivated so many of their masters. Loyalty may be put to the test at every level as *King Lear* exemplifies.

The language of this play is full of references to service given or withheld. At its heart is the concept of the bond, particularly in the sense of the natural ties that bind together child and parent and widen out into a larger social nexus of loyalties. Are these bonds claimable as of right, the play asks, or must they be freely entered into to be valid? To the Roman mind the answer would have been self-evident. *King Lear* however, suggests that it is service willingly tendered in adversity that ennobles. The Fool counsels Kent: 'Let go thy hold when a great wheel runs down a hill, lest it break thy neck with following' (*Lear* II.iv.69) though neither heeds the advice. Together wiith Edgar and Cordelia they epitomise true service, as does Cornwall's man at Gloucester's blinding.

I have served you ever since I was a child;
But better service have I never done you
Than now to bid you hold.

(*Lear* III.vii.71)

Like others of his kind in the Roman plays he dies seeking to affirm his loyalty. Even the farmer's dog barking at the intruder in Lear's brief anecdote[18] attests to a constancy so lacking in the 'superserviceable rogue' Oswald, that 'bawd in way of good service' as Kent calls him in his tirade.[19] Edmund's 'services are bound' to Nature.[20] In other words, he disclaims all obligation to others, dedicating himself to that same self-interest which the Fool in theory advocates but abjures in practice, loyalty constantly overriding common sense. In Enorbarbus' case the reverse applies:

Mine honesty and I begin to square.
The loyalty well held to fools does make

Our faith mere folly.

(Ant. III.xiii.41)

Montaigne's view, however, was rather different.

> The bond that holdes me by the law of honestie seemeth to me much
> more urgent and forcible than that of civill compulsion.... I would
> much rather breake the prison of a wall or of the lawes than the bond
> of my word.[21]

Although this 'civill compulsion' underpropped to a considerable
degree the Roman social hierarchy, Shakespeare prefers to envisage
service and obligation as more of a two way process. It is Antony's
generosity towards those who serve him that inspires their devotion rather
than Ciceronian notions of *officium*. The imagery he employs in his speech
to the servants, marital rather than martial, underlines the reciprocal nature
of what Henry VIII calls the 'bond of duty',[22] and helps to link the political
and emotional areas of the play.

> Mine honest friends,
> I turn you not away but, like a master
> Married to your good service, stay till death.

(Ant. IV.ii.28)

As Paul Cantor points out, with the transition from Republic to Empire,
we see, in the Roman plays, 'the relationship of master and servant replace
the relationship of city and citizen...[putting] a new emphasis on personal
fidelity as a virtue.'[23] The adulation of his followers serves to increase
Antony's self-esteem, enhancing that image of his former greatness to
which he clings with increasing tenacity as it slips steadily out of align-
ment with circumstance. Lear, on the other hand, in seeking to
'disclaim...propinquity and property of blood'[24] denies such reciprocity
and, in so doing, unleashes the forces of catastrophic disintegration
consequent upon the rupturing of such bonds.

In English the word 'service' makes no distinction of status, embracing
equally the general and the slave. The Latin language did not possess a
word with such sweeping connotations, a fact that reflects a very different
set of values in matters of dutifulness and loyalty. By its very nature
slavery is not conducive to that selflessness which, for Shakespeare, was
the essential feature of the dutiful man or woman. It is a quality exemplified by Orlando's faithful old retainer, Adam, who limps 'many a weary
step...in pure love' after his master and even offers him, in his hour of

need, the 'five hundred crowns' he has saved for his old age, exhibiting a generosity more in the Antony than the Enobarbus mould. Orlando pays him this poignant tribute:

> O good old man, how well in thee appears
> The constant service of the antique world
> When service sweat for duty not for meed.

(AYL. II.iii.56)

The speech suggests that Shakespeare had a somewhat rosy-tinted view of antiquity. The Roman slave sweated under compulsion, occasionally for reward but rarely, one imagines, from a sense of pure duty. Cicero's meditations on the theme of moral obligation were not written with such an underclass in mind.

Shakespeare, though, saw the issue in much broader terms. When Othello reminds Lodovico that he has 'done the state some service' and when the citizen urges his fellows, during the candidacy of Coriolanus, to 'Consider...what services he has done for his country'[25] we feel that we are being invited to consider a concept of duty which is, in essence, indistinguishable from that to be found in a Lucius or an Adam, servants who reflect, in microcosm, that same sense of selfless obligation which motivates their masters.

Often Shakespearean servants are given orders which, if carried out, would violate the dictates of conscience. In *The Winter's Tale* Paulina flatly refuses Leontes' crazed command to commit his infant to the fire[26] breaking her vow of allegiance and risking her own life with her defiance but, in the end, earning his heartfelt gratitude for her service. Pisanio – 'a constant knave/Not to be shak'd' according to the Queen'[27] – would rather 'choke' himself than prove untrue to his Romano-British master, Posthumus. He too must disobey in order to be loyal. Like Clitus, Dardanius and Volumnius, he rejects the proferred sword and refuses to employ it as he is bidden.

> If it be so to do good service, never
> Let me be counted serviceable.

(Cym. III.ii.14)

We are reminded of Eros who went further still in his devotion and, true to his name, died for love of Antony, ironically prefiguring the nature of his master's own death shortly afterwards.

Suffering is the frequent reward of service. Antigonus saves the infant Perdita at the cost of a hideous death at the paws of a bear.[28] 'Guildenstern

145

and Rosencrantz go to't'[29] as the Fool to his 'bed at noon'.[30] The Dromio twins are kicked and beaten by their masters at frequent intervals.

> I have served him from the hour of my nativity to this instant, and
> have nothing at his hands for my service but blows,
>
> > *(Err.* IV.iv.27)

laments the one from Ephesus, consoling himself with the reflection that 'servants must their masters' minds fulfil',[31] as though this were some immutable law of the universe. It is this patient suffering that endears Horatio to Hamlet. Duty faithfully performed in the teeth of hardship seldom fails to engage Shakespeare's imagination. Witness his sympathy for the lot of the common soldier. The 'band of brothers' at Agincourt spring immediately to mind. Less well known are the moving words of the anonymous English sentry at the siege of Orleans:

> > Thus are poor servitors,
> When others sleep upon their quiet beds,
> Constrain'd to watch in darkness, rain and cold.
>
> > *(1H.VI* II.1.5)

There is a quiet heroism lurking even in that least martial of soldiers, Feeble, the woman's tailor.

> A man can die but once. We owe God a death.... No man's too good
> to serve his prince, and, let it go which way it will, he that dies this
> year is quit for the next.
>
> > *(2H.IV* III.ii.229)

One hears a Roman echo in his words reminiscent of Casca's Stoic sentiment:

> Why, he that cuts off twenty years of life
> Cuts off so many years of fearing death.
>
> > *(Caes.* III.i.101)

False service – *obsequium* in its negative sense – correspondingly evokes Shakespeare's strongest detestation. Iago is a notable case in point.

> We cannot be all masters, nor all masters
> Cannot be truly follow'd. You shall mark
> Many a duteous and knee-crooking knave

That, doting on his own obsequious bondage,
Wears out his time much like his master's ass,
For nought but provender, and when he's old, cashier'd.
Whip me such honest knaves: other there are
Who, trimm'd in forms and visages of duty,
Keep yet their hearts attending on themselves.

(Oth. I.i.42)

Sycophantic courtiers are particularly loathsome in Shakespeare's eyes, men like Oswald who turn 'With every gale and vary of their masters' (*Lear* II.ii.76) and the 'lapwing' Osric who 'did comply with his dug before he sucked it' (*Ham.* V.ii.184).

Belarius, Cymbeline's disillusioned courtier, who has escaped to the freedom of the Welsh mountains, reminds his adopted sons that

>...service is not service, so being done,
But being so allowed.

(Cym. III.iii.16)

Mark Antony's contempt for the obsequious, disloyal follower is poured out in a cluster of images that is characteristically Shakespearean:

>The hearts
That spaniel'd me at heels, to whom I gave
Their wishes, do discandy, melt their sweets
On blossoming Caesar.

(Ant. IV.xii.20)

Here three of the playwright's particular dislikes – fawning dogs, stickiness and a sickly, cloying assault upon the taste buds – come together to convey a moral revulsion that is expressed in powerfully physical terms.

Henry VI envisages allegiance as a feather tossed to and fro in the breeze

>And yielding to another when it blows,
Commanded always by the greater gust.

(3H.VI III.i.86)

The imagery here is hardly applicable to Enobarbus, a far more substantial figure than any of the fickle subjects Henry has in mind, but even he, Antony's most loyal officer, torn between duty and self-preservation, eventually opts for the latter course. Even in his betrayal, however, he remains ruefully aware that loyal service in the teeth of danger is the stuff of which Roman history is made.

> ...he that can endure
> To follow with allegiance a fall'n lord
> Does conquer him that did his master conquer,
> And earns a place i'the story.

(*Ant.* III.xiii.43)

Notes

1. II.vii.60.
2. V.vi.96.
3. IV.vi.18.
4. IV.ix.22.
5. I.iv.43.
6. III.i.255.
7. Enobarbus, Eros, Charmian, Iras and (in *Caes.*) Titinius.
8. Marcus Porcius Cato, 234-149 BC. According to Plutarch he treated his agricultural slaves like beasts of burden, declaring that they should be working or asleep. Plutarch: *Cato the Elder*, 5 and 21.
9. Whether the slaves themselves would have endorsed this viewpoint we shall, of course, never know.
10. *On Anger* 3.29.
11. *De Officiis* 1.13.
12. See, for example, Varro: *Agriculture* 1.17 quoted in Thomas Wiedemann: *Greek and Roman Slavery* (Croom Helm, 1981) p. 140.
13. See Dio 54.21.
14. In *The Tempest* and *The Comedy of Errors*.
15. *Comment on Psalm 99* 7 PL 37, 1275.
16. *De Beneficiis* III 28.
17. *Justinian Digest* I.V.4.
18. IV.vi.152.
19. II.ii.13-22.
20. I.ii.1.
21. *Essays* VI 40-1.
22. *H.VIII* III.ii.188.
23. *Shakespeare's Rome* (Cornell, 1976) p. 152.
24. I.i.112.
25. *Oth.* V.ii.339 and *Cor.* I.i.30.

26. *Wint.* II.iii.92-129.
27. *Cym.* I.vi.75.
28. *Wint.* III.iii.58.
29. *Ham.* V.ii.56.
30. *Lear* III.vi.85.
31. *Err.* IV.ii.113.

10

Love

However widely Shakespeare ranged among his classical source material for *Antony and Cleopatra*, he would have found little if any sympathy shown towards the famous lovers. Plutarch, upon whom he leaned most heavily, regarded them as degenerate in the extreme. North's translation describes Antony as a 'dissolute man' whose 'ill name to intice men's wives' made the nobility 'hate him for his naughty life'.[1] Horace and Virgil endorse this view, regarding it as axiomatic that his love for Cleopatra undermined both his physical and his moral strength, though one should remember that they were avowed apologists for the Augustan regime. Most scathing of Antony's critics was Cicero whose *Second Philippic* confronts him with a virulent denunciation that springs from the bitterest personal antipathy:

> You are a drink-sodden, sex-obsessed wreck.... In the Assembly, in full public view, we watched a man in high office of state spewing into his own lap and flooding the platform with vomit that stank of wine.... Day after day your revolting orgies carried on...until the house reverberated with the din of drunkards and the walls and pavements ran with drink.[2]

Cleopatra fares little better. Plutarch considers her love for Antony to be no different from her previous amours with Caesar and Pompey, all of them merely tactical manoeuvrings inspired by her political ambition. It was, he writes, 'the last and extremest mischief of all other which lighted on Antony'.[3] Horace goes further, describing her as a *fatale monstrum* or Fury.[4]

Medieval writers, by and large, maintained this disapproving stance. Dante assigned Cleopatra to the second circle of Hell with Dido, Helen and Semiramis, all women whose lechery had overcome their reason, while Boccaccio described Antony as a man 'dragged into infamy by his unbridled lust.'[5] Chaucer, in *The Legend of Good Women*, though more sympathetic towards the lovers' plight, regards Antony as a man so ensnared by his raging desire 'That al the world he sette at no value' (l. 599). Cleopatra he calls a 'martyr' in recognition of her courageous end.

> Anon the nadderes gonne hire for to stynge,
> And she hire deth receyveth with good cheere.

> (l. 698)

Only with the evolution of the Courtly Love ethic, together with those literary conventions that we now label 'Petrarchan', do we find any radical reassessment of the values involved in the relationship and, for the first time, a recognition that the celebrated affair might contain elements that were ennobling and even magnificent. Spenser, in the *Faerie Queene*, is torn betweeen the two traditions. Like Chaucer he marvels at

> ...beauty's lovely bait, that doth procure
> Great warriors oft their rigour to represse
> And mighty hands forget their manlinesse,

> (V.viii.i)

but the tone of the next stanza conveys a thrilling awareness that perhaps the world may indeed be governed by the lover's heart.

> And so did warlike Antony neglect
> The world's whole rule for Cleopatra's sight.
> Such wondrous power hath women's faire aspect
> To captive men and make them all the world reject.

It is not that the ancients were unaware of beauty's charms, of course, far from it. Plutarch himself makes an observation that pre-empts Petrarch by well over a thousand years: 'The soul of a lover lives in another body and not in his own' he remarks, describing Antony's flight from Actium, though the romantic effect of his words is somewhat negated by the image that follows, at least in North's translation:

> He was so carried away with the vaine love of this woman as if he had beene glued unto her and that she could not have removed without moving of him also.[6]

It is, however, a momentary lapse on Plutarch's part. The tenor of his account conveys the idea of passion as a 'sweete poysoun'. Plato called lust 'a horse of the mind' because of its tendency to run out of control and North's rendering employs the resounding phrase: 'the unreyned lust of concupiscence', a sentiment that is typically Roman in its implications.[7]

The Stoics and the Epicureans both regarded love as a form of madness, almost a mental disease. The standard Roman epithet was *insanus*.[8] Love was supremely irrational and, taken to extremes, threatened order and stability. Let poets indulge in it if they would. In statesmen it was an affliction to be mocked or pitied. Cicero, a great believer in moral restraint as a virtue in itself, warned of the dire consequences that ensued when appetites ran riot. The controlling hand of reason must always be applied.[9] Animals are motivated solely by physical pleasure, he argued, but man has the gift of reason. 'The man who is too prone to succumb to sensual delights should beware of becoming an animal himself', he opined darkly in the *De Officiis*.[10]

In Shakespeare's play, Enobarbus is the principal spokesman for this Roman view of love. 'The tears live in an onion', he tells Antony, 'that should water [his] sorrow' at Fulvia's death.[11] By the Roman code, to show emotion, even at the death of a wife, is to suggest weakness and deficiency. Later he says censoriously that Antony

> ...would make his will
Lord of his reason.

> (*Ant.* III.xiii.4)

He contemptuously dismisses his love for Cleopatra as a minor ailment, calling it 'the itch of his affection', though it is, he concedes, powerful enough to 'have nick'd his captainship'.[12]

The play's opening line establishes the Roman stance.

Nay but this dotage of our general's...

Three of the first four words carry negative connotations, Shakespeare telling the audience at the outset to expect Roman moderation and common sense to be weighed against the irrational force of love. Bottom, that most improbable of romantic lovers, pointed out that 'Reason and love keep little company together' (*MND.* III.i.138) and his observation might serve as a synopsis of the tragedy. The marriage to Octavia is founded upon reason rather than love and founders upon the same implacable rock. In the words of Ovid:

Conscience and common sense and all Love's enemies
Will be dragged along with hands tied behind their backs.[13]

Rome's dignified orderliness seems incompatible with passionate love
and yet the very precariousness of the protagonists' love, in fact, ensures
its endurance, paradoxically.[14]

The theme of *amor* does not bulk large in the totality of extant Roman
literature but it enjoyed a spectacular, if shortlived, flowering in the latter
days of the Republic and at the beginning of the Empire, precisely the
period covered by Shakespeare's two 'Antony' plays.

Horace, like Cicero, felt that passion should be an indulgence left to
the young. In the older man *libido* becomes an absurdity. It is a game of
musical chairs, not something to be taken too seriously. He would no doubt
have endorsed Rosalind's dry comment in *As You Like It*: 'Men have
died…and worms have eaten them – but not for love!'[15] Ovid echoes this
irreverent attitude but extends it further. For him love is a fascination, even
an artistic pursuit. His celebrations of promiscuity were felt by Augustus
to undermine his new edicts against adultery and in consequence, it is said,
his books were banned from libraries and the poet himself sent into exile
on the shores of the Black Sea. Even Ovid, however, sometimes kept both
feet on the ground, conceding cheerfully that 'love yields to business: be
busy and you are safe.'[16] Frivolity, in the end, must give way to the solemn
concerns of politics once the young have had their fling. The lustful youth
was urged to expend his energies upon tarts and prostitutes, a course of
action advocated with particular vehemence by Cato and by Terence.[17]

Marriage, in Roman thinking, was not a matter of passion but a means
toward the formation of alliances advantageous in the world of public
affairs. Certain of the love elegists themselves employed terms such as
nugae and *lusus* – trifles or playthings – to describe their writings, their
self-deprecation making it clear that they did not expect these outpourings
to be considered alongside verse devoted to more serious themes. Again
we may turn to Enobarbus to represent the characteristically Roman point
of view:

Under a compelling cause let women die: it were pity to cast them
away for nothing, though between them and a great cause they
should be esteemed nothing.

(*Ant.* I.ii.134)

One hears in his words another echo of Cicero.

We were not created by nature to spend our time in frivolous jesting…. Frivolity has its place…but as a means of recreation when serious and important matters have been attended to.

(De Officiis I.29.103)

The ridiculous contortions inflicted upon humankind by such unseemly indulgences provided entertainment for the gods, we are told. Ovid's comment to this effect in the *Ars Amatoria* is translated by Shakespeare, almost word for word, in Juliet's gentle teasing of Romeo on the balcony:

> At lovers' perjuries
They say Jove laughs.[18]

(Rom. II.ii.92)

'The sweete, wittie soul of Ovid lives in mellifluous and honey-tongued Shakespeare', wrote the schoolmaster Francis Meres in *Palladis Tamia*.[19] Later in the same passage he compares Shakespeare to Catullus as among 'the best lyrick poets…the most passionate among us to bemoane the perplexities of love'.

Catullus, together with Propertius and Tibullus, defied the traditional Roman attitude towards the passions. For them love was no game but life's most serious occupation.[20] Catullus loved in the teeth of common sense, torn, in his feelings for Lesbia, between ecstasy and pain. '*Odi et amo*', he wrote in one celebrated verse.[21]

> I hate, yet love: you ask how this may be.
Who knows? I feel its truth and agony.

(Carmina lxxxv)

Like Antony he struggles against his mistress' allure, breaking away from her only to be drawn back by her irresistible magnetism. 'A woman's words to her lover should be written in wind and running water', Catullus says,[22] and we are reminded of Antony's baffled despair at Cleopatra's desertion of him at Actium.

> Betray'd I am.
O this false soul of Egypt! this grave charm
Whose eye beck'd forth my wars and call'd them home;
Whose bosom was my crownet, my chief end,
Like a right gipsy, hath at fast and loose
Beguil'd me, to the very heart of loss.

(Ant. IV.xii.24)

Catullus' work contains a fervour comparable to that of Robert Burns. He is the first writer to chronicle, in all its sharp intensity, through a whole series of poems, one particular love affair and his influence upon the Renaissance was profound. Petrarch is greatly indebted to him and both Shakespeare and Marlowe, among many others, fell beneath his spell.

Tibullus, like Antony, finds that the claims of love are as alluring as the prospect of military fame.

Here among the brawls of love, I am general and valiant soldier.[23]

Militia amoris, the service of love, detains both from more literal battle-fields.

Propertius, who has been likened to Byron and Rossetti, was a great romantic well over a millennium before such a concept came to be recognised.[24] His tempestuous affair with 'Cynthia' prompted the most passionate amatory verse to be found – in European literature at least – before the late middle ages. All orthodox Roman values he throws to the wind in his blind obsession with his mistress. Like Shakespeare's lovers he asserts his passion's own rationale, its own validity. 'Conquered nations mean nothing to one in love', he declared, his feelings for Cynthia outweighing all considerations of wealth, power and nobility. He surrenders himself totally to *amor* and has no wish to be rescued from its grip. In his frenzied desire he comes close to madness, feeling the torments of a Tantalus. The frustrated lover finds that 'the water deceives his thirst, ever moving away from his parched lips'.[25]

It is a situation that would have appalled the conventional Roman mind with its staid insistence upon order, balance and proportion – a mind, in fact, like Philo's who, in the play's opening speech, informs us that Antony's infatuation

> ...reneges all temper
> And is become the bellows and the fan
> To cool a gipsy's lust.

> (*Ant.* I.i.8)

The metaphor suggests that the sexual act simultaneously quenches and rekindles desire, as though the lover is a Sisyphus condemned to roll a rock up a hill whose summit is unattainable. Hamlet recalls his mother's passion for his dead father in similar terms:

> Why, she would hang on him
> As if increase of appetite had grown

By what it fed on.

(*Ham.* I.ii.143)

Again it falls to Enobarbus to express Rome's bewilderment – not untinged with awe – at Cleopatra's limitless fascination.

> Age cannot wither her, nor custom stale
> Her infinite variety: other women cloy
> The appetites they feed, but she makes hungry
> Where most she satisfies.

(*Ant.* II.ii.235)

Whatever the source of her mysterious allure it is a matter of some convenience for Pompey, another of sound Roman temperament.

> Let witchcraft join with beauty, lust with both,
> Tie up the libertine in a field of feasts,
> Keep his brain fuming.

(*Ant.* II.i.22)

This sexual paranoia will, he hopes, detain 'the ne'er-lust-wearied Antony' safely in Egypt, 'proroguing' his Roman honour and thus leaving the seas to him.[26] From the traditional Roman standpoint it is the fulfilment of the prophecy Venus makes on the death of Adonis when, in Shakespeare's early poem, she says of love:

> It shall be raging mad and silly mild,
> Make the young old, the old become a child.

(*V & A* 1151)

Antony experiences this madness more than once during the course of the play. 'The shirt of Nessus is upon me!' (*Ant.* IV.xii.43) he cries out,[27] for example, when the 'triple-turn'd whore' deserts him at the height of battle.

Troilus, forced to confront a still more devastating betrayal of love, probes the nature of rationality's collapse:

> O madness of discourse,
> That cause sets up with and against itself!
> Bifold authority! Where reason can revolt
> Without perdition, and loss assume all reason
> Without revolt. This is, and is not, Cressid.

(*Troil.* V.ii.141)

Like Tibullus he is faced with a 'traitoress, but, though traitoress, still beloved'.[28]

To Antony we may apply, in reverse, Brutus' celebrated comment about Caesar:

> I have not known when his affections sway'd
> More than his reason.
>
> (*Caes.* II.i.20)

In the later play, received Roman wisdom is flouted at every turn. Antony's challenge to these conventional values reflects the sense that, in the process of establishing the Empire, the old Republican certainties are beginning to dissolve. *Antony and Cleopatra* contains much harking back to the Republic. Octavius, for example, recalls how Antony once, in time of famine, subsisted upon horse urine, hedge berries and the bark of trees, bearing the privation 'like a soldier'.[29] Now, in his 'dotage', he feasts kings in Alexandria and lets a woman wear the sword with which he overcame Brutus and Cassius at Philippi.[30] The *virtus* cult is undermined and Stoicism gives way to dissipation. Philo invites us to watch

> The triple pillar of the world transform'd
> Into a strumpet's fool.
>
> (*Ant.* I.i.12)

Antony has fallen short of the rigorous Roman ideal as he himself admits to Octavia: 'I have not kept my square' (*Ant.* II.iii.6).

As the play progresses, however, we see an alternative value system emerge. The 'squareness' of Octavian Rome comes to seem increasingly unappealing. Grey, efficient, solid, linear, its attractions pall beside the colourful, fluid world of warmth and feeling that Egypt represents and out of which the lovers create their own private raison d'être. High Octavian principle degenerates, by contrast, into shabby compromise and expediency. Roman firmness now comes to seem tedious and sterile against the lovers' quicksilver world of the imagination.

Octavius' own world can be measured, indeed it is circumscribed, predicated upon calculation, security and limit. Antony, on the other hand, finds beggary in that which can be reckoned.[31]

The earlier works are not without their questioning of Roman values, but here Shakespeare subjects them to the intensest scrutiny and finds them deeply flawed. There is no doubting the relentless practicality of the Roman system. Organised, cautious and industrious, Octavius epitomises the virtues of his people. Will-power and obedience ally themselves to seriousness, discipline and moderation. Individuality is always subordinate to the larger interests of the state. He has a weightiness, dignity and self-control which is impressive, certainly, but highly unromantic. By comparison with Egyptian *brio* Rome seems staid and dull. Octavius is called, by Thidias, 'the universal landlord'[32] and the phrase suits him well. His personality, like his sister's, is 'cold and sickly', lending 'narrow measure' to his rare words of approbation.[33] Antony's generous warmth had, we are told, 'no winter in't' but was autumnal, growing (like his lust) 'the more by reaping'.[34] When, near the end, Cleopatra declares "tis paltry to be Caesar' and reduces Octavius to the status of 'ass unpolicied' we readily find in him and all he represents that very 'diminution' of which Enobarbus spoke in condemning Antony.[35]

Unlike that of his more successful counterpart, however, Antony's stature grows, posthumously, in the final act, achieving through the lens of Cleopatra's soaring rhapsodies, a god-like aura. By comparison Octavius seems strictly earthbound and unheroic. When he says to Maecenas:

> Within our files there are,
> Of those that serv'd Mark Antony but late
> Enough to fetch him in. See it done.

> (*Ant.* IV.i.12)

he refers, of course, to units of his army and not to the systematised documentation of the modern administrator but, by an etymological quirk, the latter sense would not be inappropriate, for he is every inch the efficient bureaucrat.

There are, it should be said, two Antonies. 'A Roman thought hath struck him' (*Ant.* I.ii.80), observes Cleopatra with a certain irony. He switches easily from Egyptian back to Roman mode, even his syntax changing to the measured rhythms and careful articulation appropriate to this context, as Julian Markels points out in his perceptive study of the play.[36]

The marriage to Octavia is the essence of Roman statesmanship. Devotion to Cleopatra does not make him any the better able to endure the bitterness of military defeat, although it is his despair at her supposed death rather than his soldierly honour that propels him the final step towards his very Roman suicide.

In both the lovers, passion and politics are inextricably mingled – indeed each becomes, in some sense, an expression of the other. Cleopatra understands her partner's need to maintain his Roman honour, irksome to her though its consequences are. Antony's status as 'world sharer' earns her chronicle as well as his, and in it her love for him is spectacularly affirmed.

I made these wars for Egypt and the queen
Whose heart I thought I had, for she had mine.

(Ant. IV.xiv.15)

It is ironic that Cleopatra should undermine those Roman virtues in her lover which she most admires, only to assume, at the end, that marble constancy[37] which for so long eluded Antony. Her own stoic death emphasises the inseparability of love and power in the play. The poison takes her with Antony's name upon her lips and the crown of Egypt upon her head. How characteristically Shakespearean a touch that it should have slipped a little out of true.

The choice between love and worldly power is an impossible one for either of them to make which is why, ultimately, they refuse to choose at all. In seeking to inhabit both worlds they are crushed between the two. But then, as Ovid wrote in the *Amores*:

Love on a plate soon palls –
Like eating too much cake...
If you want what's easy to get,
Pick leaves off trees, drink Tiber water![38]

Roman tradition, as we have seen, insisted in excluding *amor* from the pursuit of statesmanship. The softer feelings had no place in public affairs of any kind. On a battlefield they are preposterous. To be defeated in the normal way is shame enough. Antony's humiliation, like his love, 'o'erflows the measure'.

Now I must
To the young man send humble treaties, dodge
And palter in the shifts of lowness, who
With half the bulk o'the world play'd as I pleas'd,
Making and marring fortunes. You did know
How much you were my conqueror, and that
My sword, made weak by my affection, would
Obey it on all cause.

(Ant. III.xi.62)

In Antony, manliness and love refuse to be made incompatible. Cleopatra's 'Pardon! Pardon!' is swiftly answered.

Fall not a tear, I say. One of them rates
All that is won and lost. Give me a kiss.

Even this repays me.

(*Ant.* III.xi.69)

It is not a sentiment to be found in the earlier Roman plays, nor does Coriolanus arrive at the recognition until just before the end.

O, a kiss
Long as my exile, sweet as my revenge!

(*Cor.* V.iii.44)

One is reminded of Macduff's words on hearing that his wife and children have been slaughtered by Macbeth. 'Dispute it like a man!' Malcolm urges, to receive the striking answer:

I shall do so;
But I must also feel it as a man.

(*Mac.* IV.iii.221)

The passage points towards Shakespeare's growing dissatisfaction with that hard-edged austerity which previously engaged his admiration. Where was the room for human warmth in the Roman code? Even John Calvin, not most people's idea of a sentimentalist, had commented upon this deficiency:

We observe then how completely the Romans were without natural affection, loving neither their wives nor the female sex...[39]

Confronted by his mother, wife and child, Coriolanus' stubborn *virtus* finally yields, and he is forced to the realisation that 'doves' eyes...can make gods forsworn'. To his discomfiture he feels his Roman hardness start to dissolve.

I melt and am not
Of stronger earth than others.

(*Cor.* V.iii.28)

This imagery of melting is the key motif in *Antony and Cleopatra*. Indeed it might well be argued that in no play of Shakespeare's is more meaning conveyed by one particular strand of metaphor.

Rome has a massive firmness and solidity, an austere grandeur which lacks the capacity to accommodate itself to the urgings of the heart as opposed to the head. Its values are frozen in the past, marmoreal, statuesque. They tower forbiddingly over each new generation which feels, in its turn, daunted by the legacy it has been bequeathed, as though a weight is bearing down upon its shoulders, pressurising it towards conformity. Octavia epitomises this intimidating petrifaction. 'Cold and still' as she is,

> She shows a body, rather than a life,
> A statue, than a breather.

(Ant. III.ii.20)

She represents that 'squareness' which her husband, by his own admission, has failed to keep. Against this measured angularity we find juxtaposed images of fluidity and evanescence. The positive manner in which this 'Egyptian' imagery is presented leaves little doubt as to where Shakespeare's sympathies lie. Roman firmness and linearity have come to seem rigid, tedious and sterile.

At Egypt's heart is her mercurial Queen. '*Varium et mutabile semper femina*,' wrote Virgil in the *Aeneid*.[40] 'Woman was ever fickle and volatile.' Aeneas is referring to Dido, Queen of Carthage, Cleopatra's *alter ego* it might be said. Her love is uncontainable, spilling over far beyond the 'bourn' that, teasingly, she sets down for it in the opening scene. If Rome is the sea wall then Cleopatra is the turbulent sea. Water is her element. Her power depends upon a navy not an infantry. Our most vivid picture of her, painted again by Enobarbus, depicts her on the River Cydnus, her barge rowed by silver oars

> Which to the tune of flutes kept stroke and made
> The water which they beat to follow faster
> As amorous of their strokes.

(Ant. II.ii.199)

There is, as Susan Snyder has demonstrated,[41] a purposelessness and a frivolity in the movements we associate with Egypt – drifting, fanning, floating, hopping – which contrasts tellingly with Roman stolidity and stasis. Skittishness and caprice are in the very air which, but for the laws of physics, would have

> ...gone to gaze on Cleopatra too
> And made a gap in nature.

(Ant. II.ii.218)

Antony's whimsical observation of the sky reflects his uneasiness at the shifting nature of the values in this Egyptian world from which hard-edged restraint is so markedly absent.

> Sometimes we see a cloud that's dragonish,
> A vapour sometime, like a bear or lion...
> That which is now a horse, even with a thought
> The rack dislimns, and makes it indistinct
> As water is in water.

(Ant. IV.xiv.2-11)

Enobarbus' lame response – 'It does, my lord' – conveys a characteristic Roman bewilderment in the face of what appears to him a moral free-for-all. Antony shares this perplexity, wrestling with its implications but never able to find the firm ground upon which Octavius stands.

> What our contempts doth often hurl from us
> We wish it ours again. The present pleasure,
> By revolution lowering, does become
> The opposite of itself.

(Ant. I.ii.120)

Such insecurity is the inevitable concomitant, Shakespeare seems to imply, of that intense outpouring of passionate feeling which dominates the play and which is so alien to the Roman cast of mind as revealed in earlier texts such as *Titus Andronicus* and *Julius Caesar*. A love like Antony's and Cleopatra's cannot be built upon secure foundations but bobs upon a swaying tide of precariousness and ambiguity. The play's central image is dissolution and mutability, as we have seen. The lovers, like the cloud, are unable to 'hold this visible shape',[42] losing distinction in a way that recalls *The Phoenix and the Turtle.*

> So they lov'd, as love in twain
> Had the essence but in one:
> Two distincts, division none;
> Number there in love was slain.

Love unlocks a power to pass beyond the physical limitations of the self, Shakespeare suggests.

> Then must thou needs find out new heaven, new earth.

(Ant. I.i.17)

It is an idea that would have been incomprehensible in Rome.

Like the moon and the Nile – both important emblems in the play – the lovers are in perpetual flux and yet, underlying this, is a deeper constancy than that embodied by Octavian rigorousness. By overflowing its bounds the Nile fertilises the surrounding land. New life emerges from the slime, putrescence being another mode of melting.

> Lay me stark-nak'd, and let the water-flies
> Blow me into abhorring,
>
> (Ant. V.ii.59)

proclaims Cleopatra in a vehement flight of rhetoric. She must, emblematically, decay into the fluidity of the river in order to be reborn as 'fire and air'.

Poets like Tibullus and Propertius, possessed as they were by love, regarded it as slavery and imprisonment. In Shakespeare's hands, however, it becomes release. Just as, in its setting, *Antony and Cleopatra* ranges far more widely than any of the other Roman plays, – spanning, in purely geographic terms, most of the known world, – so, equally, in the values it affirms, we recognise a much broader vision, a more comprehensive sensibility.

Here defeat can be liberating, victory a hollow mockery as it is for Octavius in Cleopatra's monument. Antony's suicide differs fundamentally from those of Brutus and Cassius. Theirs are relatively straightforward deeds, true to the spirit of the Roman honour code, but Antony's death serves many ends in one.[43] Like them he dies, in part, to avoid the humiliation of defeat and with an eye to his posterity,

> ...a Roman by a Roman
> Valiantly vanquish'd.
>
> (Ant. IV.xv.57)

Thus far, at least, he conforms to the tradition of Stoic fortitude and heroism. His suicide, additionally, like Cleopatra's, 'Shackles accidents and bolts up change' (*Ant.* V.ii.6). In a world of dynamism and fluctuation they are finally at rest. Not for them the *Pax Augusta*, stretching ahead, flat, methodical and colourless, but the more vibrant fixity of myth.

> No grave upon the earth shall clip in it
> A pair so famous,
>
> (Ant. V.ii.357)

Octavius declares with unconscious ambiguity. Uniquely among Shakespeare's Romans they die for love[44] in true romantic vein, like a Romeo and a Juliet, while, at the same time, affirming their *virtus* and their Stoic spirit. Suicide is the ultimate validation of their love.

Unlike their Roman predecessors they envisage a personal survival beyond the grave.

> Stay for me
> Where souls do couch on flowers, we'll hand in hand
> And with our sprightly port make the ghosts gaze.

> (*Ant.* IV.xiv.50)

They die to be mystically reunited, as in a marriage of fire and air, and to find a constancy denied to them in the turbulence of this life. Antony runs like a bridegroom to a lover's bed while Cleopatra completes the wedding ceremony:

> Husband, I come:
> Now to that name my courage prove my title.

> (*Ant.* V.ii.286)

Love and death form a 'knot intrinsicate'.[45] Earlier she has been all 'winds and waters', as Enobarbus reports. One is reminded of a line in *Venus and Adonis*:

> For men have marble, women waxen minds.

> (*V & A* 1240)

Whatever her earlier vacilliation, however, she becomes 'marble constant' in making away with herself 'after the high Roman fashion'.[46] Like Antony she combines cold fortitude with hot, erotic flame.

> We have no friend
> But resolution and the briefest end.

> (*Ant.* IV.xv.90)

Shakespeare's choice of the word 'resolution' here ingeniously encapsulates the essence of the play. Through the firm 'resolve' of her suicide her problems will be 'resolved', or melted, in the 'resolution' of her life from Octavian substance to an insubstantiality that belongs to a dimension of the imagination of which such as he can have no inkling.

Only Propertius, of Roman poets, envisages love's power to transcend death in any personal sense.

> Others may clasp thee now – soon I alone;
> Thou shalt be mine and mingle bone with bone.[47]

His elegies, with their mysterious loveliness, their eerie glamour, are quite alien to the Roman cast of mind as we traditionally understand it. Like Shakespeare's famous couple, he feels passion so intensely that he cannot believe even death will bring it to an end. There must be something beyond.

> Not so lightly has Cupid clung to my eyes
> That my dust could forget and be free of love.[48]

'There is a world elsewhere',[49] as Coriolanus discovers, both in the geographical sense and as an alternative to the harsh *virtus* code. Antony, too, makes choices between 'Octavian' values – by which criteria he is 'the abstract of all faults/That all men follow'[50] – and the intuitions of the leaping heart. Though he clings to the remnants of his *Romanitas*, it is the roman*tic* impulse which takes possession of him. Shakespeare suggests that the political world is irredeemably flawed and that it must yield before the higher claims of a personal commitment and devotion. We are confronted with the startling thought that the love of two individuals can outweigh piled centuries of disembodied state.

> Let Rome in Tiber melt, and the wide arch
> Of the rang'd empire fall! Here is my space,
> Kingdoms are clay: our dungy earth alike
> Feeds beast as man; the nobleness of life
> Is to do thus. [*He embraces Cleopatra.*]

> (*Ant.* I.i.33)

Rome 'melts' for him as it does for Coriolanus, when, finally, he too becomes sufficiently 'a gosling to obey instinct' and, implicitly, to reject those 'colder reasons'[51] that governed his behaviour to that point.

> I will appear in blood.
> I, and my sword, will earn our chronicle.

> (*Ant.* III.xiii.175)

The words are Antony's, yet might easily be mistaken for Coriolanus'. Antony, though, fights that he may 'return once more/To kiss these lips' and, on the eve of battle, calls for yet 'one other gaudy night'.[52]

Both men agonise about their identity. Coriolanus is conscious of being forced into a charade in which his true self becomes a mockery while Antony feels the need for defiant assertion of his selfhood.

I am Antony yet!

(*Ant.* III.xiii.93)

Like other Roman leaders, he speaks of himself frequently in the third person as though somehow to mythologise his own image. Indeed he goes further, claiming Hercules as his ancestor[53] and identifying himself with Aeneas, another heroic figure to break from the arms of a weeping African queen.[54]

The lovers, in a sense, dissolve into the higher reality of each other as an escape from the painful isolation of their own separate subjectivity. The exchange of clothes during what Octavius calls their 'lascivious wassails'[55] may be seen as an external symbol of this merging. Octavius accuses Antony of effeminacy, declaring that he

...is not more manlike
Than Cleopatra; nor the queen of Ptolemy
More womanly than he.

(*Ant.* I.iv.5)

It is a charge not levelled against any other of Shakespeare's Romans and, in itself, indicative of the very different view of *virtus* – manliness – that predominates in this play.

What the classical world saw as weakness and decadence in Antony, Shakespeare presents as a superior strength. It is his love for Cleopatra that earns his place in posterity rather than his triumphs on the battlefield. It is not, however, a question merely of joining the Roman pantheon of fame or becoming, like Julius Caesar, some 'glorious star'.[56] Here love challenges time in a far more personal sense.

Antony and Cleopatra inhabit a realm of idealisation that has little in common with the other Roman plays, quarrelling with the mundane in their search for a superior reality. The Queen insists that

...to imagine
An Antony were nature's piece, 'gainst fancy,
Condemning shadows quite.

(*Ant.* V.ii.98)

166

Even fantasy balks at the task entrusted to it in recreating her dead lover. We are now 'past the size of dreaming'.[57]

In their search for absolute value in their love the pair run up against the cruel paradox so cogently expressed by Troilus whose aching idealism is strongly reminiscent of their own:

> This is the monstruosity in love, lady, that the will is infinite and the act confin'd; that the desire is boundless and the act a slave to limit.
>
> (*Troil.* III.ii.77)

In *Antony and Cleopatra*, however, the lovers deny measure and limitation, regarding them as Octavian territory. Caesar may have the world if they may have each other.

> Ah but a man's reach should exceed his grasp
> Or what's a heaven for?

wrote Robert Browning.[58] In this play, though, reach seems endlessly extensible, the lovers bursting through conventional constraint and glimpsing a kind of heaven that lies beyond. 'Measure' itself overflows as early as the second line. 'Octavian' quantification is denied with a wild abandon that recalls Catullus' most famous poem to Lesbia.

> Give me a thousand kisses – more!
> A hundred yet: add to the score
> A second thousand kisses: then
> Another hundred, and again
> A thousand more, a hundred still,
> So many thousands we fulfil...[59]

For Shakespeare's lovers even such extravagant reckoning is the merest beggary. It is, therefore, peculiarly apt that, in the play's final moments, the coldly prosaic Octavius, the very epitome of Roman-ness, should be touched to lyricism by this ardent flame as he stands, wondering, by Cleopatra's throne. It is as though he recognises in the dead Queen a nobility that overshadows his own.

> She looks like sleep,
> As she would catch another Antony
> In her strong toil of grace.
>
> (*Ant.* V.ii.344)

The ambivalent image of the 'toil' or net suggests her power to catch and hold an Antony in life or to let him slip, fluid, through the mesh like wind and water, to follow after and be reunited with her wherever she has gone.

The haunting words of Brutus spring to mind: 'I shall find time, Cassius, I shall find time' (*Caes.* V.iii.103). Northrop Frye defined the heroic as 'something infinite imprisoned in the finite'[60] and in *Antony and Cleopatra* Shakespeare is much concerned with the transcending of time's limitation. He takes issue with Plutarch, who declared that Antony

> ...yeelded him selfe to goe with Cleopatra into Alexandria, where he spent and lost in childish sports and idle pastimes the most pretious thing a man can spende and that is, time.[61]

In the other Roman plays the emphasis is heavily on the past. Here, by contrast, Shakespeare searches for an accommodation between austere, illustrious history and the urgent immediacy of love. Works such as *Titus Andronicus* and *Julius Caesar* represent Rome as monolithic permanence, sheer durability, as well as encouraging us to look forward to its semi-mystical destiny, as Virgil does in the *Aeneid*. It has, therefore, a timelessness of its own.

In this later play, however, Shakespeare is concerned with what, in *Sonnet 15*, he calls 'crowning the present'.

> Make war against proportion'd course of time.

> (*RL.* 774)

Lucrece's demand is answered in *Antony and Cleopatra*. Time, like other aspects of quantification, exists to be defied. Antony, in particular, seeks refuge from the mocking reminders of his former greatness, earning Octavius' contemptuous comparison with

> ...boys, who being mature in knowledge,
> Pawn their experience to their present pleasure
> And so rebel to judgement.

> (*Ant.* I.iv.31)

He, for his part, urges Octavius to 'be a child o'the time'.[62] 'Possess it', answers Caesar, and this is what Antony sets out to do.

> There's not a minute of our lives should stretch
> Without some pleasure now.

> (*Ant.* I.i.46)

he tells Cleopatra, as though he has in mind Horace's famous maxim:

Harvest the day and leave as little as you can for tomorrow.[63]

Feste's poignant song strikes a similar note in *Twelfth Night*:

What is love? 'Tis not hereafter;
Present joy hath present laughter.

(*Tw. N.* II.iii.46)

'All length is torture'[64] to Antony who will foreshorten time into a permanent 'now', a word which occurs forty-five times in the play. His preoccupation is shared by Cleopatra who feels a desperate need to locate him in the present moment:

Where think'st thou he is now? Stands he or sits he?
Or does he walk? Or is he on his horse?

(*Ant.* I.v.19)

Her crowning ambition is to lose herself totally in the immediacy of him:

O my oblivion is a very Antony
And I am all forgotten.

(*Ant.* I.iii.90)

'I must stay his time',[65] she resolves, and in Alexandria the pair live their lives up to the hilt. The lamps burn late, as they do in the Boar's Head tavern, another world of garish anarchy. 'What a devil hast *thou* to do with the time of the day?' (*1H.IV* I.ii.6) says Hal to Falstaff as though he existed in a different dimension from the one encompassing ordinary men. Time, in other words, may be experiential and not dependent upon some disembodied clock.

The lovers absorb each moment with a fullness, an intensity, that is totally subjective, dissolving, as it were, potentiality out from the frozen world the Octavias inhabit into the passionate heat of actualisation. What Ulysses calls 'envious and calumniating time'[66] may be cheated not in prolongation but in its opposite, that is by speeding the fleet-foot moment on its way. It is the philosophy expounded in Andrew Marvell's famous lines:

Rather at once our time devour
Than languish in his slow-chapt power;

Let us roll all our strength and all
Our sweetness up into one ball,
And tear our pleasures with rough strife
Thorough the iron gates of life:
Thus, though we cannot make our sun
Stand still, yet we will make him run![67]

Octavius imagines he can thwart time by exhibiting Cleopatra in his victory parade.

> Her life in Rome
> Would be eternal in our triumph.

(Ant. V.i.66)

But he is wrong. Time belongs to the lovers.

> Eternity was in our lips and eyes.

(Ant. I.iii.35)

'Eternity *was*.' The temporal paradox cuts direct to the heart of the play. Rome's statuesque grandeur looms above the lovers, cold and inexorable as an iceberg. In its huge shadow they rush together, to disappear in a blaze of splendour that is inversely proportionate to its duration in 'measurable' time. As Friar Lawrence tells their younger selves:

> These violent delights have violent ends,
> And in their triumphs die, like fire and powder
> Which, as they kiss, consume.

(Rom. II.vi.19)

At the last the assembled Romans stand blinking in the incandescent afterglow of a passion they can never begin to comprehend.

Notes

1. pp. 154-61.
2. III.6; XXV.63; XLI.104-5.
3. pp. 36-7.
4. *Odes* 1.37, 21.
5. *De Casibus Virorum et Feminarum Illustrium* (1355-60), a work which eventually formed the basis for William Baldwin's compilation of

verse biographies: *The Mirror for Magistrates* (1559) which, in its turn, almost certainly provided Shakespeare with material for his plays.

6. The passage is quoted in the Arden edition of *Antony and Cleopatra* (edn M.R. Ridley, Methuen, 1954) pp. 365-6.

7. See Arden edn, appendix p. 255.

8. For example, Cicero: *Tusc.* 4, 72 ff. and Horace: *Satires* i.2.48.

9. See, for instance, *De Officiis* 1.29.102.

10. 1.29.105.

11. I.ii.167.

12. III.xiii.7-8.

13. *Amores* II.i.x trans. Guy Lee.

14. See Paul Cantor: *Shakespeare's Rome* (Cornell, 1976) p. 159.

15. IV.i.101.

16. *Remedia Amoris* 143.

17. See, for example, Terence: *Adelphi* 32-3.

18. Cf. *Ars Amatoria* 633. *Iuppiter exalto periuria ridet amantum.*

19. A collection of miscellaneous essays published in 1598.

20. Though, arguably, this was to some extent a pose, an intellectual game played by the fashionable *poetae novi.*

21. Cf. *Cym.* III.v.71.

22. *Carmina* xx.

23. I.i.76 trans. Walter Lyne.

24. 'Romantic' derives from the term 'romance', a literary genre much preoccupied with heroines and 'courtly love', a set of attitudes which developed, it seems, in S.E. France during the 12th century. Many of these works were originally written in the Provençal or 'Romanic' language, a vernacular form of medieval Latin, hence the tenuous link with the word 'Roman'. Ironically perhaps, the two words seem, in other respects, antithetical.

25. *Ut liquor arenti fallat ab ore sitim.*

26. II.i.24-38.

27. IV.xii.43. Nessus, the centaur, was fatally injured by Hercules' poisoned arrow. Before dying, Nessus gave his blood-soaked shirt to Hercules' wife, Deianira, claiming it to be a love charm. It later brought about Hercules' painful death. The story is recounted in *Metamorphoses* ix.

28. *Perfida, sed quamvis perfida cara tamen* (III.6.56).

29. I.iv.61-70.

30. *Caes.* II.v.23.

31. I.i.15.

32. III.xiii.72.

33. III.iv.7-8.

34. V.ii.86.

35. V.ii.2; V.ii.306; III.xiii.198.
36. *The Pillar of the World* (Ohio State University Press, 1968) p. 19.
37. V.ii.238.
38. II.xviii and xix trans. Guy Lee.
39. *Commentaries on the Book of Daniel* (trans. Frederic Myers, 1852) II 349.
40. IV 569.
41. *Patterns of Motion in Antony and Cleopatra, Shakespeare Survey* 30 (1980).
42. IV.xiv.14.
43. It is also worth noting that his suicide, unlike their efficient dispatch, is a botched, ill-managed affair. Perhaps, symbolically, it is the equivalent of his partner's tilted crown (V.ii.317).
44. Though, of course, they die with a number of other considerations in their minds as well.
45. V.ii.146.
46. IV.xv.87.
47. IV.vii. trans. J.W. Duff.
48. I.xix. trans. Walter Lyne.
49. III.iii.135.
50. I.iv.9.
51. *Cor.* V.iii.35 and V.iii.86.
52. *Ant.* III.xiii.173-83.
53. IV.xii.44.
54. *Aeneid* IV. xiv.53.
55. II.v.19-23.
56. *1H.VI* I.i.55. See *Metamorphoses* xv.
57. V.ii.97.
58. *Andrea del Sarto.*
59. *Vivamus mea Lesbia* trans. A.M. Duff.
60. *Fools of Time* (University of Toronto Press, 1967) p. 5.
61. Plutarch: *Life of Mark Antony* 28 (trans. Sir Thomas North).
62. II.vii.98.
63. *Carpe diem, quam minimum credula postero*, Horace 3.28 trans. D. West.
64. IV.xiv.46.
65. III.xiii.155.
66. *Troil.* III.iii.174.
67. *To His Coy Mistress.*

11

Cymbeline and Synthesis

Shakespeare's changing attitude towards the Roman world and its values finds final expression in *Cymbeline*, written, it seems, within a year or two of *Antony and Cleopatra* and *Coriolanus*.[1] The play is very different in most respects from the five previous works in the sequence – if sequence it can legitimately be called. Some might even argue that *Cymbeline* should not be considered a 'Roman' play at all. It is true that, of its twenty-eight scenes, only three are set in Rome itself, but Romans feature prominently in a further nine and their names are frequently on people's lips throughout the remainder of the text. Indeed many of the Celtic Britons are already 'Romanised' to a considerable degree, as their Latinate names suggest. Cymbeline himself, for example, was brought up – and 'knighted' – at Augustus' court. For all Imogen's claim that

> I'th'world's volume
> Our Britain seems as of it, but not in't.
> In a great pool, a swan's nest.

(Cym. III.iv.139)

there is no doubt that the islands are very much, in fact, a part of the Roman orbit as is made clear when, the very next day, Caius Lucius lands at Milford Haven with his legions.

Historically the events of *Cymbeline* follow on from those of *Antony and Cleopatra*. According to Holinshed,[2] the British King ascended the throne in 33 BC, three years before the lovers' suicides. The events of Shakespeare's play take place, it seems, some twenty or more years into Cymbeline's reign,[3] in the middle of the *Pax Augusta* and a decade or so before the birth of Christ.

Antony and Cleopatra is frequently recalled not only in the many

173

references to Augustan Rome but also in the stress laid upon time, ripeness and regeneration, themes we associate with the earlier tragedy as well as with the quartet of 'late' plays or 'romances' of which Cymbeline forms a part.[4] In the mellower light of this last phase of Shakespeare's career, time ceases to be enemy to love and becomes, instead, its midwife. Octavius' 'strong toil of grace'[5] may be reinterpreted as the painful labour necessary to give birth to that divine mercy brought into the world during his reign by the Nativity in Bethlehem.

The word 'grace', with its powerful Christian connotations, is now clearly very much in Shakespeare's mind, occurring with striking frequency in his maturest works.[6] One is reminded of Coriolanus' first greeting to his wife: 'My gracious silence, hail!' (*Cor.* II.i.74), words which look forward to the intercession scene, to Virgilia's mute entreaty and to the melting of stubborn *virtus* in compassion.

Cleopatra, we recall, liked to appear dressed as Isis,[7] goddess of the earth, whose tears for her lost lover, Osiris, caused the Nile to overflow, bringing with it both fertility and destruction. Each new year's growth may be seen, in this mythic context, as a celebration of the redemptive power of love.

The four 'romances' conclude, like the earlier comedies, not so much with an end as with a fresh beginning. Marina, Imogen, Perdita and Miranda – all 'lost' in various senses of the word – are 'rediscovered' in the final act, bringing back the spring to the earth in bonds of love. When, near the end of *The Tempest*, Propero pronounces that

> The rarer action is
> In virtue than in vengeance,

(Temp. V.i.27)

the sense of the word 'virtue' has travelled a very long way from its Roman origin as 'manly fortitude'. Shakespeare is now thinking in terms of the Christian *caritas*.

Again it is *Antony and Cleopatra* which acts as the bridge from the earlier Roman texts to this final vision. Ripeness and rotting, as we have seen, become, in Egypt, part of the same creative cycle. In *Sonnet 86* Shakespeare's 'ripe thoughts' are 'inhearsed' in his brain, 'Making their tomb the womb wherein they grew.' It is a process that Touchstone meditates upon in *As You Like It*.

> And so from hour to hour we ripe and ripe
> And then, from hour to hour, we rot and rot;
> And thereby hangs a tale.

(AYL. II.vii.25)

Rottenness in Nile terms is fecundity. When aboard his barge, Pompey protests that 'This is not yet an Alexandrian feast' (*Ant.* II.vii.94). Antony's reply: 'It ripens towards it' contains the same expansiveness that we find in Cleopatra's description of his 'bounty':

> There was no winter in't: an autumn 'twas
> That grew the more by reaping.

> (*Ant.* V.ii.86)

Here, essentialised, is a comic vision not encountered in the earlier Roman texts.

Posthumus 'in's spring became a harvest'.[8] In his relationship with Imogen there are echoes of Antony's with Cleopatra.

> To his mistress,
> (For whom he now is banish'd) her own price
> Proclaims how she esteem'd him; and his virtue
> By her election may be truly read
> What kind of man he is.

> (*Cym.* I.i.50)

True to his name, Posthumus, apparently decapitated, is restored to life at the end, as is the spotless reputation of his wife. 'Hang there like fruit, my soul!' (*Cym.* V.v.264) he cries, embracing her, and his words carry profound implications of creative continuity, reminding us that Imogen is 'alone the Arabian bird'[9] or phoenix, as Antony was in the eyes of Agrippa.[10] The fabulous bird, with its cycle of self-immolation and resurrection, symbolises the power of love, in its Christian context, to bring about forgiveness and reconciliation, as it does in the final act of all four plays.

It is not an intellectual process. 'Love's reason's beyond reason', explains Arviragus to Belarius.[11] It is a sentiment as foreign to the *mos maiorum* as what Iachimo calls – in another passage strikingly reminiscent of *Antony and Cleopatra* –

> The cloyed will,
> That satiate yet unsatisfied desire, that tub
> Both fill'd and running.

> (*Cym.* I.vii.47)

His typically Roman contempt for romantic excess is like the attitude towards Desdemona and Othello exhibited by his precursor, Iago, to whom it is merely 'a lust of the blood and a permission of the will'.[12]

Iachimo inhabits simultaneously two very different worlds. Shakespeare seems undecided as to whether his villain is an ancient Roman or a Renaissance Italian. The action of the play takes place entirely within the reign of Augustus Caesar and Iachimo seems to have contact with the imperial court.

> Some dozen Romans of us...have mingled sums
> To buy a present for the emperor.

> (*Cym*. I.vii.106)

He is apparently familiar with the Capitol[13] and later leads, by the mandate of the Senate, a detachment of soldiers in Caius Lucius' expedition to Wales. Nevertheless he is referred to as '*Signior* Iachimo'[14] and 'Italian fiend',[15] mixes with Frenchmen, Dutchmen and Spaniards,[16] and boasts of his 'Italian brain'[17] in a passage that suggests the Tudor idea of the 'Machiavel' (as well as raising distant echoes of Aaron the Moor in *Titus Andronicus*).

There are other such anachronisms. When Imogen, on receipt of her husband's letter, protests 'That drug-damn'd Italy hath out-craftied him' (*Cym*. III.iv.15) her words call to mind the age of Cesare Borgia rather than classical Rome. The reference to 'Romish stews'[18] has the ring of that Protestant bigotry to be found in *Doctor Faustus*. By comparison, the striking clock mark two[19] seems of small account.

Nor are the play's bewildering swerves confined to the temporal plane. Posthumus shifts effortlessly from Briton to Roman and back again, as he does from nobleman to common soldier. It seems he is equally at home in all these guises. When we are told that

> He sits 'mongst men like a descended god;
> He hath a kind of honour sets him off,
> More than a mortal seeming....

> (*Cym*. I.vii.169)

Roman heroes such as Caesar and Mark Antony spring to mind[20] and one may recall, in particular, Cominius' description of Coriolanus – another exile – in Antium.

> He is their god; he leads them like a thing
> Made by some other deity than Nature
> That shapes men better.

> (*Cor*. IV.vi.90)

There are, in *Cymbeline*, so many echoes of the earlier Roman works that it is possible to regard the play as a conscious retrospect on Shakespeare's part. Perhaps, some eighteen years after the writing of *Titus Andronicus*, he set out to subsume his 'Roman' thoughts into one comprehensive vision as a means of arriving at a final verdict on their significance.

More probably, as he turned again to Roman history, cherished fragments drifted up, unbidden, from the far recesses of the mind to fall into new patterns on the page.

Posthumus' ill-advised vaunting of his wife's chastity is strongly reminiscent of Collatine's boast about the sexual inviolability of Lucrece. Indeed the events of Shakespeare's narrative poem are relived in Iachimo's soliloquy in the bedchamber:

> Our Tarquin thus
> Did softly press the rushes, ere he waken'd
> The chastity he wounded.

> (*Cym*. II.ii.12)

Beside the sleeping Imogen Iachimo finds 'The tale of Tereus', the page turned down 'where Philomel gave up'.[21] This notorious rape, as recounted by Ovid in the *Metamorphoses*,[22] reminds us of the hideous assault upon Lavinia and her subsequent mutilation in *Titus Andronicus* where, in Act IV, the same book is instrumental in bringing her ravishers to justice.

There are further similarities between the two plays. The boorish Cloten has much in common with Chiron and Demetrius, all three suffering gory death followed by dismemberment. Unlike her two unfortunate predecessors, Imogen survives unmolested despite the efforts of the Queen, Cloten's mother, to bring about her downfall, much as Tamora, another queen, abetted the designs of her own two rapist sons. The fact that 'constancy' may now 'stand...safe'[23] is in tune with the more optimistic note sounded in this latter stage of Shakespeare's career.

The tapestry in Imogen's chamber, as vividly recollected by Iachimo, depicts

> Proud Cleopatra, when she met her Roman,
> And Cydnus swell'd above the banks...

> (*Cym*. II.iv.70)

Enobarbus' famous set-piece is immediately brought back to mind. A later reference to the venomous 'worms of Nile'[24] provides another sharp reminder of the earlier play, as does Imogen's speech over what she takes to be the dead body of her husband:

...this is his hand:
His foot Mercurial: his Martial thigh:
The brawns of Hercules...

(*Cym.* IV.ii.309)

She too seeks her own death but feels more qualms than a Brutus, a Cassius or an Antony, adherents to a harsher moral code.

...Against self-slaughter
There is a prohibition so divine
That cravens my weak hand.

(*Cym.* III.iv.77)

Like them, however, she urges a servant to carry out the deed:

Come, here's my heart...
Obedient as the scabbard... Prithee, dispatch:
The lamb entreats the butcher.

(*Cym.* III.iv.79-98)

Again the outcome is different. Pissanio refuses the proferred sword and she lives on, as does Posthumus despite also seeking his own demise:

...and so, great powers,
If you will take this audit, take this life,
And cancel these cold bonds.

(*Cym.* V.iv.26)

His words have the authentic ring of Roman Stoicism and are followed immediately by a vision of his illustrious father, Sicilius Leonatus (the 'lion-born'), in warrior garb, and his dead brothers, parading their wounds in *Coriolanus* fashion. But, despite appearances, the world of *Cymbeline* is not that of the other Roman plays. Sicilius condemns Jupiter for lack of *caritas* towards his son:

Why hast thou thus adjourn'd
The graces for his merits due,
Being all to dolours turn'd?

Thy crystal window ope; look out;
No longer exercise
Upon a valiant race thy harsh

And potent injuries.

(Cym. V.iv.78)

The language here, with its allusions to 'grace' and 'merit' in its call for forgivenesss, has markedly Christian overtones not met with in the earlier works with which we have been concerned.

The character of Caius Lucius is particularly interesting. We first encounter him as an ambassador sent from Rome to demand the tribute which Cymbeline has 'left untender'd'.[25] Lucius shows a quiet strength, retaining his dignity in the face of the insults hurled at him by his Celtic hosts. When, eventually, he pronounces 'war and confusion in Caesar's name'[26] it is done with an evident reluctance to fight which we have not previously noted as a Roman attribute. Towards the end of the play Lucius returns to Britain, this time as the general commanding Augustus' army. When captured and sentenced to death his calm courage and nobility are very reminiscent of Marcus Brutus':

> But since the gods
> Will have it thus, that nothing but our lives
> May be call'd ransom, let it come: sufficeth
> A Roman with a Roman's heart can suffer.

(Cym. V.v.78)

Like Brutus, too, he shows a tender concern for his young page, the aptly-named 'Fidele', begging Cymbeline to spare 'his' life. Brutus' servant-boy is also a Lucius, and the reversal seems too neat not to have been intentional. When we recall that there are two further Luciuses in *Titus Andronicus*, both of whom are instrumental, like their *Cymbeline* namesake, in bringing about some sort of reconciliation at the end of the play, it would seem to be stretching coincidence too far if we suppose that the choice of names is purely fortuitous. In *Titus* the older Lucius is made emperor. He it is who shows mercy – not a quality that proliferates in the play – towards Aaron's bastard child and takes steps 'To heal Rome's harms and wipe away her woe' (*Tit. A.* V.iii.148). In the final scene he calls to him his son, the younger Lucius:

> Come hither, boy; come, come and learn of us
> To melt in showers...

(Tit. A. V.iii.160)

a passage that anticipates the later plays.

There may be, in the name's etymology, a suggestion of light.

179

Certainly, in *Julius Caesar*, with candle and music, Lucius brings light into Brutus' life both literally and metaphorically,[27] just as his counterparts in the other plays help to lighten the darkness that would otherwise prevail in the final scenes.

At the end of *Cymbeline* the soothsayer, Philharmonus, speaks of the Roman eagle vanishing into the sunbeams and of a British king 'which shines here in the west'.[28] There is a bright optimism which we have not found previously in Shakespeare's contemplation of the Roman world.

We sense a divine providence at work in the shaping of British history. The soothsayer's name itself would have reminded a contemporary audience of that harmonising process embarked upon by James the First. The new Stuart dynasty had been seen by some as the fulfilment of Merlin's prophecies about the unification of the realm. James shrewdly exploited such notions, declaring himself a second Arthur sent to restore Britain to her former glories. In 1608, very possibly during the writing of *Cymbeline*, he created his son Prince of Wales and the same year the English and Scottish crowns were united by Act of Parliament. Significantly, Shakespeare has Augustus' legions land at Milford Haven, the very spot where Henry Richmond, James' great grandfather, was detined to step ashore and initiate another supposedly golden age. Contemporary apologists drew elaborate parallels between Augustan times and the new Jacobean era.

James adopted the title 'Jacobus Pacificus', proclaiming himself a peacemaker in the Augustan mould and publishing a tract subtitled 'Great Britain's Blessings'. His *Pax Britannica*, as he termed it, is mirrored at the end of *Cymbeline* when the King announces:

> My peace we will begin: and Caius Lucius,
> Although the victor, we submit to Caesar,
> And to the Roman empire; promising
> To pay our wonted tribute.

> (*Cym.* V.v.460)

The two races are reunited after their long separation. According to tradition the Romans and the British had both descended from the royal house of Troy – the former from Aeneas and the latter from his great-grandson Brute. The playwright Thomas Dekker, in a fit of sycophancy, went so far as to call James 'Brute's grand grandsire'.[29]

> The time of universal peace in near:
> Prove this a prosperous day, the three-nook'd world
> Shall bear the olive freely.

> (*Ant.* IV.vi.5)

proclaims Octavius at Alexandria. Though it would probably be fanciful to read into the unusual phrase 'three-nook'd' a veiled reference to the newly united Britain – consisting of England, Scotland and Ireland – such a detail would not be inconsistent with the way Shakespeare's mind appears to have been working towards the end of his career.

Holinshed, his primary source for the historical background of *Cymbeline*,[30] asserts that it was part of God's great design for Christ to be born during a time of peace in both Britain and Rome. The date duly chosen, the thirty-fourth year of Cymbeline's reign and the twenty-eighth of Augustus', falls some dozen or so years into the *Pax Augusta*, in commemoration of which the Senate had erected a monument[31] depicting Aeneas making grateful sacrifice upon seeing the portent of his future home in Italy.

> What time th'eternall Lord in fleshly slime
> Enwombed was, from wretched Adam's line
> To purge away the guilt of sinfull crime:
> Of joyous memorie of happy time,
> That heavenly grace so plenteously display'd...

as Spenser puts it, describing Kimberline's reign in *The Faerie Queene*,[32] a poem which probably influenced Shakespeare in his researches for the play.

It was, by tradition, a golden age and the imagery bears this out.

> Golden lads and girls all must,
> As chimney-sweepers, come to dust

> (*Cym*. IV.ii.262)

laments Guiderius in his famous dirge, but Posthumus, after his visitation from Jupiter, is conscious of having been afforded a 'golden chance' whereby he is 'steep'd in favours' far beyond his deserving.[33] God's grace is incommensurate with merit. In it there lies a 'virtue' or special power that is regenerative and strengthening. The First Gentleman attributes such a gift to Posthumus in the opening scene, but it is not until Act Five that we see it put to effect when he says to Iachimo:

> Kneel not to me:
> The power that I have on you is to spare you:
> The malice towards you, to forgive you.

> (*Cym*. V.v.418)

Cymbeline himself sounds the note of reconciliation in his pronouncement: 'Pardon's the word to all' (*Cym.* V.v.423).

The British are fiercely patriotic, confronting their more powerful
enemy with a bravado that occasionally echoes *Henry V*.

> We will nothing pay for wearing our own noses.

> (*Cym.* III.i.14)

Allied to martial courage we find, here too, humility and compassion –
qualities not much encountered in the other Roman plays. There is a
startling magnanimity in the King's attitude towards his defeated enemy.

> Although the victor, we submit to Caesar
> And to the Roman empire, promising
> To pay our wonted tribute.

> (*Cym.* V.v.461)

These New Testament values could hardly be further from the flinty ethos
of *Titus Andronicus* with which Shakespeare began his Roman explora-
tions. The Soothsayer attributes the accord to heavenly intervention:

> The fingers of the powers above do tune
> The harmony of this peace.

> (*Cym.* V.v.467)

Cymbeline's paying of tribute to Caesar is, in Shakespeare's eyes,
clearly a matter of immense significance, as the supernatural visitations
serve to emphasise.

> Our subjects, sir,
> Will not endure his yoke.

> (*Cym.* III.v.5)

Cymbeline tells Augustus' representative and there is an ambiguity in his
choice of word. 'Yoke' implies restriction, even enslavement which, of
course, the British can never accept. However, as they later realise, it also
suggests a joining of strengths, enabling great deeds to be carried out that
could not be accomplished in separation. (*Cym.* III.i.23)

> A kind of conquest
> Caesar made here, but made not his brag
> Of 'Came and saw and overcame'.[34]

Again the words are somewhat equivocal, the Queen being apparently torn between a grudging admiration for Roman achievement and her innate British patriotism.

> Till the injurious Romans did extort
> This tribute from us, we were free

(Cym. III.i.48)

complains Cymbeline in the middle of the play, only to perform his amazing volte-face at the end. The British, it could be said, lack consistency. Even Posthumus' honour, like Cloten's, sometimes seem to be 'nothing but mutation'.[35]

The Romans, too, have their limitations.

> If Caesar can hide the sun from us with a blanket, or put the moon
> in his pocket, we will pay him tribute for light.

(Cym. III.i.43)

Cloten's irony serves to prick the bubble of Rome's pretentiousness, just as the backward glances towards Julius Caesar, 'whose remembrance yet/Lives in men's eyes'[36] suggest that, with the collapse of the Republic, something has been lost – a view we encountered in *Antony and Cleopatra*.

The relationship between Rome and Britain is discussed, obliquely, in the Welsh mountain scenes. Guiderius and Arviragus, the Celtic princes, have grown up in touch with nature, far from the sophisticated court and civilisation. The superiority of this pastoral way of life is an important theme of the late romances, being argued at length, for example, in *The Winter's Tale*.[37] Here the implication seems to be that the British possess a rugged vigour, allied to an intuitive mysticism, which Shakespeare finds heroic despite its occasional gaucheness and naivety. Britain is young, optimistic, visionary where Rome, rooted in its glorious past, lacks flexibility and imagination. The brothers represent natural man, being

>   ...as gentle
> As zephyrs blowing below the violet...
> ...and yet as rough...as the rud'st wind...
>   'Tis wonder
> That an invisible instinct should frame them
> To royalty unlearn'd, honour untaught,
> Civility not seen from other, valour
> That wildly grows on them, but yields a crop

As if it had been sow'd.

(*Cym.* IV.ii.171-81)

What is missing are the sterling Roman qualities such as decorum, discipline, organisation and rationality, although something of this has already rubbed off on the British from earlier contact with the invaders.

> Our countrymen
> Are men more order'd than when Julius Caesar
> Smil'd at their lack of skill, but found their courage
> Worthy his frowning at. Their discipline
> (Now wing-led with their courages) will make known
> To their approvers they are people such
> That mend upon the world.

(*Cym.* II.iv.20)

Like the brother princes, Britain at the play's close is reabsorbed into the larger world of Roman civilisation. Jupiter prophesies that the lopped branches 'from a stately cedar' shall, as part of the 'mending' process, 'be jointed to the old stock and freshly grow'.[38]

Just as Henry, by marrying the French Princess Katherine, unites two warring nations so, in *Cymbeline*, at the end

> A Roman and a British ensign wave
> Friendly together.

(*Cym.* V.v.481)

The two great races, after their long separation, are finally reconciled as fate decreed. The Roman eagle, phoenix-like, flies into the sun to renew his youth while the British, reinvigorated from Rome's cultural roots, 'set...forward' towards their glorious Jacobean future.

> The imperial Caesar should again unite
> His favour with the radiant Cymbeline.

(*Cym.* V.v.475)

Antony and Cleopatra concluded with the words 'great solemnity' and *Coriolanus* with 'noble memory', the audience being left to ponder upon Rome's grandeur and its glorious history. *Cymbeline*, by contrast, ends with the assertion that never was there 'such a peace'. Shakespeare, after two decades of examining Roman values, arrives finally at the idea of synthesis. Rome's power, tempered with justice and moderation, accommodates itself to the new Christian ethic. It could be called a renaissance.

Notes

1. The consensus of opinion points towards 1609. Although there are numerous references to Rome in Shakespeare's last play, *Henry VIII*, these are, of course, to the Roman Catholic Church.
2. See note 30 below.
3. See *Cym.* I.i.61-2.
4. *Pericles* (1607-8); *Cymbeline* (1609); *The Winter's Tale* (1610-11); and *The Tempest* (1611).
5. *Ant.* V.ii.346.
6. At least sixty times in this late quartet of plays.
7. See, for example, III.vi.17.
8. I.i.46.
9. *Cym.* I.vii.17.
10. *Ant.* III.ii.12.
11. *Cym.* IV.ii.22.
12. *Oth.* I.ii.335.
13. I.vii.106.
14. I.v.170.
15. V.v.210.
16. I.v.
17. V.v.196.
18. I.viii.152.
19. V.v.153. The striking clock mark one is, of course, in *Julius Caesar*.
20. Cf. *Caes.* I.ii.133-6 and *Ant.* V.ii.82-6
21. II.ii.45.
22. *Metamorphoses* VI.450-670.
23. *Cym.* I.v.123.
24. *Cym.* III.iv.36.
25. *Cym.* III.i.10.
26. III.ii.66.
27. *Caes.* II.i.35; IV.iii.157 (s.d.); IV.iii.265.
28. *Cym.* V.v.477.
29. *Magnificent Entertainment* 1603.
30. Raphael Holinshed: *Chronicles of England, Scotlande and Ire-lande.. from the First Inhabiting to the Conquest* 1577 (enlarged 1587).
31. The *Ara Pacis Augustae*, still preserved in Rome.

32. II.x.50.

33. V.iv.130.

34. Cf. *AYL*. V.ii.30.

35. IV.ii.133.

36. III.i.2.

37. See, in particular, the lengthy IV.iv.

38. *Cym.* V.iv.140-3. The imagery of grafting makes another interest-ing link with *The Winter's Tale*. See, for instance, *Wint.* IV.iv.79-103.

Bibliography

Primary

Augustine, St, *The City of God* (Loeb Classical Library, 1957-72)
Bacon, Francis, *The Advancement of Learning*, A. Johnston (ed.) (Oxford University Press, 1974)
———— *Essays*, W.A. Armstrong (ed.) (Athlone, 1975)
Baldwin, William, *A Treatise of Moral Philosophy* (London, 1547)
———— *A Mirror for Magistrates* (London, 1559)
Boccaccio, Giovanni, *De Casibus Virorum et Feminarum Illustrium* (Florence, 1535-60)
Calvin, John, *Commentaries on the Book of Daniel*, trans. F. Myers (Edinburgh, 1852)
Castiglione, Baldassare, *The Courtier*, trans. Thomas Hoby, Tudor Translations (London, 1905)
Catullus, *Poems*, K. Quinn (ed.) (Macmillan, 1970)
Chapman, George, *Bussy D'Ambois*, N. Brooke (ed.) (Manchester University Press, 1980)
Chaucer, Geoffrey, *The Legend of Good Women*, Complete Works, F. Robinson (ed.) (Oxford University Press, 1957)
———— *The Knight's Tale*
———— *The Monk's Tale*
Cicero, *De Amicitia*, H. Gould and J. Whiteley (eds) (Bristol Classical Press, 1983)
———— *De Officiis*, trans. W. Miller (Loeb Classical Library, 1913)
———— *De Inventione*, trans. H. Hubbell (Loeb Classical Library, 1949)
———— *Pro Plancio, Orationes*, A. Clark and W. Peterson (eds) (Oxford University Press, 1905-11)
———— *De Oratore*, trans. E. Sutton and H. Rackham (Loeb Classical Library, 1948)
———— *De Divinatione, De Natura Deorum*, trans. H. Rackham (Loeb Classical Library, 1933)
———— *Second Philippic*, J. Denniston (ed.) (Bristol Classical Press, 1978)
———— *Ad Atticum*, trans. E. Winstedt (Loeb Classical Library, 1912-18)

———— *Pro Murena*, C. Macdonald (ed.) (Bristol Classical Press, 1982)
———— *Pro Caelio*, trans. J. Freese and R. Gardner (Loeb Classical Library, 1958)
———— *De Legibus*, trans. C.W. Keyes (Loeb Classical Library, 1928)
———— *Tusculanarum Quaestionum*, trans. E. King (Loeb Classical Library, 1945)
Du Vair, Guillaume, *Moral Philosophy of the Stoicks*, trans. T. James (London, 1598)
Elyot, Thomas, *The Boke Named the Governour*, 1531 (Dent, 1907)
Ennius, Quintus, *Annals*, trans. E. Stuart (Loeb Classical Library, 1925)
Erasmus, Desiderius, *The Education of a Christian Prince*, 1576, trans. L. Born (New York, 1904)
———— *The Praise of Folly*, 1509, trans. B. Radice (Penguin, 1971)
Gentillet, Innocent, *Contre-Machiavel*, 1576, trans. S. Patericke (London, 1602)
Holinshed, Raphael, *Chronicles*, A. Nicoll (ed.) (Dent, 1927)
Homer, *The Iliad*, trans. G. Chapman, 1611, A. Nicoll (ed.) (Routledge, 1957)
Hooker, Richard, *Of the Laws of Ecclesiastical Polity* (Harvard University Press, 1977-81)
Horace, *Satires*, trans. N. Rudd (Penguin, 1973)
———— *Odes*, trans. W. Shepherd (Penguin, 1983)
———— *Epistles*, O. Dilke (ed.) (Methuen, 1961)
Jonson, Ben, *Catiline*, W. Bolton and J. Gardner (eds) (University of Nebraska Press, 1983)
———— *Sejanus*, J. Barish (ed.) (Yale University Press, 1965)
Juvenal, *Satires*, N. Rudd and E. Courtney (eds) (Bristol Classical Press, 1977)
Lipsius, Justus, *Two Bookes of Constancie*, trans. J. Stradling (London, 1594)
Livy, *Ab Urbe Condita*, trans. P. Holland (London, 1600)
Lyly, John, *Endimion*, 1591, *Complete Works*, R. Bond (ed.) (Oxford University Press, 1967)
———— *Euphues: the Anatomy of Wit* (1578)
Lynne, Walter (ed.), *The Three Books of Chronicles* (London, 1550)
Machiavelli, Niccolo, *The Prince*, trans. G. Bull (Penguin, 1970)
———— *Discourses*, E. Crick (ed.), trans. L. Walker (Penguin, 1983)
Marlowe, Christopher, *Hero and Leander, Complete Poems*, S. Orgel (ed.) (Penguin, 1986)
Meres, Francis, *Palladis Tamia* (London, 1598)
Montaigne, Michel de, *Essays*, trans. J. Florio, 1603 (Dent, 1965)
Ovid, *Amores*, J. Barsby (ed.) (Bristol Classical Press, 1979)
———— *Ars Amatoria*, S. Hollis (ed.) (Oxford University Press, 1977)
———— *Remedia Amoris, Erotic Poems*, P. Green (ed.) (Penguin, 1982)
———— *Fasti*, trans. J. Frazer (Loeb Classical Library, 1931)

———— *Heroides*, trans. G. Showerman (Loeb Classical Library, 1931)

———— *Metamorphoses*, trans. A. Golding (London, 1567) and M. Innes (Penguin, 1955)

Painter, William, *The Palace of Pleasure*, 1566 (Dover Publications, 1967)

Petrarch, *Il Canzoniere*, trans. M. Bishop (Greenwood Publications, 1980)

Petronius, *Satyricon*, trans. J. Sullivan (Penguin, 1977)

Pliny the Elder, *Naturalis Historia*, Excerpts, trans. P. Holland; P. Turner (ed.) (Centaur, 1962)

Pliny the Younger, *Fifty Letters*, A. White (ed.) (Oxford University Press, 1969)

Plutarch, *Lives*, trans. Sir Thomas North (London, 1579) – relevant extracts quoted in appendices to Arden editions of Roman plays

Propertius, *Elegies*, W. Camps (ed.) (Bristol Classical Press, 1985)

Reynolds, Richard, *Chronicles of Noble Emperours of the Romaines* (London, 1571)

Sallust, *Bellum Catilinae*, P. McGushin (ed.) (Bristol Classical Press, 1980)

————*Bellum Iugurthinum*, L. Watkiss (ed.) (Bristol Classical Press, 1984)

Seneca, *Dialogues*, L. Reynolds (ed.) (Oxford University Press, 1977)

———— *De Clementia*, J. Basore (ed.) (Loeb Classical Library, 1932)

———— *De Beneficiis*, J. Basore (ed.) (Loeb Classical Library, 1935)

———— *Thyestes*, R. Tarrant (ed.) (Scholars' Press, 1985)

———— *Hercules Oetaeus*, *Tragedies*, trans. F. Miller (Loeb Classical Library, 1917)

Sidney, Philip, *Arcadia* (Kent State University Press, 1971)

———— *In Defence of Poesie*, J. Van Dorsten (ed.) (Oxford University Press, 1971)

Spenser, Edmund, *The Faerie Queene*, D. Davis (ed.) (Dent, 1985)

Terence, *Adelphi*, R. Martin (ed.) (Cambridge University Press, 1976)

Tibullus, *Elegies*, trans. G. Lee (Cairns, 1982)

Virgil, *Aeneid*, trans. Earl of Surrey (London, 1557)

———— *Georgics*, trans. R. Wells (Carcanet, 1982)

Secondary

Adcock, F., *Roman Political Ideas and Practice* (University of Michigan Press, 1959)

Allen, B.M., *Augustus Caesar* (London, 1937)

Allen, D.C., *Some Observations on the Rape of Lucrece* (*Shakespeare Survey* 15, 1962)

Allen, H.S., *The Age of Erasmus* (Oxford University Press, 1914)

Altheim, F., *A History of Roman Religion* (London, 1938)

Anson, J., *Shakespeare's Stoic Pride* (*Shakespeare Survey* 19, 1966)

Arnold, E.V., *Roman Stoicism* (Cambridge University Press, 1911)

Arnott, P., *An Introduction to the Roman World* (Macmillan, 1970)

Bailey, C. (ed.), *The Legacy of Rome* (Oxford University Press, 1947)

Balsdon, J.P., *Roman Women* (Bodley Head, 1962)

Barroll, J.L., *Shakespeare and Roman History* (*Modern Language Review* 53, 1958)

Barrow, R.H., *The Romans* (Penguin, 1949)

Barton, A., *Livy, Machiavelli and Shakespeare's Coriolanus* (*Shakespeare Survey* 38, 1985)

Bolgar, R., *The Classical Heritage and Its Beneficiaries* (Cambridge University Press, 1954)

Boren, H., *Roman Society* (D.C. Heath, Toronto, 1977)

Brockbank, J.P., *History and Histrionics in Cymbeline* (*Shakespeare Survey* 11, 1958)

Brooke, N., *Shakespeare's Early Tragedies* (Methuen, 1968)

Brooke, T., *Shakespeare's Plutarch* (London, 1909)

Bulman, J.C., *The Heroic Idiom of Shakespearean Tragedy* (Associated University Press, 1985)

Campbell, O.J., *Shakespeare's Satire* (New York, 1943)

Cantor, P., *Shakespeare's Rome* (Cornell, 1976)

Carcopino, J., *Daily Life in Ancient Rome* (Penguin, 1956)

Cary, M., *et al.* (eds), *The Oxford Classical Dictionary* (Oxford University Press, 1949)

Charney, M., *Shakespeare's Roman Plays* (Cambridge University Press, 1961)

Chaudhuri, S., *Infirm Glory – Shakespeare and the Renaissance Image of Man* (Oxford University Press, 1981)

Christ, K., *The Romans* (Chatto & Windus, 1984)

Clarke, M.L., *The Roman Mind* (London, 1956)

Council, N., *When Honour's at the Stake* (Allen & Unwin, 1973)

Crook, J.A., *Law and Life of Rome* (Macmillan, 1978)

De Burgh, W.G., *The Legacy of the Ancient World* (Penguin, 1953)

Dixon, S., *The Roman Mother* (Croom Helm, 1988)

Duff, J.W., *A Literary History of Rome* (Benn, 1964)

Earl, D., *The Moral and Political Tradition of Rome* (Thames & Hudson, 1967)

—————— *The Political Thought of Sallust* (Cambridge University Press, 1961)

Farnham, W., *Shakespeare's Tragic Frontier* (Cambridge University Press, 1950)

Fluchère, H., *Shakespeare* (Longman, 1953)

Fowler, W., *Social Life at Rome in the Age of Cicero* (Macmillan, 1922)

Frank, T., *Catullus and Horace* (New York, 1928)

French, M., *Shakespeare's Division of Experience* (Cape, 1982)

Frye, N., *Fools of Time* (University of Toronto Press, 1967)

Gardner, J., *Women in Roman Law and Society* (Croom Helm, 1986)

Gilmore, M., *The World of Humanism 1453-1517* (Harper, 1952)

Goldman, M., *Characterising Coriolanus* (*Shakespeare Survey* 10, 1957)

Grant, M., *Roman Literature* (London, 1958)

Grimal, P., *The Civilisation of Rome* (Allen & Unwin, 1963)

Grudin, R., *Mighty Opposites – Shakespeare and Renaissance Contrariety* (University of California Press, 1979)

Hadas, M., *A History of Rome* (Bell, 1958)

Hallett, J., *Fathers and Daughters in Roman Society* (Princeton University Press, 1984)

Hamilton, E., *The Roman Way* (New York, 1932)

Hammond, M., *The Augustan Principate* (Harvard University Press, 1933)

Hankins, J., *Backgrounds of Shakespeare's Plays* (Harvester, 1978)

Highet, G., *The Classical Tradition: Greek and Roman Influences on Western Literature* (Oxford University Press, 1949)

Hill, H., *The Roman Middle Class in the Republican Period* (Blackwell, 1952)

Hill, R., *The Composition of Titus Andronicus* (*Shakespeare Survey* 10, 1957)

Holzknecht, K., *The Backgrounds of Shakespeare's Plays* (New York, 1950)

Honigman, E., *Shakespeare's Plutarch* (*Shakespeare Quarterly* 10, 1959)

Horowitz, D., *Shakespeare – An Existentialist View* (Tavistock, 1965)

Hubbard, M., *Propertius* (Duckworth, 1974)

Huffman, C., *Coriolanus in Context* (Bucknell University Press, 1972)

Hulse, S., *A Piece of Skilful Painting in Shakespeare's Lucrece* (*Shakespeare Survey* 31, 1978)

Hyde, W., *Paganism to Christianity in the Roman Empire* (Philadelphia, 1946)

Jones, E., *Stuart Cymbeline* (Essays in Criticism, Vol. II, 1961)

Kahn, C., *The Rape in Shakespeare's Lucrece* (*Shakespeare Survey* 9, 1976)

Kay and Jacobs, *Shakespeare's Romances Reconsidered* (University of Nebraska Press, 1986)

Kenney, E., *Cambridge History of Classical Literature* (Cambridge University Press, 1982)

Kerenyi, C., *The Religion of the Greeks and the Romans* (Thames & Hudson, 1962)

Kerrigan, J., *Keats and Lucrece* (*Shakespeare Survey* 41, 1989)

Kilvert, I., *Makers of Rome* (Penguin, 1965)

Knight, G.W., *The Imperial Theme* (Methuen, 1931)

―――― *The Crown of Life* (Methuen, 1947)

Kristeller, P., *The Classics and Renaissance Thought* (Cambridge University Press, 1955)

Law, R., *The Roman Background of Titus Andronicus* (*Studies in Philology* 40, 1943)

Lees, F., *Coriolanus, Aristotle and Bacon* (*Review of English Studies*, 1950)

Lewis, N., and Reinhold, M., *Roman Civilisation* (Harper & Row, 1966)

Liebeschuelz, J., *Continuity and Change in Roman Religion* (Oxford University Press, 1979)

Long, M., *The Unnatural Scene* (Methuen, 1976)

Lyne, R., *Latin Love Poets from Catullus to Horace* (Oxford University Press, 1980)

McCallum, M., *Shakespeare's Roman Plays and their Background* (Russell, 1967)

McKendrick, *The Roman Mind At Work* (Princeton University Press, 1958)

McNeir, W., *Shakespeare's Julius Caesar: A Tragedy Without a Hero* (Mainz, 1971)

Magnus, L., *English Literature in its Foreign Relations* (London, 1927)

Markels, J., *The Pillar of the World* (Ohio State University Press, 1968)

Massey, M., and Moreland, P., *Slavery in Ancient Rome* (Macmillan, 1978)

Miola, R., *Shakespeare's Rome* (Cambridge University Press, 1983)

Mitchell, C., *Coriolanus: Power as Honour* (*Shakespeare Survey* 1, 1965)

Muir, K., *Shakespeare's Comic Sequence* (Liverpool University Press, 1979)

Nicolet, C., *The World of the Citizen in Republican Rome* (Batsford, 1980)

Ornstein, R., *Seneca and the Political Drama of Julius Caesar* (*Journal of English & Germanic Philology* Vol. 57, 1958)

Osborne, J., *A Place Calling Itself Rome* (Faber, 1973)

Palmer, J., *Political Characters of Shakespeare* (Macmillan, 1945)

Phillips, J., *The State in Shakespeare's Greek and Roman Plays* (Octagon, 1971)

Platt, A., *Rome and Romans According to Shakespeare* (University Press of America, 1983)

Price, H., *The Authorship of Titus Andronicus* (*Journal of English and Germanic Philology* Vol. 47, 1948)

Quinn, K., *Catullus: An Interpretation* (Batsford, 1972)

Quinones, R., *The Renaissance Discovery of Time* (Harvard University Press, 1972)

Raaflaub, K., *Social Struggles in Ancient Rome* (University of California Press, 1986)

Rabkin, N., *Shakespeare and the Common Understanding* (New York, 1967)

Reynolds, L., and Wilson, N., *Scribes and Scholars: A Guide to the Transmission of Greek and Latin Literature* (Oxford University Press, 1968)

Ribner, I., *Patterns in Shakespearean Tragedy* (Methuen, 1979)

Riemer, A., *A Reading of Shakespeare's Antony and Cleopatra* (Sydney, 1968)

Rist, J., *Stoic Philosophy* (Cambridge University Press, 1969)

—————— *The Stoics* (Cambridge University Press, 1978)

Roberts, A., *Mark Antony* (Malvern, 1988)

Rossiter, A., *Angel With Horns* (Longman, 1961)

Rouse, W. (ed.), *Shakespeare's Ovid: Golding's Translation of the Metamorphoses* (London, 1961)

Russell, B., *History of Western Philosophy* (Allen & Unwin, 1946)

Sandbach, F., *The Stoics* (Chatto & Windus, 1975; Bristol Classical Press, 1989)

Schoenbaum, S., *Shakespeare – A Compact Documentary Life* (Oxford University Press, 1977)

Scullard, H., *A History of the Roman World 753 to 146 BC* (Methuen, 1935)

—————— *Roman Politics* (Oxford University Press, 1951)

—————— *Festivals and Ceremonies of the Roman Republic* (Thames & Hudson, 1981)

Shanzer, E., *The Problem of Julius Caesar* (*Shakespeare Quarterly* 6, 1955)

Siegel, P., *Shakespeare in His Time and Ours* (Indiana University Press, 1968)

—————— *Shakespeare's English and Roman History Plays* (Associated University Press, 1986)

Simmons, J., *Shakespeare's Pagan World* (Harvester, 1974)

Sinnigen and Boak, *A History of Rome to AD 565* (Macmillan, 1977)

Smith, R., *The Failure of the Roman Republic* (Cambridge University Press, 1955)

Snyder, S., *Patterns of Motion in Antony and Cleopatra* (*Shakespeare Survey* 30, 1980)

Sommers, A., *Wilderness of Tigers: Structure and Symbolism in Titus Andronicus*, Essays in Criticism, Vol. 10 (1960)

Spencer, T., *Shakespeare and the Nature of Man* (New York, 1961)

Spencer, T.R., *Shakespeare and the Elizabethan Romans* (*Shakespeare Survey* 10, 1957)

Stapfer, P., *Shakespeare and Classical Antiquity* (West, 1973)

Stewart, J., *Character and Motive in Shakespeare* (London, 1949)

Stirling, B., *The Populace in Shakespeare* (Columbia University Press, 1949)

Stobart, J., *The Grandeur That Was Rome* (London, 1934)

Syme, R., *The Roman Revolution* (Oxford University Press, 1939)

Taylor, L., *Party Politics in the Age of Caesar* (University of California Press, 1949)

Thayer, C., *Shakespearean Politics* (Ohio University Press, 1983)

Thompson, A., *Philomel in Titus Andronicus and Cymbeline* (*Shakespeare Survey* 31, 1978)

Thomson, J., *The Classical Background of English Literature* (Allen & Unwin, 1948)

———— *Shakespeare and the Classics* (Allen & Unwin, 1952)

Tillyard, E., *Shakespeare's Last Plays* (Chatto & Windus, 1938)

Traversi, D., *Shakespeare – The Last Phase* (Hollis & Carter, 1954)

———— *Shakespeare – The Roman Plays* (London, 1963)

Vawter, M., *Division 'tween Our Souls: Shakespeare's Stoic Brutus* (*Shakespeare Studies* Vol. III, University of South Carolina Press)

Velz, J., *Shakespeare and the Classical Tradition* (Minneapolis, 1968)

———— *The Ancient World in Shakespeare* (*Shakespeare Survey* 31, 1978)

———— *Clemency, Will and Just Cause in Julius Caesar* (*Shakespeare Survey* 22, 1969)

Vyvyan, J., *Shakespeare and the Rose of Love* (Chatto & Windus, 1960)

Waddy, L., *Pax Romana and World Peace* (New York, 1950)

Wagenvoort, H., *Pietas* (E.J. Brill, Leiden, 1980)

Waith, E., *The Metamorphosis of Violence in Titus Andronicus* (*Shakespeare Survey* 10, 1957)

———— *The Herculean Hero* (Chatto & Windus, 1962)

Watson, C., *Shakespeare and the Renaissance Concept of Honour* (Princeton University Press, 1961)

Weitz, M., *Literature Without Philosophy* (*Shakespeare Survey* 28, 1975)

Wells, C., *The Northern Star: Shakespeare and the Theme of Constancy* (Blackthorn, 1989)

Whitaker, V., *Shakespeare's Use of Learning* (San Marino, California, 1953)

White, R., *Innocent Victims: Poetic Injustice in Shakespearean Tragedy* (Athlone, 1986)

Wiedemann, T., *Greek and Roman Slavery* (Croom Helm, 1981)

Wilkinson, L., *Horace and His Lyric Poetry* (Cambridge University Press, 1951)

Wilson, D., *Shakespeare's 'Small Latin' – How Much?* (*Shakespeare Survey* 10, 1957)

Wirszubski, C., *Libertas as a Political Idea* (Cambridge University Press, 1960)

Wiseman, T., *New Men in the Roman Senate* (Oxford University Press, 1971)

Wolf, W., *The Escape from Mutability in Antony and Cleopatra* (*Shakespeare Quarterly* 33, 1982)

Yates, F., *Shakespeare's Last Plays* (Routledge and Kegan Paul, 1975)

Zeeveld, W., *The Temper of Shakespeare's Thought* (Yale University Press, 1974)

Appendix:
Shakespeare's Classical Reading

As a pupil at Stratford Grammar School – which he must surely have been, despite the lack of documentary proof – Shakespeare would have devoted more time to the study of Latin than to any other element of the curriculum. The scene in *Merry Wives* in which the schoolmaster, Sir Hugh Evans, tests a student on his Latin grammar gives us a good idea of what such teaching involved.

Cicero was widely studied in Tudor schools, both for his moral philosophy and for his exemplary prose style. Shakespeare would have encountered the *De Officiis* and the *De Amicitia* in the original Latin, though English versions had been available since Robert Whytinton's translation of 1534.

Virgil was regarded as the greatest of the Classical poets, the *Aeneid* having been first translated into English by the Earl of Surrey in 1557, a version which introduced blank verse to the language at the same time and may therefore have been doubly influential upon Shakespeare who can hardly have been unacquainted with it. Chapman's translation of Homer's *Iliad* started to appear in 1598 and is another important literary landmark that is unlikely to have escaped Shakespeare's attention.

The influence of Ovid upon English poetry of the period was even greater. Shakespeare unquestionably owes him an enormous debt. It is certain that he studied the *Metamorphoses*, probably working mainly from Golding's celebrated translation of 1567 and referring to the Latin text when he felt the need. Francis Meres, writing in 1598, declared that 'the sweet, witty soul of Ovid lies in mellifluous and honey-tongued Shakespeare; within his *Venus and Adonis*, his *Lucrece* and his sugared Sonnets among his private friends.' The Bodleian Library possesses a Latin copy of the *Metamorphoses* with what many believe to be the playwright's own signature upon its fly-leaf.

Seneca's influence upon Tudor drama is well known, his revenge tragedies, in particular, making a huge impact. Both *Titus Andronicus* and

Hamlet show clear evidence of Shakespeare's familiarity with these texts.

His Roman history Shakespeare took almost exclusively from Plutarch, whose interest lay in the examination of character and motivation rather than in Senecan brutality. Sir Thomas North's translation of the *Lives* – via Amyot's French version from the original Greek – is in itself a major literary achievement and Shakespeare borrowed much of its style and attitudes as well as raw material for his plots.

This brief summary would be incomplete without mention of Montaigne whose *Essays* (1571-92) are so steeped in the Classics that scarcely a page is without its quotations from the ancient authors who were his meat and drink. Shakespeare probably had access to John Florio's translation in manuscript well before it found its way into print in 1603.

Index